The City
in African-American
Literature

The City
in African-American
Literature

Edited and with an Introduction by

Yoshinobu Hakutani and Robert Butler

Madison • Teaneck
Fairleigh Dickinson University Press
London and Toronto: Associated University Presses

by Associated University Presses, Inc.

Associated University Presses
440 Forsgate Drive
Cranbury, NJ 08512

Associated University Presses
25 Sicilian Avenue
London WC1A 2QH, England

Associated University Presses
P.O. Box 338, Port Credit
Mississauga, Ontario
Canada L5G 4L8

The paper used in this publication meets the requirements
of the American National Standard for Permanence of Paper
for Printed Library Materials Z39.48-1984.

Library of Congress Cataloging-in-Publication Data

The city in African-American literature / edited and with an
  introduction by Yoshinobu Hakutani and Robert Butler.
      p.   cm.
  Includes bibliographical references and index.
  ISBN 0-8386-3565-2 (alk. paper)
    1. American literature—Afro-American authors—History and
criticism.   2. City and town life in literature.   3. Cities and
towns in literature.   4. Afro-Americans in literature.
  I. Hakutani, Yoshinobu.   II. Butler, Robert.
  PS169.C57C58   1995
  810.9'321732—dc20   94-17251
                                                        CIP

SECOND PRINTING 1996

PRINTED IN THE UNITED STATES OF AMERICA

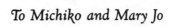

To Michiko and Mary Jo

Contents

Introduction

YOSHINOBU HAKUTANI AND ROBERT BUTLER

Morton and Lucia White observed in *The Intellectual versus the City* that "For a variety of reasons our most celebrated thinkers have expressed different degrees of ambivalence and animosity toward the city." Citing an "anti-urban roar" in "our national literary pantheon" which included writers such as Jefferson, Emerson, Thoreau, Hawthorne, Melville, Poe, and Henry Adams, they concluded that there is nothing in our national literature like "the Greek attachment to the *polis* or the French writer's affection for Paris." Examining a wide range of American writers who they feel make up "the core of our intellectual history," Morton and Lucia White claim that "It would be extremely difficult to cull from their writings a large anthology of poetry or social philosophy in celebration of American urban life."[1]

However, a substantial reversal of this anti-urban drive in American literature may be found in African-American writing, a literary tradition which has frequently been critical of the values expressed in mainstream American literature. While one of the central drives in our classic literature has been a nearly reflexive desire to move away from the complexity and supposed corruption of cities toward idealized non-urban settings such as Cooper's West, Thoreau's woods, Melville's seas, Whitman's open road, and Twain's river, very often the opposite has been true in African-American letters. To be sure, many important black texts such as Washington's *Up from Slavery,* Dunbar's *Lyrics from Lowly Life,* and Alice Walker's *The Third Life of Grange Copeland* express a deep suspicion of city life, but the main tradition of black American literature has been persistently pro-urban in vision. *The Narrative of the Life of Frederick Douglass,* for example, portrays the rural South as a plantation culture intent on exploiting and then destroying black people, but it envisions the city as a place of deliverance. W. E. B. Du Bois, born in a small village in western Massachusetts, likewise discovered greatly expanded possibilities for development in cities such as Boston and Atlanta. James Weldon Johnson, perceiving New York for the first time in 1899, enthusiasti-

9

cally embraced the modern American city as a place of renewal: "the glimpse of life I caught during our last two or three weeks in New York . . . showed me a new world, an alluring world, a tempting world of greatly lessened restraints, a world of fascinating perils; but above all, a world of tremendous artistic potentialities."[2]

Langston Hughes would later help to fulfill these potentialities in his celebrations of Harlem, a city which fired his imagination and became the center of his life and art. His first view of New York in 1925 is remarkably similar to Johnson's earlier evocation of that city: "There is no thrill in all the world like entering, for the first time, New York Harbor . . . New York is truly the dream city—city of towers near God, city of hopes and visions."[3] Richard Wright's vision of Chicago is split between wonder and terror, but it is always preferable to the rural alternatives in Mississippi which Wright so categorically rejected. A "fabulous . . . indescribable city," Chicago was both a brutally naturalistic environment which could crush Bigger Thomas and also a world of "high idealism"[4] which could help to liberate the narrator of *Black Boy* and *American Hunger*. Never romanticized, it nevertheless provided Wright with a compelling symbol of American identity, the larger world for which he hungered. And when Wright despaired of achieving human identity in the United States, he renewed his search for selfhood in Paris.

Much important African-American literature which has emerged since the Depression has also been largely urban in character. Although never hesitant to criticize the negative aspects of American city life, it has only rarely suggested that pastoral alternatives to the city exist for black people. This large and significant body of literature, moreover, contains some surprising celebrations of city life. James Baldwin's best fiction is rooted in New York, a place of extraordinary beauty as well as pain. Claude Brown's *Manchild in the Promised Land,* which set out to tell the story of "the first urban generation of Negroes," is careful to point out that black people in the city are "better off"[5] than their counterparts in the rural South because the city, for all its corruptions and violence, has the vitality and educational possibilities necessary for the "better life" Brown himself achieved. Amiri Baraka's 1981 essay "Black Literature and the Afro-American Nation: The Urban Voice" argues that, from the Harlem Renaissance onward, black literature has been "urban shaped," producing a uniquely "black urban consciousness." While careful not to gloss over the problems of black people in American cities, he predicts that the setting for black liberation will be the city: "But if the cities represent higher levels of perception and sophistication for us in America, they must be the focal point of yet more advanced levels of struggle."[6] And Toni Morrison, although stressing that the American city in general has often induced a sense of "alienation" in many black writers, nevertheless adds that modern black literature is suffused with an "affection" for "the village within" the city, black neighborhoods which are repositories for life-sustaining "community values."[7] Gwendolyn Brooks's poetry often celebrates this sense of cultural unity within the black neighborhoods of South Chicago, and a "village" of black life can be found even in Gloria Naylor's *The Women of Brewster Place*. Despite the urban horrors which that book so painfully details, some hope is affirmed at the end of the novel by the emergence of community spirit symbolized by the tearing down of ghetto walls and the preparations for a block party.

One way to explain this surprisingly positive image of the city in African-American literature is to examine the historical experience of black people in America. From the very outset, black people were denied imaginative access to a pre-urban homeland in Africa because the institution of slavery did everything possible to stamp out the memory of that world. And the actual experience of slaves in America did not permit them the luxury of romantically imagining the non-urban settings which are so mythically prominent in the fictions of Cooper, Melville, and Twain. As Huckleberry Finn and Jim sadly discover, the territories ahead could be truly liberating only for white people. In the era following the literal end of slavery, new strategies for reinslavement were devised in the South where codes of segregation and the practice of sharecropping were to make it impossible for black people to establish a positive image of rural life which could serve as a counterbalance to the pull of the cities.

The black writer, therefore, has usually found it inappropriate to envision idealized non-urban space as a relief from the pressures of urban living. As Blyden Jackson has pointed out, black literature from its beginning has been urban in outlook because rural life has been so strongly linked in the black imagination with slavery and post-Civil War forms of racial discrimination that black writers were drawn to portray city life as a way to counter Southern stereotypes with more liberating images of black experience in the urban North. For Jackson, this is particularly true of African-American fiction: "The Negro novel is a city novel. It almost always has been."[8]

The city, therefore, has been a crucial symbol in black literature and that literature has been remarkable for the rich variety of ways it has used urban settings and themes. Because of this, the city in African-American literature resists any simple categorizations and neat generalizations. A. Robert Lee, in discussing literary portraits of Harlem, stresses this important point:

The only *fact* about Harlem . . . may be its intractability, its undiminished refusal to be accommodated by any single explanation. That, one supposes and readily celebrates, accounts for why there have been so many Harlems on the mind—be they expressed in the novel or in any of the abundant other forms inspired by the enduring black First City of America.[9]

LeRoi Jones likewise cautioned against applying simplistic abstractions to black cities like Harlem when he insisted that Harlem "like any other city . . . must escape *any* blank generalizations simply because it is alive, and changing each second with each breath any of its citizens take."[10]

This selection of essays, therefore, is not informed by a narrow thesis which would limit one's view of how black writers have presented the city; rather, it contains many different perspectives on the black city. The impression emerging from this book is that the city has been—and continues to be—a live subject for black American writers, inspiring a rich diversity of literary visions of the city as it is captured by black writers from different times, places, backgrounds, and angles of perception. For example, the predominantly hopeful images of the city contained in slave narratives contrast sharply with later naturalistic accounts of urban reality expressed in novels such as Willard Motley's *Knock on Any Door* and Ann Petry's *The Street*. The socially diverse ethnic neighborhood of Marita Bonner's *Frye Street and Environs* is quite different from the teeming ghetto portrayed in Claude Brown's *Manchild in the Promised Land*. In the same way, Richard Wright's Chicago is distinct from James Baldwin's Harlem. Even when black writers living in similar time periods focus on the same city, they often develop radically different literary visions of that city. No one, for example, would mistake Ellison's distinctively surrealistic depiction of Harlem for Malcolm X's grittily mimetic portrait of that same place.

* * * * * *

Robert Butler's "The City as Liberating Space in *Life and Times of Frederick Douglass*" considers Douglass's book a "paradigmatic" text in African-American literature because it sharply challenged the pastoral vision of much mainstream American literature and suggested a new direction for black writers which was largely urban in character. Douglass discredits standard pastoral settings such as the farm, the forest, and the small town, while associating the city with various forms of human liberation. Although he is careful not to romanticize the American city, Douglass nevertheless insists that pastoral dreams have always been at odds with black realities in America and that the American city, for all of its limitations, can be a liberating new space for black people.

Donald B. Gibson's "The Harlem Renaissance City: Its Multi-Illusionary Dimension" stresses how black writers used this urban space to create many new directions in black literature. Gibson is careful to warn readers that the city which emerges in Harlem Renaissance literature cannot be adequately grasped in terms of any monolithic generalization which reduces the city to either a "good" or "evil" place. Instead, Gibson argues "The city is not just one or two things; it is a multiplicity of combinations of forces, of entities, of alliances; it is as much as imagination will allow." The urban literature of the Harlem Renaissance, thus grounded in a vision of city life that was complex and many-sided, continued to influence black literature long after the end of the 1920s. Questioning the assumptions of writers like Nathan Huggins who claimed that the Harlem Renaissance "failed" because it was premised upon ideas which were naive and romantic, Gibson argues that the Harlem Renaissance left a legacy for black writers which endures to the present.

The next two essays focus on two very different aspects of Richard Wright's urban vision. Yoshinobu Hakutani's "The City and Richard Wright's Quest for Freedom" examines Wright's belief that the movement of black people from the rural South to the urban North was the pivotal event in modern black history, because it allowed black people access to new forms of freedom which could empower them to achieve new lives. Although he never hesitates to point out the pathological features of American urban life, Wright nevertheless stresses in *Native Son*, *Black Boy*, and *The Outsider* that the city created the possibility of not only personal transformation but economic, social, and political transformation as well. Jack B. Moore's "No Street Numbers in Accra," however, records Wright's disenchantment with the African city and his subsequent recoil from certain aspects of modern African life. Moore stresses that the African cities which Wright describes in *Black Power* demonstrated "the difficulty or impossibility of overcoming deterministic environmental and social forces that trap individuals and entire societies. In this hostile scheme the city is a power that seems to drag humanity down with it through its own disorder and decay."

Essays by Eberhard Brüning and Michel Fabre explore the impact of two European cities upon major black writers. Brüning's "*Stadtluft macht frei!*: African-American Writers and Berlin (1892–1932)" surveys the responses of various Anglo- and African-American writers to Berlin, from the late-nineteenth century to the beginning of World War II, stressing the particular importance of Berlin for W. E. B. Du

Bois, Claude McKay, and Langston Hughes. For each of these black writers, Berlin was a symbol of a better life, as Brüning says, "an alternative to the restrictions and narrowness of the rural south of the United States." Fabre's "Richard Wright's Paris" likewise stresses how a European city functioned mainly as a positive environment for an important black writer. Like many expatriates, Wright often felt at home in Paris, for "in his eyes Paris represented French culture, and he could admire it and, within time, enjoy the beauty of age-old monuments without being awed by them." But because Wright was severely critical of French colonial policies in Africa, he felt uncomfortable with certain aspects of Parisian life and never fully accommodated himself to that city. Like his fictional character Fishbelly Tucker, Wright "lived in Paris but he was not really of it." As Fabre stresses, Wright "was satisfied with celebrating the better aspects of Parisian life ... while limiting his use of Paris as a setting to what he was most conversant with—the circles and groups, mostly American and black" which could provide him with "his alien home outside his homeland."

James Baldwin also fled the American city to live in Paris and, like Wright, presented a complexly split view of urban life in America. Fred L. Standley's "'But the City Was Real': James Baldwin's Literary Milieu" carefully explores this ambivalence. On the one hand, Baldwin viewed Harlem as "one of the only places I'm really at home in the world" because it was a rich embodiment of his own personal and cultural history, providing him with a sense of identity as an African-American man. But, on the other hand, he envisioned Harlem as a powerful emblem of how black citizens have been systematically excluded from the promises of American life and trapped into a ghetto which he described as "some enormous, cunning, and murderous beast, ready to devour, impossible to escape." Unlike most critics who have either ignored the city in Baldwin's work or minimized its importance, Standley argues that Baldwin himself was "the product of an urban environment" and that the city is of central importance in Baldwin's work.

Like James Baldwin, John A. Williams saw the city as a vivid reflector of the historical experience of African-American people in the twentieth century. Priscilla Ramsey's "John A. Williams: The Black American Narrative and the City" examines Williams's portrayal of the American city as a "nightmare world" which reduces black people to lives of isolation, fragmentation, and entrapment. Resisting the temptation to posit a hopeful alternative in pastoral space which often characterizes mainstream American fiction, Williams provides his oppressed heroes with a viable alternative to American urban life in the European city, for it is in places like Amsterdam and Paris that they can find what Ramsey describes as "their greatest sense of freedom and unconstricted movement."

In contrast to African-American writers such as Wright, Baldwin, and Williams, who dealt with city life at home as well as abroad, William Attaway and Willard Motley restricted themselves to social issues arising from black life in American cities. Attaway's novels describe a historical reality, focusing on the migration of black people in the South to the industrial North. Attaway shows, as John Conder says, that "racial conflict, a reality in the South, is but a mask conceal-ing the underlying reality of class conflict in the North, a battle engen-dered there by economic forces spawned by industrialization." For Conder, Motley's *Knock on Any Door* treats the problems which Atta-way focuses on: Chicago is a duplicate of the Pittsburgh Attaway has depicted. Motley's fiction thus portrays the social problems in Chicago which black people in the South inevitably face when they settle in the northern cities. Even though Motley's *Knock on Any Door* de-scribes Italian-Americans living in Chicago, the theme applies to a generic novel of the city: Motley suggests that, regardless of race, man is often destroyed or damaged by the urban environment More importantly, however, Motley's fiction suggests that, as Conder con-cludes, "if conditions make victims of us all, the conditions for victim-ization appear in rural areas as well as cities," but that "the odds for achieving self-realization are on the side of cities, not rural areas."

Robert Butler's "The City as Psychological Frontier in Ralph El-lison's *Invisible Man* and Charles Johnson's *Faith and the Good Thing*" also emphasizes that the city offers the possibility of self-realization for black people. Ellison himself, like the hero of *Invisible Man,* eventu-ally came to see the city in existential terms as a rite of initiation for which he had to be his own guide and instructor. Similarly, New York becomes for Ellison's invisible man a journey without a map leading to self-discovery and self-creation. This eventually brings him to an existential underground, which is an extraordinary symbol of the lim-itless frontiers of the mind. In the same way, Charles Johnson's Faith Cross ultimately experiences the northern city as an open space offer-ing her limitless possibilities for personal growth and social develop-ment. For both Ellison and Johnson the modern city is what the West is in mainstream American literature, an indeterminate open space creating the independence, freedom, and mobility necessary for achieving genuine selfhood.

If Ellison and Johnson imagine the city as a psychological frontier offering the possibility of renewal for black people, Gloria Naylor voices a persistent worry that the city may be a trap for African-

Americans. Michael F. Lynch's "The Wall and the Mirror in the Promised Land: The City in the Novels of Gloria Naylor" argues that Naylor's black characters can raise their standards of living in industrial cities, but they often become, in turn, victims of materialism. Black citizens of Linden Hills, as Lynch notes, "fail to develop a strong sense of self because . . . they dismiss knowledge of self in the interest of acquisition and advancement." Some of Naylor's characters, however, succeed in achieving identity and self-knowledge. Like Tish and Fonny in Baldwin's *If Beale Street Could Talk,* they reject the romantic quest for innocence and seek interdependence, love, and understanding. Ann Petry's *The Street* also deals with the social and economic forces of the city as does Naylor's *The Women of Brewster Place,* but Petry's novel is more than a *roman a thèse.* It strikes the reader, as Larry R. Andrews observes, "above all as an act of imagination and literary art" seldom seen in a naturalistic novel. Petry is superb in depicting "the powerful physical way in which the city assaults the characters' senses through concrete detail." For Andrews, Petry's surrealistic technique is reminiscent of "the urban evocations of Poe and Dickens . . . the great modern portrayals of the city—the St. Petersburg of Gogol, Dostoevsky, and Bely . . . and the Harlem of Ellison's *Invisible Man.*"

Whether through naturalism or surrealism, the portrayal of black life in the city is often focused on one's quest for identity and freedom. It is hardly surprising, then, that science fiction by black American writers also treat such themes. The cityscapes described by Samuel R. Delany are characterized by their flexibility, variety, and futurity. As Donald M. Hassler says, "these cities are, indeed, multiplex." Delany's *Triton,* for example, is a contemporary city where "variety, even deviant behavior flourishes." What is remarkable about Delany's science fiction is that while Delany is a relentless realist rather than a fantasist, he remains a pastoral poet who "acknowledges that both the issues and the answers . . . carry within them a large portion of mystery that can never be teased out either tentatively or laboriously." And, at times, Delany's writing reminds one that many black American writers have had in their career a strong affinity for Marxism.

While a majority of the African-American writers discussed in this book seek, and often find, identity and humanity in the city for their fictive characters, others also seek but do not find such values. The writers of the Harlem Renaissance portrayed the urban world with exuberance and hope, but the black dramatists of the American sixties described it with violence and frustration. The cityscapes of Ed Bullins, Amiri Baraka, and Adrienne Kennedy, as Robert L. Tener shows, imply that "there is even the sense that the city is some diabolical

instrument or machine for killing that even as it possesses its inhabitants sets out to destroy them."

* * * * * *

Although African-American literature has been largely urban in
outlook, surprisingly little attention has been paid by literary histori-
ans and critics to how the city is portrayed in black writing. No single
book on the subject exists, although there are several more specialized
studies on the Harlem Renaissance, most notably Nathan Huggins's
Harlem Renaissance, Amritjit Singh's *The Novels of the Harlem Renaissance*, Houston Baker's *Modernism and the Harlem Renaissance*,
and James de Jongh's *Vicious Modernism: Black Harlem and the Literary Imagination*. But the impact of other important cities in black
literature has not been examined sufficiently. Much more needs to be
written on how Chicago has functioned in African-American literature. We also need to know more about the unique ways in which
black women writers have depicted the city: some like Marita Bonner
and Paule Marshall recoil from urban reality while others like Nella
Larsen and Gloria Naylor respond to the city in terms of a complex
ambivalence. The Southern city, the European city, and pre-Harlem
New York also await the sustained attentions of literary critics. Careful studies of how Anglo- and African-American writers differ in their
portrayal of city life also are needed.

This selection of essays, therefore, is intended to encourage a wide
range of further study in this crucial aspect of African-American literature. As Hazel Carby has observed recently, black urban writing
has been a "neglected tradition" because critics and scholars have
focused most of their attentions on the "rural folk tradition" in black
literature. "Contemporary critical theory," Carby suggests, "has . . .
produced a discourse that romanticizes the folk roots of Afro-
American culture and denies the transformative power of both historical and urban consciousness."[11] It is time now to address this imbalance in African-American literary studies and begin a careful and
sustained study of how the city functions in that literature.

Many people helped us in preparing this book, but we would like
to thank particularly the Research Councils of Kent State University
and Canisius College for giving us grants-in-aid.

NOTES

1. Morton and Lucia White, *The Intellectual versus the City* (Cambridge: Harvard University Press, 1962), 1–3.

2. James Weldon Johnson, *Along This Way* (New York: Viking Press, 1933), 152.

3. Quoted in Arnold Rampersad, *The Life of Langston Hughes, 1902–1941: I Too Sing America, 1* (New York: Oxford University Press, 1986), 50.

4. Richard Wright, "How 'Bigger' Was Born," *Native Son* (New York: Harper, 1940), xxvi. Michel Fabre in *The Unfinished Quest of Richard Wright* (New York: William Morrow, 1973) points out that Chicago, for all the difficulties it created for Wright, still gave him a radically new life which freed his spirit. Characterizing Wright's Chicago as "still the teeming, ever-expanding city that Carl Sandburg had immortalized" (74), Fabre observes that Chicago gave Wright crucially important opportunities not possible in his prior life.

5. Claude Brown, *Manchild in the Promised Land* (New York: New American Library, 1965), vii–viii. In his one trip away from New York when he visits relatives in the rural South, Brown is bored with and alienated by country living. He returns to New York with great relief: "Down South was sure a crazy place and it was good to be going back to New York" (52).

6. Amiri Baraka, "Black Literature and the Afro-American Nation: The Urban Voice," *Literature and the Urban Experience: Essays on the City and Literature,* eds. Michael C. Jaye and Ann Chalmers Watts (New Brunswick, N.J.: Rutgers University Press, 1981), 148–58.

7. Toni Morrison, "City Limits, Village Values: Concepts of the Neighborhood in Black Fiction," in *Literature and the Urban Experience: Essays on the City and Literature,* ed. Michael C. Jaye and Ann Chalmers Watts (New Brunswick, N.J.: Rutgers University Press, 1981), 37–38.

8. Blyden Jackson, *The Waiting Years: Essays on Negro American Literature* (Baton Rouge: Louisiana State University Press, 1976), 180.

9. A. Robert Lee, "Harlem on My Mind: Fictions of a Black Metropolis," in *The American City: Cultural and Literary Perspectives,* ed. Graham Clarke (New York: St. Martin's Press, 1988), 83.

10. LeRoi Jones, *Home: Social Essays* (New York: Apollo Press, 1966), 145.

11. Hazel Carby, "The Historical Novel of Slavery" in *Slavery and the Literary Imagination,* ed. Deborah McDowell and Arnold Rampersad (Baltimore and London: Johns Hopkins University Press, 1989), 140.

The City
in African-American
Literature

1

The City as Liberating Space in *Life and Times of Frederick Douglass*

ROBERT BUTLER

1

Frederick Douglass was driven by a deeply felt need to tell the story of his life and wrote that story in various forms throughout his career. Beginning with *The Narrative of the Life of Frederick Douglass* (1845), Douglass wrote three more major versions of his autobiography: *My Bondage and My Freedom* (1855), the first edition of *Life and Times of Frederick Douglass* (1881), and a revised edition of *Life and Times* (1892) three years before his death. Examining the classic literature written by mainstream American writers during this crucial period from the 1840s to the early 1890s, one immediately becomes aware of a striking contrast between Douglass's vision of American life and the way it is portrayed in classic books like Cooper's *The Deerslayer* (1841), Melville's *Moby-Dick* (1851), Thoreau's *Walden* (1854), Twain's *Adventures of Huckleberry Finn* (1884), and Whitman's final version of *Leaves of Grass* (1892). These texts written by white writers are mainly pastoral in outlook because they often equate confinement and moral evil with social reality and idealize non-urban space as physically liberating and morally good. But Douglass's autobiographies emphatically reverse this sort of symbolic geography, attacking pastoral locations such as the farm, the woods, and the village as places of human enslavement and praising the city as a new space, offering various forms of liberation for black people.[1]

Each version of his autobiography, for example, begins with a description of rural Talbot County, Maryland, which sharply inverts the way such a setting is usually portrayed in American pastoral litera-

21

ture. Its soil is "worn-out, sandy, desertlike" and its inhabitants clearly reflect such depletion, being described as "spiritless" and stricken with "ague and fever."[2] Images of stasis complete this dismal picture—the Choptank River is presented as "the laziest and muddiest of streams" and the white population is "indolent and drunken" (27). Wherever rural life is presented in the early chapters it is described unromantically as a morally evil, physically depleted world which traps all people, black and white. Colonel Lloyd's plantation is characterized by "monotony and languor" (39), broken only by slaves drunkenly carousing at Christmas time in the "filth and wallowing" (148) which their white masters encourage as a way of deflecting and exhausting any rebellious energies they might have. Political and social order is maintained in such a world by carefully locking everyone into a place in a hierarchical system: "The idea of rank and station was rigidly maintained on this estate" (44). Douglass therefore sees this rural world as an immense prison, a "house of bondage" (71). At times, he describes it in religious terms as a kind of hell, "a horrible pit" (86) reducing the slave's life to endless punishment.

Unlike Huck Finn, who can retreat into the woods of Jackson's Island to gain relief from such a restrictive society, Douglass finds matters get worse when he leaves the social world of the plantation and enters a state of nature in the woods. After the oxen he is driving to Covey's farm break away from him, he finds himself "all alone in a thick wood to which I was a stranger" (119) and he is soon severely whipped there by Covey as a punishment for allowing the oxen to escape. Nature in this episode is clearly presented as Hobbesian, not Wordsworthian, as Covey rushes at him with "the savage fierceness of a wolf" (121) and flogs him with the branch of a gum tree.

Another standard pastoral location, the small village, also fails him when he is transferred from Colonel Lloyd's plantation to live with the Aulds at St. Michael's. The small village, so often romanticized in English and American literature as a place of simplicity and virtue, becomes for Douglass another form of slavery he had known earlier. It is "highly unfavorable to morals, industry, and manners" since its "ignorant population" is noted for its "coarseness, vulgarity and an ignorant disregard for the social improvement of the place" (103). Both an "unsaintly" and "unsightly" place, it is a world which threatens Douglass with regular beatings by the "Negro-breaker" Covey and also starves him to the point where he must steal food in order to survive. One of the most degrading episodes of Douglass's slave experience occurs at St. Michael's when he sees his master Thomas Auld cruelly whip a "lame and maimed" (112) slave woman, all the while reciting Scripture with "blood-chilling blasphemy" (112).

Whereas Thoreau in *Walden* leaves the city to achieve salvation in the woods and Huck Finn must try to find a new life by rejecting society and lighting out to the unspoiled West, Douglass seeks his salvation by rejecting pastoral space altogether and pursuing a radically new life in the city. When he is told by his master that he will be moved to Baltimore to serve as a slave in Thomas Auld's house, he receives such news with "ecstasy" (73) and he later considers his move to the city as one of the pivotal moments of his life:

> I may say here that I regard my removal from Col. Lloyd's plantation as one of the most interesting and fortunate events in my life. Viewing it in the light of human likelihoods, it is quite probable that but for the mere experience of being thus removed, before the rigors of slavery had fully fastened upon me, before my young spirit had been crushed under the iron control of the slave-driver, I might have continued in slavery until emancipated by the war. (75)

Even though he is outwardly degraded by being made a "present" (75) to Auld's young son Tommy, he is inwardly transformed by his living in a city. The very nature of urban life—even a southern city which legally and morally endorses slavery—loosens the bonds which imprisoned him in rural life. The maritime economy of Baltimore opens it to the world beyond the South and the more Douglass sees of this world, the more he is inspired by it to see himself as a person, not a slave.

Moreover, the kind of work he does in the city is quite different from the soul-numbing, body-destroying labor of the plantation. The house work he does for the Aulds makes far fewer physical demands on him and gives him the leisure time he was denied at Col. Lloyd's plantation and Covey's farm. He later discovers that slaves in Baltimore have much more economic independence than their white counterparts in the rural South, for they can, with the permission of their masters, "hire their own time" (188) by contracting to do work for pay with people other than their masters. By thus becoming "master of his own time" (189) a few hours during the week, Douglass can get a real sense of economic and moral freedom for the first time in his life. He also can experience the ennobling power of work, laboring now for his own sense of profit and achievement rather than the good of a slavemaster who exploits him. Furthermore, he can save at least part of the money he earns to help him accumulate enough cash to flee the South and establish himself in the North.

It is little wonder, therefore, that Douglass experiences Baltimore as a kind of liberating frontier, an urban equivalent to the pastoral space which frees traditional white heroes such as Cooper's Natty Bumppo and the persona of Whitman's "Song of Myself." Passing through Annapolis on his way to Baltimore, he thinks "So the great world was opening to me and I was eagerly acquainting myself with its lessons" (74). Indeed, it is in the city that Douglass's mind is awakened and begins to break the psychological shackles which rural slavery had placed upon him. The most important "lesson" he learns in Baltimore is the "new and special" revelation (74) that whites do not want black people to become literate because they realize that the entire slave system is grounded in ignorance and will topple if slaves acquire the education necessary for them to see slavery for what it is and then rebel against it. A crucial point in Douglass's life in Baltimore occurs when his mistress, who never owned slaves prior to her marriage, introduces him to the "mystery" and "wonderful art" (78) of reading. She is later forbidden by her husband to engage in such activity because he realizes "If you teach him to read, he'll want to know how to write, and this accomplished, he'll be running away with himself" (79). When Douglass discovers this vital link between literacy and freedom, he "understood the direct pathway from slavery to freedom" (79). Thus knowledge necessarily brings him to the crucial awareness that slavery is neither a part of the natural order of things nor a punishment imposed upon blacks by God, but is instead an arbitrary and artificial system used by whites to exploit blacks:

> Nature never intended that men or women should be either slaves or slaveholders, and nothing but rigid training long persisted in, can perfect the character of the one or the other. (81)

Armed with this knowledge, Douglass can begin to liberate himself by "retraining" himself as a person instead of a slave. Baltimore, because it frees him of the systematic control which whites exert over blacks in the absolutely closed world of the plantation, is a good place for Douglass to begin the education which ultimately helps to liberate him because it is a relatively open world where he can see himself and his environment in fresh ways. Teaching himself to read when he capitalizes on Mrs. Auld's early lessons by talking to white children with whom he plays, Douglass finds that his eyes are gradually opened to the "horrible pit" (86) of slavery. Once empowered with the ability to read, he can grope toward a way of escaping from the South's closed system of exploitation. Whereas the plantation gave him no access to the free world outside of the South because it severely limited his awareness of that world, the "city newspaper" (89) in Baltimore, appropriately called *The Baltimore American,* provides him daily knowledge of the larger American world beyond the South which offers him the possibility of certain kinds of liberation. By reading the newspaper, Douglass acquires valuable knowledge of the free states, many of which he was simply unaware of while living on Col. Lloyd's plantation, and he also finds out about the "grand movement" (89) of abolitionism. Douglass therefore "read[s] with avidity," finding "hope in those words" (89) of the Baltimore papers. For such words not only contain a "terrible denunciation of slavery" (89) but also point the way to freedom in the northern city.

Although Douglass is removed from Baltimore when Thomas Auld has a misunderstanding with his father and is forced to send him to St. Michael's where he is once again victimized by plantation slavery, his experience in Baltimore keeps him alive as a human being. His "Baltimore dreams" (143) of becoming a free man allow him to van-quish Covey who tries to break him as a person by reducing him to "beast-like stupor" (124). Douglass's ability to read and write has nurtured within him a human conception of himself and also has enabled him to unite with other blacks by teaching them about the evils of slavery and inspiring in them a resolve to escape. Even though their plan for escape fails and Douglass ends up for a time in the village jail where he suffers "a life of living death" (174), he is reborn when his master sends him back to Baltimore instead of selling him to a slave trader who would consign him to the plantations of Alabama.

Douglass's second stay in Baltimore enables him to escape to the North for two reasons: 1) It puts him in close daily contact with trains and ships which can be the literal means of his leaving the South, and 2) it continues his process of education. Although his master at St. Michael's feels that "city life" has affected Douglass "perniciously" (112) because it has "ruined him for every good purpose" (113), pre-cisely the opposite is the case, for urban life has given Douglass a basis to create a human self and then move to the North where this self can be nurtured in a more open public world. When Douglass returns to Baltimore he learns the valuable trade of ship caulker, which he can use later to support himself in New Bedford. He also can "increase [his] little stock of education which had been at a dead stand still since [his] removal from Baltimore" (185) by reading books. Moreover, his daily contacts with freemen in various jobs in Baltimore induce in him a strong conviction that he is "equal to them in nature and attachments" (186).

He cleverly uses an urbane mastery of language which he develops in Baltimore to accomplish his escape by borrowing a sailor's "free papers" (198) and then using them to gain passage on a train bound for Philadelphia. Because the conductor checking these papers fails to read them carefully and Douglass's "knowledge of ships and sailors' talk" (199) gained by working in city shipyards helps him to convincingly impersonate a sailor, he gains his freedom by using language more skillfully than does his white oppressor. As Ellison's invisible man would later say of Douglass, he was a man who liberated himself after "he had talked his way from slavery to a government ministry."[3]

2

The remainder of *Life and Times of Frederick Douglass* is a journey through increasingly more liberating forms of urban space. Although he is careful not to idealize the numerous cities he comes to experience and stresses at many times that various forms of racism do indeed flourish in the urban North, he nevertheless argues that the northern city for him is a liberating new world because it provides him with the freedom, independence, and mobility he needs to transform himself from a slave named Frederick Bailey to a free man named Frederick Douglass. As Douglass comes to understand slavery, he realizes that one of its most crippling features was the intense fear of movement induced in American slaves because they usually equated motion with being separated from family and friends and then being sold to plantation owners of the "far South" where slavery took especially harsh forms:

> The people of the North, and free people generally, I think, have less attachment to the places where they are born and brought up than had the slaves. Their freedom to come and go, to be here or there, as they list, prevents any extravagant attachment to any one particular place. On the contrary, the slave was a fixture; he had no choice, no goal, but was pegged down to one single spot, and must take his root there or nowhere. The idea of removal elsewhere came generally in the form of a threat, and in punishment for a crime. It was therefore attended with fear and dread. The enthusiasm which animates the bosoms of young freemen, when they contemplate a life in the far west, or in some distant country, where they expect to rise to wealth and distinction, could have no place in the thought of a slave . . . . His going out into the world was like a man going into the tomb, who, with open eyes, sees himself buried out of sight and hearing of wife, children, and friends of kindred tie. (97)

What the city provided Douglass was a new space through which he could confidently move as he sought new possibilities. For Douglass, the city is not the kind of "tomb" which Melville's Bartleby succumbs to, nor is it the kind of hell which torments Hawthorne's Robin Moli-neux or Poe's nameless man of the crowd. Rather, it is a womb offering new life. As he moves through a series of cities, he experiences dra-matic growth because he is able to appropriate for himself increasingly more significant aspects of urban space: he starts out as a picaresque wanderer, becomes a menial worker on the margins of city life, then turns into an important citizen, and finally becomes an urban leader. As he moves through urban space he thus undergoes a number of transformations of the self, in much the same way as traditional American heroes have experienced conversion as they identify with various forms of pastoral open space by going to sea, retreating to the woods, journeying on a river, or embarking on an open road.

Douglass's first moment of conversion takes place when he enters New York after escaping from Baltimore:

> My free life began on the third of September, 1838. On the morning of the fourth of that month, after an anxious and most perilous but safe journey, I found myself in the big city of New York, a *free man*, one more added to the mighty throng which, like the confused waves of a troubled sea, surged to and fro between the lofty walls of Broadway. Though daz-zled with the wonders which met me on every hand, my thoughts could not be much withdrawn from my strange situation. For the moment the dreams of my youth and the hopes of my manhood were completely ful-filled. The bonds that held me to "old master" were now broken. (202)

The city here is a liberating world because it not only separates the hero from a restrictive past dominated by "old master" but also gives him the fluid, indeterminate space he needs to define himself in fresh terms. Douglass here sees New York as a spacious "sea" and swimming in that sea "dazzled [him] with the wonders." As a result, he feels that he has "escaped from a den of hungry lions" (202) and enthusiastically exclaims "A new world had opened for me" (202).

Douglass, however, soon qualifies this nearly mythic view of New York when he is forced to deal with its harsher realities on a daily basis. The impersonality of the city makes him feel "a sense of loneli-ness and insecurity" (203), and he also comes to realize that many Southerners and bounty hunters lurk in the city and will return him to slavery if they discover his true situation. But he nevertheless stresses that New York is a key to his freedom, for it is there that he meets a black man named Stuart who introduces him to David Rug-gles, an officer in the Underground Railway. Ruggles makes arrange-ments for him to go to New Bedford, a much safer place because it is a progressive city, influenced strongly by the abolitionist movement. While in New Bedford, Douglass is protected by laws which specify that "no slaveholder can take a slave out of New Bedford" (209), and he also is encouraged by the fact that the political system is relatively open to black people. Furthermore, New Bedford is a center of pros-perity which Douglass claims is "the richest city in the union" (207) in terms of per capita income. He easily finds work there to support himself and his wife, whom he marries on the very day he begins to live in New Bedford. This city therefore becomes "a striking and gratifying contrast" (208) to everything Douglass has known in the South, for he sees "in New Bedford the nearest approach to freedom and equality that I had ever seen" (208).

New Bedford becomes for Douglass a rationally ordered city which contrasts very sharply with the irrational world of southern slavery. Unlike the South which is premised upon "brute force," New Bedford is an enlightened place based upon the "educated mind" (208). Labor there has a "superior mental character" (208) because it derives from the rational self-interest of the worker rather than the dark compul-sions of the slave system. Work in New Bedford, therefore, "went smoothly as well-oiled machinery" (208), a dramatic contrast to the inefficiency and violence which he associates with slave labor. Doug-lass also finds New Bedford to be a place which offers him better opportunities for formal and informal education than any other place in which he has lived. Black and white children attend the same public schools, "apparently without objection from any quarter" (209), and Douglass finds rich possibilities for his own self-education. He often reads while working, nailing a newspaper to a post near the bellows he operates. He also is deeply affected by William Lloyd Garrison's ideas on abolition when he attends Garrison's lectures in Liberty Hall and later reads his newspaper, The Liberator. Indeed, he feels that Garrison's "paper took a place in my heart second only to the Bible" (213). Inspired by Garrison's example, he becomes an orator when he addresses black people regularly at the Second Street school-house and also gives a speech at an antislavery convention arranged by Garrison on Nantucket.

New Bedford, like New York, therefore enables Douglass to experi-ence dramatic personal and social growth. His new role of orator and his new work for the Massachusetts Anti-Slavery Society give him a fresh conception of himself:

Here opened for me a new life—a life for which I had no preparation. Mr. Collins used to say when introducing me to an audience, I was a "graduate from the peculiar institution with a diploma on my back." The three years of my freedom had been spent in the hard school of adversity. My hands seemed furnished with something like a leather coating, and I had marked myself for a life of rough labor, suited to the roughness of my hands, as a means of supporting my family and rearing my children.

Young, ardent, and hopeful, I entered upon this new life in a full gush of unsuspecting enthusiasm. The cause was good, the men who engaged in it were good, the means to attain its triumph good. Heaven's blessing must attend all, and freedom must soon be given to the millions pining under a ruthless bondage. My whole heart went with his holy cause. For a time I was made to forget that my skin was dark and my hair crisped. (216)

Douglass eventually discovered that his work for the Massachusetts Anti-Slavery Society "had its shadows also, as well as its sunbeams" (216), for such work often brought him in contact with racist whites who indeed reminded him in many ways that his skin was dark and tried to deprive him of his rights as an American citizen. For example, he was often submitted to the indignities of traveling Jim Crow cars while riding trains to antislavery conventions and sometimes encountered violent resistance to his speeches by people overtaken by what he called the "mobocratic spirit" (227). Moreover, he eventually had a serious falling out with Garrison and other white abolitionists over the goals and strategies of the antislavery movement. But he never lost his sense of himself as a participant in a "holy cause" while working against slavery and saw such work as providing him with a transformation of self into an important statesman. For if his journey to New York allowed him to become a "graduate from the peculiar institution" of slavery, his journey to New Bedford empowered him to grow beyond a menial worker committed to a "life of rough labor," and become a public person, an orator, teacher, and leader who could help to execute a divinely overseen plan to liberate black people from slavery.

When white people in the abolitionist movement tried to restrict his role by suggesting that he tone down some of his ideas and use a more pronounced southern black accent so as not to appear to be "too learned" (218) to predominantly white audiences, Douglass grew increasingly more uncomfortable with such restrictions and eventually went his own way. He spent two years abroad after publication of his *Narrative of the Life of Frederick Douglass* in 1845, partly because he felt that agents of his former slave master would return him to slavery. In 1847 he returned to the United States, only after British friends bought his freedom. He was intent on setting up an independent black press in Boston, but he moved to Rochester in 1848 when support for the project in Boston did not materialize.

Douglass's long stay in Rochester initiated another important phase of his life: as an activist who printed an independent paper, a member

of the Underground Railroad who helped many ex-slaves escape to
Canada, and an important black political leader who rose to national
prominence. Rochester, although never romanticized by Douglass, satisfied him more deeply than any other place in which he had lived.
Admitting that there were certainly "thorns" in his "pathway" (267)
during the twenty-five years he lived in Rochester, most notably his
daughter being barred from attending a private girls' school and various forms of segregation on public accommodations, Douglass, nevertheless, saw his move to Rochester as an important step in his life:

> Notwithstanding what I said of the adverse reaction exhibited by some of
> its citizens at my selection of Rochester as the place to establish my paper,
> and the trouble in educational matters just referred to, that selection was
> in many respects very fortunate. The city was and still is the center of a
> virtuous, intelligent, enterprising, liberal, and growing population. . . . It
> is on the line of New York Central Railroad—a line that, with its connec-
> tions, spans the whole country. . . .
>   . . . I know of no place in the Union where I could have located at that
> time with less resistance, or received a larger measure of cooperation and
> assistance, and I now look back to my life and labors there with no unal-
> loyed satisfaction, and having spent a quarter of a century among its
> people, I shall always feel more at home there than anywhere else in this
> country. (269–70)

The physical location of Rochester was ideally suited for Douglass's
work as a "stationmaster" on the Underground Railroad, and its position on the New York Central rail line connected Douglass with all
other parts of the country. The city's well-educated and "liberal"
populace supported Douglass's growth as an orator, writer, and political leader. Rochester, therefore, became the place where the process
of Douglass's transformation from a lowly slave to an important public
figure is completed, the "home" which was in harmony with his true
character and allowed him to assume the role of a national leader.

Douglass's national prominence is underscored by his moving late
in his life from Rochester to Washington, D.C. While living in Washington he assumed a number of important public roles, including U.S.
marshal for the District of Columbia, recorder of deeds, and U.S.
consul to Haiti. When telling the story of his Washington years,
Douglass is acutely aware of how his status as an important public
figure in the nation's capital contrasts remarkably with his earlier
status as a slave on a southern plantation. Speaking enthusiastically
of his new position as U.S. marshal, he says:

> I felt myself standing on new ground, on a height never before trodden
> by any of my people, one heretofore occupied only by members of the

Caucasian race. . . . Personally, it was a striking contrast to my earlier
condition. Yonder I was an unlettered slave toiling under the lash of Covey,
the Negro-breaker; here I was the United Marshal of the capital of the
nation. (518)

This contrast between the rurally enslaved Frederick Bailey and the
nationally prominent Frederick Douglass at the "height" of life in the
nation's capital reinforces Douglass's heroic image of himself as a self-
made man who can provide a model of success for his people. Whereas
slavery has reduced him to the status of an invisible man in a "dark
corner" of the "dark domain" (39) in the plantation South, his life
in Washington gives him visibility and importance, making him a
representative American figure. Presiding as U.S. marshal at the presi-
dential inauguration of 1877, he feels that he is "part of a great national event" (517). In his later public roles in Washington he feels
that he is an important "witness and advocate" (511) for black people
in America. As a public official he envisions his personal life in nearly
epic terms, as "the thin edge of the wedge to open for my people a way
in many directions and places never before occupied by them" (514).

Douglass's vision of himself and the city has one more important
dimension: his response to the city abroad. He went abroad twice,
first in 1845 when he stayed in England and Ireland to escape the
danger of being returned to Maryland as a slave, and also in 1886
when he and his second wife visited England, France, Italy, and Egypt.
Douglass considered both visits to be important parts of his life because each significantly expanded his vision of himself and his place
in the world. His earlier trip to England and Ireland confirmed his
vocation to be a political figure who could, like the Irish politician
Daniel O'Connell, use his pen and voice to liberate his people. His
second trip abroad, which he considered "a milestone in my experience
and journey of life" (557), also was crucial because it gave him a sense
of participating in a Western culture that was broader and deeper
than the American society which at the time was exacting a heavy
price for his marrying a white woman. His European trip of 1886,
therefore, gave him a temporary respite from "color prejudice and
proscription at home," enabling him to "walk the world unquestioned,
a man among men" (590).

The "space" that Ireland and England provide him is decidedly
urban in character. During his 1845 trip, Douglass devotes almost no
attention to describing the famous countrysides of Ireland and England, concentrating instead on life in Dublin and London. Likewise,
his impressions in 1886 focus on "the great old city of Avignon" (566),
the "great city of Naples" (578), and the "grand old city" (569) of

Genoa. He is especially enthusiastic about the "Eternal City" (572) of Rome, beholding it in "ever-increasing wonder and amazement" (572). He gives some attention to the pastoral beauties of the French countryside, the sublimity of Mt. Vesuvius, and the remarkable deserts he observes when he passes through the Suez Canal, but main attention is given to the great cities of Western civilization. Again, he measures his dramatic growth as a person by contrasting his experience in London, Paris, and Rome with his earlier condition of slavery in the rural South:

> To think that I, once a slave on the Eastern shore of Maryland, was experiencing all this was well calculated to intensify my feeling of good fortune by reason of contrast, if nothing more. A few years back my Sundays were spent on the banks of the Chesapeake Bay, bemoaning my condition and looking out from the farm of Edward Covey. . . . Now I was enjoying what the wisest and the best of the world have bestowed for the wisest and best to enjoy. (588)

Douglass's experience in European cities, therefore, offers him new transformations, making it possible to transcend altogether the role of slave which the rural South imposed upon him. It also allowed him to go well beyond the status as a worker he enjoyed in Baltimore, the status of an escaped slave in New Bedford, and even the status of an important public servant in Rochester and Washington, D.C. For in London, Paris, Rome, and other famous European cities, he joins the ranks of "the wisest and the best." He becomes what he always wanted to be, "a man among men."

There are only three times in the book where Douglass succumbs to the pastoral impulse, and he quickly corrects himself in each case. After the Civil War is over he naively thinks that the struggle against slavery is finished and his "voice is no longer needed" (373). He therefore considers retiring to "a little farm and settle down to an honest living tilling the soil" (374). But this impulse quickly passes when he receives many invitations to speak at colleges, lyceums, and literary societies, and he decides to keep Rochester as his home base of operations. He is also briefly tempted to return to the rural South during Reconstruction to gain political office as a black politician, but he feels that his "life and labors in the North had unfitted me for such work" (398). Having adopted the more restrained oratorical styles of the urban North, he feels he would be considered "tame and spiritless" by the rural "masses" (398) in the South.

A more substantial pastoral impulse, however, assails Douglass when he returns briefly to Maryland after the Civil War to visit the estates of Col. Lloyd and Thomas Auld. In a chapter entitled "Time Makes All Things Equal," Douglass tries to reconcile himself with his southern past by singing the praises of the rural South and predicting that black people will be given an important role to play in the postbellum South. But this chapter is not very convincing because it is written with a "poetic force" (440) resulting in badly overwritten melodrama and sentimentality. The death bed scene where Thomas Auld is implausibly revealed as a person who "never liked slavery" (443) drips with sentimentality which completely contradicts everything said earlier about Auld. The lushly romantic descriptions of the southern setting which stress the "impressive" (448) family burial grounds and the beauties of the "great house" with its "tranquil and tranquilizing" (449) gardens also jar with the more grimly realistic descriptions of these places presented earlier in the book. But the falsest pastoral note is sounded in chapter 16 where Douglass argues strongly that emancipated black people should not emigrate to the rural North because "The South is the best locality for the Negro" (438). Douglass here adopts the same plan for post-Civil War blacks which Booker T. Washington would later propose in Up from Slavery, arguing that freed slaves are not yet ready for life in northern cities but must seek their destiny in "manual labor" (429) on southern farms.

Such an argument runs counter to the main thrust of Douglass's entire life, for it was in fleeing the mind-numbing work of southern fields and pursuing a new life in the urban North that he was able to free himself of physical and spiritual slavery. Douglass's oddly pastoral argument also flies in the face of history, for it is written at the beginning of the Reconstruction period, a time when the South began a process of re-enslaving black people by developing systems of sharecropping and segregation. When Douglass wrote the final version of Life and Times in 1892, he realized this and completely revised his expectations for black people in the rural South. By this time Douglass understood that the policies of accommodation with the South undertaken during the presidencies of Chester Arthur and Rutherford P. Hayes had returned the "spirit of slavery" (536) to the South. He also realized that the Supreme Court decision of 1883, which declared the Civil Rights Act of 1875 to be unconstitutional, had put black people at the mercy of southerners intent on depriving them of their political, social, and economic rights. Given such "national deterioration" leading to "reactionary tendencies against the black man" (539), Douglass was forced to abandon his hopes for the rural South and once again focused his attentions on the urban North as a liberating space for black citizens.

3

In *The Fall of Public Man*, Richard Sennett makes a sharp distinc-tion between the eighteenth-century "cosmopolis," an urban world in which personal identity and public reality were kept in a healthy state of "equilibrium", and the nineteenth-century city which had deteriorated to the point where urban blight and impersonality threat-ened to overwhelm the individual. Because urban reality had so un-dermined human value and aspiration, the nineteenth-century hero recoiled into the self, producing what Sennett called "the erosion of public life" and the "romantic search for self-realization" in fundamen-tally private forms of experience.

Although mainstream American fiction written during Douglass's lifetime, such as Melville's *Pierre*, Howells's *The Rise of Silas Lapham*, and Crane's *Maggie: A Girl of the Streets*, clearly verify Sennett's thesis, Douglass's autobiographies help to create a distinctive direction for black literature by recovering a faith in public life, especially as it is stimulated by and sustained by the city. Begun in the 1840s and completed in the 1890s, decades in which Sennett detects a growing rift between man's "intimate" experience of the self and the outer world of the city, Douglass's autobiographies cut against the grain of mainstream American literature. Rather than envisioning the city as what Sennett calls "dead public space,"[4] Douglass saw urban space as a flawed but viable civil world awaiting redefinition and reconstruc-tion. For him, the relationship between city and self can be mutually beneficial, for just as his personal energies could help to transform places like Rochester into a more just social world promised by civil documents such as the Bill of Rights, the city in turn could offer him a substantial social identity denied to him in the rural South.

Douglass's autobiographies, therefore, constitute what Houston Baker has called a "paradigmatic"[5] text and what James Olney has characterized as a "founding document"[6] for African-American litera-ture. Books such as Johnson's *Along This Way*, McKay's *Home to Harlem*, Wright's *Black Boy*, Hughes's *Montage of a Dream Deferred*, Baldwin's *Notes of a Native Son*, Ellison's *Invisible Man*, Malcolm X's *The Autobiography of Malcolm X*, Brooks's *A Street in Bronzeville*, and Naylor's *The Women of Brewster Place* in various ways follow the direction which Douglass helped to define, for each expresses a nearly instinctive suspicion of the American Dream as it is defined in pastoral terms and instead proposes a black version of that dream as it is enacted in the city.

Growing out of a distinctive literary tradition which Douglass helped to establish, black literature in America is strongly urban in character. For even as it aggressively criticizes certain aspects of American urban life, it is in basic agreement with Douglass's conviction that white pastoral dreams have always been at odds with black realities and that the city, for all of its limitations, can be a liberating space for black people. In this way, African-American literature has consistently challenged the modernist premise embedded in much canonical American literature that the self must always be at odds with the social, political, and cultural realities of urban life.

NOTES

1. Important slave narratives written after *The Narrative of the Life of Frederick Douglass* also tend to be strongly urban in outlook. *The Narrative of William Wells Brown* (1847) describes its narrator's escape from various forms of slavery in the South and his finding new economic and social possibilities in cities like Cleveland, Buffalo, London, and Boston. William Pennington's *The Fugitive Blacksmith* (1849) similarly concludes with the hero establishing a new life in New York after freeing himself from the "mental and spiritual darkness" of life on a Maryland plantation. William and Ellen Craft's *Running a Thousand Miles for Freedom* (1860) focuses on their flight from the "town" of Macon, Georgia, to northern cities such as Philadelphia, which they describe as "our first city of refuge," and Boston, where they are befriended by abolitionists and learn to read and write. After the passage of the Fugitive Slave Law, which made their lives in Boston precarious, they left the country and went to the English cities of Liverpool and London where they became "free from every slavish fear." In a similar way, Harriet Jacobs's *Incidents in the Life of a Slave Girl* (1861) concludes with the heroine achieving freedom, selfhood, and a home for herself and her children in a number of cities after escaping a life of slavery on a southern plantation. Emerging from the "black pit" of her past life, she discovers many new possibilities in Philadelphia, New York, and Boston.

A notable exception to this anti-pastoral motif in American slave narratives is *The Life of Josiah Henson* (1849) which tells the story of Henson establishing an all-black community in rural Canada after escaping southern slavery and passing through cities such as Cleveland and Buffalo. But, in the main, American slave narratives strongly resist this pastoral outlook. Given that white culture did everything it could to stamp out the memory of a pre-urban homeland in Africa and the actual experience of slavery in the rural South did not permit black people the luxury of romantically imagining the pastoral settings which are so mythically prominent in the writings of Cooper, Thoreau, and Twain, they were strongly inclined to see the city as the best option for establishing new lives.

2. Frederick Douglass, *Life and Times of Frederick Douglass* (New York: Collier-Macmillan, 1962), 27. All subsequent references to the text are to this edition, and page numbers appear parenthetically after the quotation.

3. Ralph Ellison, *Invisible Man* (New York: Random House, 1952), 288.

4. Richard Sennett, *The Fall of Public Man* (New York: Alfred Knopf, 1974), 18, 7, 12.

5. Houston Baker, Jr., *Singers at Daybreak: Studies in Black American Literature* (Washington, D.C.: Howard University Press, 1972), 12.

6. Deborah McDowell and Arnold Rampersad, eds. *Slavery and the Literary Imagination* (Baltimore and London: Johns Hopkins University Press, 1989), 3.

2

The Harlem Renaissance City:
Its Multi-Illusionary Dimension

DONALD B. GIBSON

Woe to the bloody city. It is all full of lies and robbery.
—Nahum 3:1

And I saw the holy city, new Jerusalem, coming down out of
heaven from God, made ready as a bride adorned for her husband.
—Rev. 21:2

God the first garden made, and the first city Cain.
—Cowley[1]

THE conception of the city figured in these representations emerges
from specific assumptions about reality, assumptions firmly fixed in
western thought and mythology, perhaps more firmly fixed in the pre-
Freudian imagination than later. In each of these conceptions the city
is imaged as a monolithic entity having an essential, definable nature.
The city *is* this or that. It is a "bloody" city possessing the infinitely
varied and variable—though all negative—characteristics belonging
to a "bloody" city. The "holy" city is solely and entirely that, pure
and without ugliness or any species of stain. The "first" city, because
of who founded it, is the outgrowth of alienation from God and
humankind; its wellsprings are bloodshed, sin, murder, fratricide, un-
godliness. Whether the city is St. John's heavenly city, Sodom, Gomorrah, Ur, Ninevah, Babel, Jerusalem, or Thebes, it is likely to be
in its representation a single-dimensioned (at best double) construct,
and to possess nothing of the multidimensionality we know it in fact
to have. When is Jerusalem anything other than "the holy city"?

Mythology and history are not always easily distinguished; each
may be an extension of the other in all manner of degree and kind.

But it is probably worthwhile to know how we are conceiving the city—on the whole or as particular cities—in any given discussion of cities. The poet Lucy Ariel Williams, in her poem "Northboun'," published in 1925[2] during the height of the Renaissance, confounds history and mythology, however intentionally. The poet seems intent upon presenting a perspective that recognized absolutely no distinction between history and mythology. "Northboun'" is written from the point of view of a black migrant prior to his journey northward. The poet makes it impossible not to know that she is not the speaker in the poem, the language of the poem's narrator, an "other," being such as to indicate clearly that the speaker could not possibly have written the poem.

> Talkin' 'bout the City whut Saint John saw—
> Chile, you oughta go to Saginaw;
> A nigger's chance is "finest kind,"
> An' pretty gals ain't hard to find.
>
> Huh! de wurl' ain't flat,
> An' de wurl ain't roun',
> Jes' one long strip
> Hangin' up and down.
> Since Norf is up,
> An' Souf is down,
> An Hebben is up,
> I'm upward boun'.

The poem's narrator does not know about the southwest and midwest, that there has previously been black migration to Arkansas, Oklahoma, Kansas, Nebraska.[3] The speaker only thinks, as, conceivably, the uninformed migrant of 1925 might, that the options are northward and urban—as they seemed to most to be. Mythological truth unseats historical truth, as the poet, through the speaker, ignores economics and refigures geography, forcing it into conformity with Christian mythology. The poet goes one step further. The fictionalized historical truth (Saginaw is better than St. John's holy city—as though the comparison were possible) displaces mythology in the mind of the simple migrant. It is, however, not only in the mind of the ignorant migrant and mythological commentators that the city is seen as singledimensioned; sophisticated modern academicians have seen it in much the same way: as a monolithic entity having essential existence. It is difficult to get beyond the limits imposed by myth, both for poet and peasant.

Consider the following observation recently made about the American city:

If, then, the American city has been seen as an image of despair and corruption, it has equally been viewed as an image of vitality and possibility. It remains, in the end, an enigma.[4]

The city is "enigma" only if it need be one or the other. If it is allowed that both visions, indeed realities, may exist within the same framework, then there is no enigma involved at all. For one economic class, the city may be a field of despair and hopelessness; for another it might well offer vitality and possibility. How interesting it would be to see what groups in New York saw despair and hopelessness and which saw vitality and possibility between black Thursday, 23 October 1929, the day the stock market crashed, and March 1932 when the market bottomed out. The city is not just one or two things; it is a multiplicity of combinations of forces, of entities, of alliances; it is as much as imagination will allow. If the devil stalks about the City of God, that is enigma. The enigma is in the contradiction occasioned by the appearance of evil in God's holy city. If the devil stalks around 135th Street and Seventh Avenue, that is no enigma, for evil has its place among many forces in, and definitions of, the modern urban environment.

The same problem exists in another recent representation of the city:

> The balance between the alluring and ugly, comprehensible and elusive, hopeful and dreary in city life would suggest that the concept of paradox offers at least one useful way of viewing the world's dominating mode of life.[5]

Again, we are only looking at "paradox" if disparity exists within the confines of a unified field of discourse. Paradox exists only if we image the city as being essentially one thing or another. Conceived in its multiplicity, the city offers contrast but not paradox. The simultaneous existence of rich and poor in the urban setting is paradoxical only if the phenomenon is considered in terms other than economic or class. Only in traditional moral terms do the categories "rich" and "poor" exist in paradoxical relation. In class terms there is no paradox, for the relation between poor and rich in capitalistic society is a perfectly logical one.

The relation between city and country is also clearly an economic relation at bottom. Sociological, psychological, and moral consequences are secondary. Characteristics traditionally felt to belong inherently to the city are not that at all. The member of the northern urban proletariat is but the rural peasant who has found his way to the city.

To them [those who championed the rural above the urban], as to Jefferson, cities were "the ulcers on the body politic." In their eyes the city spiritual was offset by the city sinister, civic splendor by civic squalor, urban virtues by urban voices, the city of light by the city of darkness.[6]

"Squalor," "vice," and "darkness" have nothing necessarily to do with cities but everything to do with economic systems and choices about how wealth is distributed.

Arna Bontemps, among the foremost writers who, as David Levering Lewis says, "migrated" to Harlem during the Renaissance of the twenties, found the city not the least bit like "a cancer on the body politic," but more like an elixir:

> They [Bontemps and other litterateurs] found that under certain conditions, "it was fun to be a Negro." In some places the autumn of 1924 may have been an unremarkable season. "In Harlem," Bontemps remarked, "it was like a foretaste of paradise. A blue haze descended at night and with it a string of fairy lights on the broad avenues."

"Harlem's air," Lewis adds, "seemed to induce a high from which no one was immune."[7]

Osofsky, who describes the same city at about the same time, seems to be talking about another place entirely, a world having absolutely no connection with not only Bontemps's world but with his whole universe:

> For those who remained permanently [in New York] the city was a strange and often hostile place—it was so noisy and unfriendly, so cold, so full of "temptations and moral perils," a "pernicious influence," a "fast and wicked place." "Many of those who come North complain of the cold and chills from the like of which they had not previously suffered."[8]

Both Osofsky and Bontemps are possessed by the mythology of the city, each believing that his description is a true one—certainly not a lie. The problem each has and the problem most commentators have had about the city—and this is especially true of the city of the Harlem Renaissance—is in seeing the city as being an essential "something" rather than being what it is: a dynamic of interrelated forces acting and reacting in relation to each other. The city not only shapes lives but is shaped by lives. Harlem made urban New York blacks; black migrants, primarily from the South, made Harlem. Of the 60,534 blacks who lived in Manhattan in 1910, only 14,300 had been born in the city.[9] Between 1920 and 1930, the black population of New York city increased nearly three hundred percent.[10] "If my race can make Harlem," one observer said, "good lord, what can't it do."[11] Without doubt the tenor of life in Harlem, as in any other city, was heavily influenced by such teeming hordes of migrants. What, then, *is* Harlem? It is an infinite multiplicity of cross- and counter-interactive factors, some of greater import than others, depending on the political orientation of the viewer.

Toni Morrison, in her approach to defining the relation of blacks to the city, suggests looking at African-Americans and the city in such a way as to avoid dichotomizing, and therefore simplifying, the issue. Her brilliant analysis allows recognition of the negative aspects of the urban experience of blacks without defining the very nature of that experience as wholly negative and of necessity pathological. She recognizes the relation between black urban life and pathology, but does not suggest that the very nature of African-American experience per se produces it. She deftly steps around the well-intentioned analysis of the African-American personality set forth by the psychologists Kardiner and Ovesey:

> The Negro, in contrast to the white, is a more unhappy person; he has a harder environment to live in, and the internal stress is greater. By "unhappy" we mean he enjoys less, he suffers more. There is not one personality trait of the Negro the source of which cannot be traced to his difficult living conditions. There are no exceptions to this rule. The final result is a wretched internal life. This does not mean he is a worse citizen. It merely means that he must be more careful and vigilant and must exercise controls of which the white man is free.[12]

Morrison knows what the average black person knows but what Kardiner and Ovesey do not: whatever the African-American is, he or she is not a walking instance of pathology. There is pain in blackness, and there is joy also. Often these are mixed to such an extent that their components are not easily distinguished.

Morrison wisely tells us that black writers (and by extension black people) do not see the same city white writers and people see, because their experiences are not the same. James, Updike, Sandburg, and Fitzgerald know a different city from that known by Langston Hughes and James Baldwin. And for good reason.

> Black people are generally viewed as patients, victims, wards, pathologies in urban settings, not as participants. And they could not share what even the poorest white factory worker or white welfare recipient could feel: that in some way the city belonged to him. Consequently, the Black artist's view of the city and his concept of its opposite, the village or country, is more telling than the predictable and rather obvious responses of main-

stream writers to post-industrial decay, dehumanization and the curtailing of individualism which they imagined existed in the city but not in the country.[13]

The city itself is repellent to black people, Morrison tells us, for its hellishness—Ellison's "underground hideout" and Wright's "nightmare violence"; but not because it is "Eliot's Wasteland" nor suggestive of "the mechanization of life." Within the city, however, exists the village, "the neighborhoods and the population of those neighborhoods":

> Harlem, the closest thing in American life as well as literature to a Black city, and a mecca for generations of Blacks, held this village quality for Black people—although on a grand scale and necessarily parochial. The hospitals, schools, and buildings they lived in were not founded nor constructed by their own people, but the relationships were clannish because there was joy and protection in the clan.[14]

The marvel of Morrison's perspective is that it accommodates a wide variety of disparate and paradoxical phenomena, doing away with the necessity of deciding whether the city is the City of God or Sodom and Gomorrah.

Many years ago when I was younger and more foolish, I set out to prove the untenable hypothesis that the city in the imaginations of black people was effectively figured as the City of God and that it was only the actual urban experience that turned it into hellish nightmare.[15] History tells us something a bit different. The conception of the northern city as the City of God never caused a single individual to raise a single foot to take one step northward. Wade tells us in his book on urban slavery that there were many good reasons that slaves preferred to live in the city. For one thing, the relation between slave and owner was under the observation of a community. If a slave was not dressed reasonably well, if she or he were undernourished or was physically abused, such facts would be known. This certainly did not protect all slaves in all cases,[16] but we know from the testimony of former slaves that the behavior of some owners was tempered by concern for reputation.[17] Work in the city was likely to be less backbreaking; there was ample opportunity for greater, more widespread social interaction than on plantations or small farms. There were more possibilities of being "hired out," of being able to work for others for wages (though these wages belonged to one's owner). There were far more opportunities to learn to read in cities simply because there was more writing to be seen and there were others around, slaves or free black people, who knew how to read and were willing to teach others.

In general one was freer in the city than in the rural situation,[18] a good practical reason for preferring it.

We probably all know that there were free blacks in the antebellum South, but we may not know how very many there were. The 1860 census tells that in that year there were 261,918 free blacks in the South. In Maryland and the District of Columbia there were 95,073; in Virginia, 58,042; in North Carolina, 30,463; and in Louisiana, 18,647.[19] These are the places containing the largest numbers of such people. Most of them lived in cities, but southern not northern ones. Although they were free to travel to the northern cities, they chose not to, despite the extraordinary difficulties and dangers free blacks encountered daily living where slavery existed.[20]

The reasons that they stayed are undoubtedly the same ones that caused the large majority of antebellum freed persons to remain in the South. The city was a magnet to ex-slaves, but, again, the southern city, not the northern one. By the 1920s, when their children and grandchildren found themselves in Harlem, they nearly all had spent some of their time previously in a southern city before making the trek north.[21] The Exodusters likewise sought no heavenly nor any other kind of city. When this first large-scale migration got underway, its destination was Arkansas, Oklahoma, Kansas, and even, for fewer migrants, Iowa and Nebraska, but to lands suitable for farming. Only the second great wave of migration brought scores of black migrants to northern cities. They came for jobs, though, not milk and honey.

Toni Morrison's understanding of relationships among black people in the city, of intragroup relations based on the model of the village, is reflected in that singularly urban phenomenon, the rent party (modeled on the quilting party, the house raising, the corn shucking?).[22]

Langston Hughes celebrates the rent party in his autobiography, The Big Sea, telling us that when he was in Harlem (during the twenties) he went to a rent party almost every Saturday night.[23] He says that they were not always occasioned by the need to pay the rent but were sometimes held for fun. I would hazard that no one ever gave a rent party for "fun." Rent parties might have been given for reasons other than paying the rent (for example paying other bills and indirectly paying the rent) and people might have had fun at them, but they were never given for fun. "Fun," in the environment of Harlem in the 1920s, meant feeling support from and relatedness to other people; feeling that one belongs somewhere in the family, somewhere in the village, somewhere in the city, somewhere in the world, somewhere in the universe. Rent parties meant literally the introduction of "strangers" into one's home—into one's "small" apartment (since rent parties were usually held in apartments) into the intimacy

of small spaces. Rent parties had the effect of reducing the size of the
largest city in the country. Such intimacy would not have been
courted unless it was felt that those entering one's private space were
somehow related, friends, known ones, and not total strangers but
brothers and sisters. They are known because they belong to the village and are communicants. And because they belonged to the village,
they knew what was and was not proper behavior. Everyone, guests
and hosts, knew that behavior would be enacted within certain unspoken but culturally agreed upon limits. The rent party was a summoning up of the past; a re-enactment and conflation with urban life
of the black village experience in the American South and Africa.[24]
Langston Hughes tells us whom he met at rent parties and suggests
as well why he went to them so very often:

> I met ladies' maids and truck drivers, laundry workers and shoe shine
> boys, seamstresses and porters. I can still hear their laughter in my ears,
> hear the soft slow music, and feel the floor shaking as the dancers danced.[25]

Interestingly enough, Hughes discusses the rent party separately from
his discussion in his autobiography of other parties in Harlem and
downtown during the Renaissance. In a section entitled "Parties,"
Hughes described the parties that he and many others in his circle
went to, which were frequently racially mixed gatherings of profes-
sionals of various kinds, writers, artists, publishers, singers, usually
given by people wealthy or famous or both. The distance between the
descriptions of these parties and the rent parties silently measures the
distance separating the working class from the bourgeoisie, a division
not sufficiently attended to in discussions of the goals of the Renaissance as articulated by Alain Locke and others. David Levering Lewis
speaks eloquently of this division:

> Saturday nights were terrific in Harlem, but rent parties every night were
> the special passion of the community. Their very existence was avoided
> or barely acknowledged by most Harlem writers. . . . With the exception
> of Langston Hughes and Wallace Thurman, almost no one—at least no one
> who recited poetry and conversed in French at Jessie Fauset's—admitted
> attending a rent party.[26]

The issue of class is not raised often enough in considerations of
the Harlem Renaissance. The economic dimension of the subject is
forced to the fore of consciousness when we consider the rent party
just as it lies submerged beneath a comment Arna Bontemps makes
in reminiscing about the time:

It did not take long to discover that I was one of many young Negroes arriving in Harlem for the first time and with many of the same thoughts and intentions. Within a year or two we began to recognize ourselves as a "group" and to become a little self-conscious about our "significance." When we were not too busy having fun, we were shown off and exhibited and presented in scores of places to all kinds of people. And we heard the sighs of wonder, amazement and sometimes admiration when it was whispered and announced that here was one of the "New Negroes."[27]

The "New Negro" is a special, elite group, more likely to be found at Carl Van Vechten's place than at a rent party. The "New Negroes" came to Harlem for quite different reasons than did most migrants; they came not for jobs but to participate in a burgeoning, stimulating literary, artistic, and intellectual climate not to be found anywhere else in the world. None of them was forced to the city by relentless economic necessity. The "New Negro" was a person who had risen high enough on the socio-economic scale as to consider pursuit of a profession unlikely to produce significant income, and whose rewards were not quickly nor easily forthcoming. These people had to have had leisure to learn to appreciate fine art, and skills highly enough developed to produce art. They were almost all from middle-class or middle-class oriented families. Every woman and man was college educated—they either had finished degrees or attended college at one time or another.[28] Carl Van Vechten emphasizes the point in a comment he makes after his newly found friend James Weldon Johnson introduces him to African-American Harlem: "In about two weeks I knew every *educated* person in Harlem. I knew them by the hundreds [my emphasis]."[29]

Alain Locke, chief public sponsor of the "New Negro" movement, never meant that integration, social and political equality would come with the development of a class of artists. No egalitarian, he meant that it would come for those who are the creators, the intellectuals, artists, and writers of the Renaissance. He spoke as though he referred to the group, but he had in mind only the "New Negroes," not the "ladies' maids and truck drivers" that Hughes hung out with at rent parties: "Indeed, by the evidence and promise of the cultured few, we are at last spiritually free, and offer through art an emancipating vision of America."[30]

Locke knew integration was coming because he saw it before his very eyes. He saw black and white interacting in unprecedented ways and on seemingly equal terms. If some saw Harlem as Eric Walrond did, "It is a house of assignation . . . this black city,"[31] Locke saw it as a "house of assimilation." Before we dismiss Locke as a misguided fool (I find his politics wanting—not his intellectual capacities), we need to image what he saw. He witnessed a phenomenon never before seen in this country: seemingly significant numbers of talented, intelligent blacks and wealthy, influential, or talented whites interacting, seemingly as equals. Never before on such a scale! He saw *that* on a personal level; literally, with his own eyes. In the wider scope he saw all the other indices (his own *The New Negro*, Toomer's *Cane*, McKay's *Home to Harlem*, and the publications of Hughes, Cullen, Hurston, Johnson, Larsen, Bontemps, Fisher, and a host of others: *The Emperor Jones*, 1920; *Shuffle Along*, 1921; *Runnin' Wild*, 1923, leaving in its wake the Charleston and the songs "I'm Just Wild about Harry" and "Love Will Find a Way"; and *Dixie to Broadway*, 1924, one of few integrated musicals, signifying, suggesting, arguing that the races were moving toward a new era of harmony).[32]

We also must consider the possibility that the good doctor Locke was intellectually sophisticated, no less naive nor optimistic than we. We might consider the possibility that he intentionally seized the day, grabbed the horns of ambiguity, directed thought and history through his own chosen channels. He knew full well that he spoke for an elite group of "New Negroes," and appropriated a rhetoric useful for pushing ahead the interests of the small group but in fact utilized the weight, the authority, of the larger group to achieve goals far more limited than those articulated. Perhaps he did not really *mean* that he expected artistic creativity to finish the work of the Civil War, to succeed where Reconstruction had failed. Perhaps he was not so naive as to suppose that the race problem could be resolved upon aesthetic grounds.

Critics such as Gilbert Osofsky, Nathan Huggins, Cary Wintz, and to a lesser extent David Levering Lewis are considering the Renaissance in two dimensional terms when they address the question, both directly and indirectly, whether the Renaissance failed.[33] It should be remembered that the vision of the Renaissance shared by Locke and the black community of writers during the time was different from the vision of those whites who came up to Harlem for a night's entertainment, for drink, drugs, sex, or whatever. Certainly the excitement generated by the forbidden or taboo was instrumental in creating some of the energy driving the Renaissance. But the New Negroes were not only "new" to the world; they were new to themselves. Huggins's view of the Renaissance is sometimes uni-dimensional when, for example, he says:

> Nobody could have anticipated the Great Depression, but the Negro renaissance was shattered by it because of naive assumptions about the centrality of culture, unrelated to economic and social realities.[34]

Surely it was not shattered "because of naive assumptions"; it would have been shattered no matter what Locke's (and he does have Locke, the aesthetician supreme, primarily in mind) assumptions were.

I would argue that though the material conditions responsible for the existence of the Renaissance changed drastically, something remained. I will avoid claiming that the "spirit" of the Renaissance prevailed and say instead that something of the energy, the village cohesion, the new sense of the existence of something worthwhile, worth talking and writing about among black people, was left to be passed on literally through the literary productions of the time. Although class antagonisms split the Garveyites away from the litterateurs, still they were each fed by the energies of the other. The spirit that allowed race pride to develop during the time was encoded in the literary productions, including those of Garvey, to be resuscitated during the sixties—though I would argue that strong strands of race pride and nationalism continued to exist well after the Renaissance; they never died out. Witness the role of black newspapers and journals in fomenting racial pride and solidarity between the end of the Renaissance and the sixties.

Whether the Renaissance succeeded or failed is an outsider's question, a question whose answer depends upon the answer the questioner seeks. None of the participants in the movement would have asked it, for the question itself presupposes an answer. Presuppositions exist: succeeded or failed in terms of what? The Renaissance would have failed if it had not left us Zora Hurston, Langston Hughes, Countee Cullen, Claude McKay, Jessie Fauset, Arna Bontemps, Nella Larsen, Rudolph Fisher, and Wallace Thurman. It also might have failed if these writers had been lost and not available to succeeding generations. Who in their right mind would consider such alternatives, success or failure, possible? Only a mode of thinking that would see the city as the city of God or the city of the devil. If Harlem is the bloody city of Nahum, "all full of lies and robbery," then the Renaissance has failed, for that description leaves out Abyssinian Baptist Church and St. Phillip's Protestant Episcopal Church. If it is "the holy city," it has likewise failed, for such a conception leaves out too much else that is of the city but not holy. It does not measure up to the original garden, Eden, nor does it fit the dimensions of the "city of Cain." It is what it is: a vast multiplicity of constantly interactive forces unable to be contained within any abstraction or construct.

NOTES

1. Abraham Cowley, "The Garden."
2. Reprinted in *The Poetry of the Negro 1746-1949*, ed. Langston Hughes and Arna Bontemps (Garden City, N.Y.: Doubleday, 1949), 144.

3. See Nell Irvin Painter, *Exodusters* (New York: Norton, 1976).

4. Introduction to *The American City*, ed. Graham Clarke (London & New York: Vision Press & St. Martin's Press, 1988), 9.

5. Christine Bolt, "The American City: Nightmare, Dream, or Irreducible Paradox?" *The American City*, 15.

6. Arthur Schlesinger, *The Rise of the City, 1878–1898* (New York: Macmillan), 81.

7. David Levering Lewis, *When Harlem Was in Vogue* (New York: Oxford, 1989), 103.

8. Gilbert Osofsky, *Harlem: The Making of a Ghetto*, 2d ed. (New York: Harper & Row, 1971), 31.

9. Lewis, *When Harlem*, 27.

10. *The American Negro Reference Book*, ed. John P. Davis (Englewood Cliffs, N.J.: Prentice-Hall, 1966), 110.

11. Osofsky, *Making of a Ghetto*, 123.

12. Abraham Kardiner and Lionel Ovesey, *The Mark of Oppression* (Cleveland & New York: World, 1962), 81.

13. Toni Morrison, "City Limits, Village Values: Concepts of the Neighborhood in Black Fiction," *Literature and the Urban Experience: Essays on the City and Literature*, ed. Michael C. Jaye and Ann C. Watts (New Brunswick, N.J.: Rutgers University Press, 1981), 37.

14. Ibid., 38.

15. "The City and the Black Writer: Mythology and Symbology," *Criterion* 7 (Spring–Summer 1969): 20–25.

16. Frederick Douglass speaks directly to this point: "Every city slaveholder is anxious to have it known of him, that he feeds his slaves well; and it is due to them to say, that most of them do give their slaves enough to eat. There are, however, some painful exceptions to this rule." See *Narrative of the Life of Frederick Douglass, An American Slave*, ed. Houston A. Baker, Jr. (New York: Penguin, 1982), 79.

17. It is clear in Harriet Jacobs's narrative, *Incidents in the Life of a Slave Girl*, ed. Jean Fagin Yellin (Cambridge: Harvard University Press, 1987), that both she and her grandmother were in great measure protected from sale and sexual abuse by public opinion in the small town of Edenton, N.C. Her grandmother uses public opinion to prevent her being sold instead of set free as she had been promised (11). Brent speaks of her grandmother's presence as standing between her and her would-be seducer: "Her presence in the neighborhood was some protection to me. Though she had been a slave, Dr. Flint was afraid of her. He dreaded her scorching rebukes. Moreover, she was known and patronized by many people; and he did not wish to have his villainy made public. It was lucky for me that I did not live on a distant plantation, but in a town" (29).

18. Douglass's testimony is again apt: "A city slave is almost a freeman, compared with a slave on the plantation. He is better fed and clothed, and enjoys privileges altogether unknown to the slave on the plantation" (*Narrative*, 79).

19. Ira Berlin, *Slaves without Masters: The Free Negro in the Antebellum South* (New York & London: Oxford University Press, 1974), 136.

20. Ibid., 90–103. It was not unusual for free blacks to be reenslaved. In some times and places persons who could not prove they were free were assumed to be slaves. Often free blacks were intentionally sold into slavery. This says nothing about disfranchisement or curtailing of rights in countless other ways.

21. Osofsky, *Making of a Ghetto*, 29.

22. Given the fact that whites' annual income was significantly higher and that

whites' rents were significantly lower than those of blacks, it is no wonder that rent parties were such a common phenomenon. "Rents, traditionally high in Harlem, reached astounding proportions in the 1920s—they skyrocketed in response to the unprecedented demand created by heavy Negro migration and settlement within a restricted geographical area. . . . In 1919 the average Harlemite paid somewhat above $21 or $22 a month for rent; by 1927 rentals had *doubled* and the 'mean average market rent for Negro tenants in a typical block' was $41.77. In 1927 Harlem Negroes paid $8 more than the typical New Yorker for a three-room apartment; $10 more for four rooms; and $7 more for five rooms, an Urban League survey noted" (Osofsky, *Making of a Ghetto*, 136).

23. Langston Hughes, *The Big Sea* (New York: Hill & Wang, 1963), 233.

24. It is probably true that the rent party was especially for Hughes a summoning up of village values. Early in Hughes's life, his biographer Arnold Rampersad tells us, Hughes "had begun to identify not his family but the poorest and most despised blacks as the object of his ultimate desire to please. He would *need* the race, and would need to appease the race, to an extent felt by few other blacks, and by no other important black writer." *The Life of Langston Hughes, 1902–1941: I, Too, Sing America* (New York: Oxford University Press, 1986), I: 22; see chap. 1, "A Kansas Boyhood."

25. Hughes, *The Big Sea*, 233.

26. Lewis, *When Harlem*, 107.

27. Quoted in Robert Hayden, "Preface to the Atheneum Edition" of *The New Negro*, ed. Alain Locke (New York: Atheneum, 1970), xi.

28. See "Biographical Notes," *The Poetry of the Negro*, 389–409.

29. Quoted in Nathan Irvin Huggins, *The Harlem Renaissance* (New York: Oxford University Press, 1971), 100.

30. Locke, *The New Negro*, 53.

31. Quoted in Osofsky, *Making of a Ghetto*, 146.

32. Cary D. Wintz observes: "at least in some ways black writers achieved a parity with their editors and with the white literary world in the late 1920s. While it is important not to read too much into this, the popularity of black writers during the hey-day of the Renaissance gave them a freedom and, at least in literary areas, an equality which has rarely been seen in any area of American life." See *Black Culture and the Harlem Renaissance* (Houston: Rice University Press, 1988), 172.

33. Houston Baker, Jr., directly discusses the question of the Renaissance's failure in *Modernism and the Harlem Renaissance* (Chicago: University of Chicago Press, 1987), 9–14. In Baker's view the Renaissance never failed but projects its influence forward in time and space beyond the twenties and into the present and far beyond the borders of the United States into the Caribbean, Africa, and South Africa. See Baker's note 71, p. 115.

34. Huggins, *Harlem Renaissance*, 303.

3

The City and Richard Wright's Quest for Freedom

YOSHINOBU HAKUTANI

ONE of the central themes in nineteenth-century American fiction was for a white man to leave his community in quest of pastoral peace of mind. Not only was he able to live in harmony with nature, but he would find a bosom friend in the stranger, a dark-skinned man from whom he learned the values of life he had never known. Natty Bumppo in James Fenimore Cooper's Leather-Stocking novels makes such friendship with Chingachgook and Hard-Heart, noble savages of the American wilderness. Ishmael in *Moby-Dick* is ritualistically wedded to Queequeg, a pagan from the South Seas. Huck Finn discovers a father figure in Jim, a runaway slave. In modern African-American fiction, on the contrary, a black man is deeply suspicious of the pastoral scene. He finds the rural South a living hell and dreams of the northern city as deliverance from racial prejudice and exclusion. Richard Wright, while being careful not to romanticize American urban life, shows that a black man who finds the city a better place to live in than the rural community which has defined his past can succeed in creating the self in the city.

Wright's desire to create the self in his own life is well documented in his autobiography *Black Boy*. His success in fictionalizing such an impulse is also evident in his other work, particularly *Native Son* and *The Outsider*. "Reduced to its simplest and most general terms," he asserts in "Blueprint for Negro Writing," "themes for Negro writers will rise from understanding the meaning of their being transplanted from a 'savage' to a 'civilized' culture in all of its social, political, economic, and emotional implications."[1] By what Wright calls the savage culture, he means the origin of black people in Africa as well as the history of slavery in the South. By the civilized culture, he implies the promised land of the American city in the North after the slaves' emancipation.

Although the motive for a white man's quest for the pastoral idylls has little to do with race, his urgent need, nonetheless, is to escape from some sort of social and emotional tension he suffers in living with other individuals. In *Moby-Dick* Ishmael confesses his motive for becoming a whale hunter: "especially whenever my hypos get such an upper hand of me, that it requires a strong moral principle to prevent me from deliberately stepping into the street, and methodically knocking people's hats off—then, I account it high time to get to sea as soon as I can."[2] The root of Ishmael's anxiety is the crush of individuals that occurs in a crowded community; Ishmael's action betrays the basic elements of national character—individualism and freedom.

If a white man wanted to exercise the rights of liberty and individuality, it would be nothing unusual in modern America that a black man also would desire to acquire such privileges. One of the causes for black men in Wright's work to move from a rural to an urban environment is precisely the absence of individuality and independence within the black community in the South. More than any other book, *Black Boy* is a criticism of the black community, where people are united by race and religion but they are not encouraged to generate the spirit of individualism. Clearly the young Wright rebelled against such tradition. For those who did not seek independence and freedom, such a community would be a haven. Ralph Ellison has observed:

> In some communities every one is "related" regardless of blood-ties. The regard shown by the group for its members, its general communal character and its cohesion are often mentioned. For by comparison with the cold impersonal relationships of the urban industrial community, its relationships are personal and warm.[3]

To Wright, however, such an environment in the South does not produce meaningful relationships among people and it is even detrimental to the creation of manhood.

The lack of individuality among black people in the South has taken a heavy toll on black character. The oppressive system, Wright observes in *12 Million Black Voices,* "created new types of behavior and new patterns of psychological reaction, welding us together into a separate unity with common characteristics of our own."[4] He provides an illustration of this behavior so familiar to plantation owners:

If a white man stopped a black on a southern road and asked: "Say,
there, boy! It's one o'clock, isn't it?" the black man would answer:
"Yessuh."

If the white man asked: "Say, it's not one o'clock, is it, boy?" the black
man would answer: "Nawsuh."

And if the white man asked: "It's ten miles to Memphis, isn't it, boy?"
the black man would answer: "Yessuh."

And if the white man asked: "It isn't ten miles to Memphis, is it, boy?"
the black man would answer: "Nawsuh."

Always we said what we thought the whites wanted us to say. (*Black
Voices* 41)

What Wright calls "the steady impact of the plantation system"
also was on the education of black children. In many southern states
the white authorities edited the textbooks which black children were
allowed to use. These textbooks automatically deleted any references
to government, constitution, voting, citizenship, and civil rights. The
school authorities uniformly stated that such foreign languages as
French, Spanish, and Latin were not suitable for black children to
learn. This provincial policy is reminiscent of the famous scene in
Adventures of Huckleberry Finn in which Jim cannot understand why
a Frenchman cannot speak English.[5] Failing to convince Jim that there
are languages other than English and cultures other than English and
American, Huck utters in frustration with a sense of irony: "I see it
warn't no use wasting words—you can't learn a nigger to argue" (79).
In *12 Million Black Voices,* Wright reports that white men "become
angry when they think that we desire to learn more than they want
us to" (64).

To Wright, the effect of white subjugation in the South was most
visible in the black communities of the Mississippi delta. By the time
he became fourteen he was able to read and write well enough to
obtain a job, in which he assisted an illiterate black insurance sales-
man. On his daily rounds to the shacks and plantations in the area,
he was appalled by the pervasiveness of segregated life: "I saw a bare,
bleak pool of black life and I hated it; the people were alike, their
homes were alike, and their farms were alike."[6] Such observations
later infuriated not only white segregationists, but many black citizens
who wrote letters to the FBI and denounced *Black Boy.* Some letters
called him "a black Nazi" and "one of the biggest spreaders of race
hatred." Another black protester complained: "I am an American Negro and proud of it because we colored people in America have come
a long way in the last seventy years. . . . We colored people don[']t
mind the truth but we do hate lies or anything that disturb[s] our
peace of mind."[7]

This absence of individuality and self-awareness among black people in the South often leads to the compromise of their character. Individually, Fishbelly and his father in The Long Dream are powerless in asserting themselves. Although they are not forced to cooperate with the white police, greed often sacrifices their moral integrity. They are fully aware that their illicit political connections will make them as wealthy as the whites. What is worse, not only politics but sex is dealt with in its sordid context: the hero's ritual of initiation into manhood is performed in a house of prostitution.[8]

Even though some black men are able to escape the southern environment and move to the industrial city in the North, they find it difficult to rid themselves of the corrupting system they have learned in the South. Jake Jackson of Lawd Today, one of the most despicable black characters Wright ever created, is tempted to do anything if he can make money. Although he is not capable of reasoning or independent observation, he is capable of deceiving others. He approves of graft as a way of life in the city for anyone to get ahead; he admires people who can profit by accepting bribes. He even envies gangsters who can wield their power to intimidate the strong and the weak alike. "I always said," Jake boasts, "that we colored folks ought to stick with the rich white folks."[9] What unites people like Fishbelly Tucker and Jake Jackson is the fact that though they can escape and, like the protagonist of Black Boy and Big Boy in "Big Boy Leaves Home," can become considerably free from the racial strictures in their lives, they ultimately fail to find themselves. Even though they are physically free of the subjugating system, mentally they have failed to become individuals with autonomy and integrity.

Wright told Irving Howe that "only through struggle could men with black skins, and for that matter, all the oppressed of the world, achieve their humanity."[10] To Wright, freedom for black people can become a reality only when all black people acquire independent visions as outsiders. No matter how courageous Silas, a black farmer in "Long Black Song," may appear, his fight against the oppressors makes little impact on the black liberation as a whole because his rebellion is motivated by a private matter.[11] The black emancipation from the rural South, Wright warns, must be accompanied by the vision of the outsider. Ely Houston, New York district attorney, in The Outsider speaks as Wright's mouthpiece:

Negroes, as they enter our culture, are going to inherit the problems we have, but with a difference. They are outsiders, and they are going to know that they have these problems. They are going to be self-conscious;

they are going to be gifted with a double vision, for, being Negroes, they are going to be both *inside* and *outside* of our culture at the same time.[12]

Houston's admonition can be easily heeded by a black intellectual like Cross Damon, but to most of Wright's uneducated black men the fear of persecution is what threatens their freedom and existence. In *Black Boy* Wright is continually at pains to show that white people had a preconceived notion of a black man's place in the South: the black man serves white people, he is likely to steal, and he cannot read or write. A black man was not likely to be executed for petty theft; there were relatively few restrictions on the subjects he was allowed to discuss with white men. Even sex and religion were the most accepted subjects of conversation, for they were the topics that did not require positive knowledge or self-assertion on the part of the black man. Interracial sex, however, was taboo, and black men risked their lives if they were caught in the act. "So volatile and tense," Wright says in "How 'Bigger' Was Born," "are these relations that if a Negro rebels against rule and taboo, he is lynched and the reason for the lynching is usually called 'rape,' that catchword which has garnered such vile connotations that it can raise a mob anywhere in the South pretty quickly, even today."[13]

This fear of persecution is most poignantly expressed in *Lawd Today*: a group of southern-born black men gaze lasciviously at the carelessly exposed thighs of a white woman sitting obliquely across the aisle on a train. The taboo of interracial sex is defined in a quatrain improvised alternately by Jake and his three companions:

> Finally, Jake rolled his eyes heavenward and sang in an undertone:
> "*Oh, Lawd, can I ever, can I ever? . . .*"
> Bob screwed up his eyes, shook his head, and answered ruefully:
> "*Naw, nigger, you can never, you can never. . . .*"
> Slim sat bolt upright, smiled, and countered hopefully:
> "*But wherever there's life there's hope. . . .*"
> Al dropped his head, frowned, and finished mournfully:
> "*And wherever there's trees there's rope.*" (96–97)

Although this scene is portrayed with humor, it represents the deepest fear any black man can have.[14]

It is well documented that the principal motive behind black people's exodus from the rural South to the industrial North is their quest for freedom and equality. Wright himself, a victim of racial prejudice and hatred in the South, fled to Chicago in search of the kind of freedom he had never experienced in the feudal South. "For the first time in our lives," he writes in *12 Million Black Voices*, "we feel human bodies, strangers whose lives and thoughts are unknown to us, pressing always close about us" (100). In stark contrast to the situation in the South where black people were not allowed to communicate freely with white citizens, the crowded and noisy apartments in the northern cities have become hubs of interracial mingling and communication, the place where the migrant black people come in close contact with "the brisk, clipped men of the North, the Bosses of Buildings." Unlike the southern landlords, the city businessmen, Wright discovered, are not "at all *indifferent*. They are deeply concerned about us, but in a new way" (100).

In the industrial city a black man functions as part of a "machine." Unlike his life in the rural South, which depends upon "the soil, the sun, the rain, or the wind," his life is controlled by what Wright calls "the grace of jobs and the brutal logic of jobs" (*Black Voices* 100). By living and working ever so closely with the white bourgeoisie, the minority workers in the city strive to learn the techniques of the bourgeoisie. Consequently, Wright notes, black workers "display a greater freedom and initiative in pushing their claims upon civilization than even do the petty bourgeoisie" ("Blueprint" 54). The harsh conditions under which black workers must produce and compete with white workers became an incentive to achieve a higher social and economic status. In short, the black man of the industrial North is given a chance to shape his own life. Economically man is a machine and his production is measured not by his race, but by his merit.

Clearly, the businessmen of the city are not concerned about the welfare of the black workers recently fled from the rural South. Like the self-proclaimed philanthropist Dalton in *Native Son,* they take an interest in the black people because their business would prosper if the black men's economic status improves. Focusing on such economic facts in the city, Wright carefully creates a character like Dalton, a symbol for the ambivalent and contradictory ways of the city. Mr. Dalton thus has given millions for social welfare, especially for the NAACP, and ostensibly donated money to buy ping-pong tables for black children. Bigger Thomas does not know this, nor is he aware that Mr. Dalton's contribution comes from the exorbitant rents charged to the black tenants living in his overcrowded and rat-infested apartments. However ironic this may be, the fact remains that Bigger feels grateful for getting a job and that, for him at least, his employer does not appear a racist. Despite the severe living conditions in which black people are placed, the fierce competitions they face,[15] and the traumas they suffer, the city nevertheless provides them with possibilities of freedom and equality.

What impressed Wright when he arrived in Chicago from the deep

South was the relative absence of discrimination. "It was strange," he writes in *American Hunger,* "to pause before a crowded newsstand and buy a newspaper without having to wait until a white man was served."[16] Although he was allowed to sit beside white men and women on a streetcar as are Jake Jackson and his black companions in *Lawd Today,* he began to feel "a different sort of tension than I had known before. I knew that this machine-city was governed by strange laws" (2). *American Hunger* also intimates an episode which suggests that some white citizens were not as much obsessed with the problems of race as southerners, and that a black man is often treated by the white citizens as an equal.[17] One time, Wright obtained employment as a porter in a Jewish delicatessen and felt he had to lie about his absence from that job to take his civil service examination for a better paying job in the post office. But it turned out that his employer would have gladly consented for him to take the examination and that he would not have had to lie about something so important and beneficial to the employee. In *The Outsider* the realistic details woven in the life of a postal worker, Cross Damon, are those of the problems caused by living in the city. Cross is not in any way handicapped in his life or work because he is a black man. He is physically and mentally a tired man; he is bored with routine work just as are his fellow workers, black or white. Because of an early and unfortunate marriage, he has to support a wife he does not love, and their children; he also has a pregnant mistress who is trying to force him to marry her. To forget his miseries he takes to drinking. But such problems have little to do with Cross's being a black man.

Earning a livelihood in industrialized society as does Cross Damon, however, takes a heavy toll of his life. Like Sartre's Mathieu, Cross finds himself in a state of incomprehensible disorder and meaninglessness. To black men such as Cross Damon and Fred Daniels of "The Man Who Lived Underground," the city takes the appearance of a labyrinthine metropolis, where the pervading mood is aimlessness, loneliness, and lack of communication. If man is treated as a machine, he is not expected to communicate or intermingle with his fellow human beings. The controlling image of Wright's city is that of a crowded place inhabited by the people, black and white, who are alienated by displacement and industrialization.

The dehumanizing influences of urban life upon non-intellectuals like Bigger Thomas make their personality warp and harden. In the heart of Chicago, Wright witnessed numerous examples of the Bigger Thomas type—nervous, fearful, frustrated. "The urban environment of Chicago," Wright recalls, "affording a more stimulating life, made the Negro Bigger Thomases react more violently than even in the

South. More than ever I began to see and understand the environmental factors which made for this extreme conduct" ("How 'Bigger' Was
Born" xv). These black youths, moreover, are alienated not only from
the white civilization, but from their own race. Based on this reality,
Bigger is depicted as "resentful toward whites, sullen, angry, ignorant,
emotionally unstable, depressed and unaccountably elated at times,
and unable even, because of his own lack of inner organization which
American oppression has fostered in him, to unite with the members
of his own race" ("How 'Bigger' Was Born" xxi).

While Bigger Thomas of *Native Son,* buttressed by Wright's own
experience in Chicago, is depicted as a hero able to transcend these
obstacles of city life and gain self-confidence, another black man, Jake
Jackson of *Lawd Today,* is presented as a degenerate character largely
unaware that industrialization and capitalism have hopelessly corrupted his soul. Wright makes it clear that while Jake is not legally a
criminal as is Bigger, Jake is a latter-day slave. If Jake is a victim of
the economic system, he is also a worshiper of the shoddy values of
the system that exploits him. Jake and Bigger are both the products
of the same civilization, but Jake, unlike Bigger, is incapable of transcending the dreadful effects of the environment.[18]

Even though the dominant influences of the urban environment
on the black men lead to dehumanization and isolation, the same
environment can provide them with avenues for transcendence. In
fact, Chicago, New York, and later Paris, unlike the southern cities,
offered Wright education, free access to libraries, political affiliation,
and introduction to realist writers such as Theodore Dreiser, Sinclair
Lewis, and John Dos Passos, and French existentialist novelists such
as Sartre and Camus. It is a well-known fact that Wright learned how
to write fiction by associating with the John Reed Club of Chicago, a
leftist writers' organization. Not only did he find intellectual stimulation in Communist philosophy, but also, as Blyden Jackson points out,
he found among the members of the Communist party the warm and
sustained relationships, the lack of which was the cause of his loneliness in the South.[19]

On the one hand, Wright's ideological fascination with communism
is overtly expressed in such early short stories as "Fire and Cloud"
and "Bright and Morning Star," which take place in the southern
environment. The chief reason Wright joined the Communist party
was not his belief in the economics of communism, nor his attraction
to trade unionism, nor his curiosity about its underground politics.
His vision was the possibility of uniting the isolated and oppressed
people all over the world. His own experience in the cities had convinced him that industrialization and commercialization lead people

to isolation and loneliness. On the other hand, his personal attraction to communism is alluded to in *The Outsider*. After accidentally gaining a new identity, Cross Damon leaves Chicago for New York, a cosmopolitan city, where he befriends a Communist couple, the Blounts, not because of sympathy for their ideology, but simply because he finds in them urbanity, liberalism, and lack of racial bigotry, the qualities he had not earlier found in white people. To a total stranger in a huge metropolis, the sudden appearance of the Blounts, who offer him food, shelter, and companionship, is indeed an oasis.

As an artist, however, Wright in his own life became disillusioned with the Communist party. To his dismay he learned that the Party insisted on discipline over truth, and that factionalism within the Party pre-empted dialogue and criticism. The Party was primarily interested in a fledgling writer as long as his imaginative ability would result in the writing of pamphlets acceptable to the Party principles. "It was inconceivable to me," he wrote, "though bred in the lap of southern hate, that a man could not have his say. I had spent a third of my life travelling from the place of my birth to the North just to talk freely, to escape the pressure of fear" (*American Hunger* 92). Not only did he find the Party practice repressive, but he realized that blind adherence to Communist ideology would leave the artist little room for concentration and reflection. "The conditions under which I had to work," Wright felt, "were what baffled them. Writing had to be done in loneliness and Communism had declared war upon human loneliness" (123).

In *The Outsider* Cross Damon murders not only the Fascist landlord, but also the Communist associate, a symbolic act of terror in asserting himself. If his New York landlord is a painful reminder of the Ku Klux Klansmen of the South, his Communist companion equally stands in the way on the road to his freedom and independence. Now with Eva, the wife of the murdered Communist, in his arms, Cross reflects on this climactic action:

> They'll think I did it because of Eva! No; Communists were not unintelligent; they could not seriously think that. There was one thing of which he was certain: they would never credit him with as much freedom to act as they had. A certain psychological blindness seemed to be the hallmark of all men who had to create their own worlds. . . . All other men were mere material for them; they could admit no rivals, no equals, other men were either above them or below them. (369)

Unlike Clyde Griffiths in Dreiser's *An American Tragedy*, a victim of the materialistic civilization, Cross Damon has learned through his murders how to exercise his will. And before death he is finally able to declare his independence.

Similarly, the last word in *Native Son* is not expressed by the white authorities who hold Bigger in jail, nor the white liberals who are sympathetic to black people. The final statement is given not by the Communist lawyer Max, but by Bigger, a black man who has at last achieved his goal in life:

> "What I killed for must've been good!" Bigger's voice was full of fren-zied anguish. "It must have been good! When a man kills, it's for some-thing. . . . I didn't know I was really alive in this world until I felt things hard enough to kill for 'em. . . . It's the truth, Mr. Max. I can say it now, 'cause I'm going to die." (392)

Bigger's dismissal of the Reverend Hammond's attempt to console the accused before the trial is also a symbolic act, which suggests the black man's rejection of religion. In the same way, Cross rejects his mother, the product of southern Negro piety.[20] Cross, like Bigger, rejects the traditional Christianity in the South, for it taught black children subservient ethics. It is only natural that Cross should rebel against such a mother, who moans, "To think I named you Cross after the Cross of Jesus" (*Outsider* 23). Both men reject religion because in a complex modern society it functions only as a ritual; it offers only irrational escape, blind flight from reality. Both men, having con-quered the forces of the urban environment, have now severed them-selves from the last remnants of the religious and political influences upon them as well. They both have become rugged individualists, the willed creators of their past, present, and future in a chaotic and hostile world.[21]

But Cross's search for meaning in his life is a departure from Big-ger's achievement of manhood. In Chicago, the problem of race, the avowed conflict between black and white people, becomes the catalyst for Bigger's manhood. In New York, the issue which torments Cross is not the conflict of race; the larger issue he faces is man's existence or annihilation. In creating Cross, Wright departed from the social issues confronting a black man and asked the universal question of what man is. In terms of plot, the accidental killing of a white woman in *Native Son* whets Bigger's creative impulses. To Cross, on the other hand, Eva, only incidentally a white woman, becomes an essence he tries to find in the meaningless existence. Cross has fallen in love with Eva because they both suffer from the same wound; she was forced to marry a man she did not love just as Cross was once married to a woman he did not love. For Cross the consummation of his love for

Eva means the ultimate purpose of his new life. It is understandable that when that goal appears within reach and yet is taken away from him, he finds only "the horror" that he had dreaded all his life (Outsider 440).

Although both men seek freedom and independence in their lives, what they find at the end of their lives, the visions which they gain before death, are poles apart. Bigger's last words, "I didn't know I was really alive in this world until I felt things hard enough to kill for 'em" (Native Son 392), signal the affirmation of life. Cross, tasting his agonizing defeat and dying, utters:

> "I wish I had some way to give the meaning of my life to others. . . . To make a bridge from man to man . . . Starting from scratch every time is . . . is no good. Tell them not to come down this road. . . . Men hate themselves and it makes them hate others. . . .We must find some way of being good to ourselves. . . . Man is all we've got. . . . But certainly differ-ent . . . We're strangers to ourselves." (Outsider 439)

Whereas Bigger's vision is full of joy and hope, Cross's is tinged with sadness and estrangement.

In general, critics have regarded Wright's philosophy in The Out-sider as existential. Noting Cross's action to kill without passion and his indifference to the emotions of others, they have called the philoso-phy of this metaphysical rebel most consistently nihilistic.[22] To some readers, moreover, Cross represents "the moral and emotional failure of the age."[23] The reason for calling Cross nihilistic lies in his unchar-acteristic remark in the novel: "Maybe man is nothing in particular" (Outsider 135). Cross's statement, however, seems to be based upon Wright's world view, the philosophy of the absurd, which was in vogue after World War II. Existentialists, and nihilists in particular, are convinced of the essential absurdity of human existence, but Cross is not. If one judges life as inherently meaningful as Cross does, then it follows that his action to seek love, friendship, and freedom on earth also is meaningful. Cross is passionately in search of order, eter-nity, and meaning. In the light of his actions in the novel, not in view of Wright's occasional philosophy, Cross ends his life as a failed humanist rather than a nihilist.

As Wright endowed Bigger Thomas with the capacity to assert his freedom and independence, Wright also endowed Cross Damon with the power to create an essence. On the one hand, Bigger, despite his lack of education, has challenged and transcended the unjust forces of the urban environment. On the other, placed under the cosmopolitan climate where he is able to shed the last vestiges of the obsolete

Christian ethics as well as the stifling Marxist ideology, Cross stumbles onto the philosophy of existentialism. Rejecting such a philosophy, however, he has instead defined his own way of life. His revolt is not so much against the nothingness and meaninglessness of existence as it is against the inability of man's attempt to make illogical phenomena logical. Despite his own failure, the revelation he gains at the end of his life suggests the possibilities of harmony and love among all men. Bigger and Cross have walked different avenues in the city, but in the end they have both been able to "uphold the concept of what it means to be human" in America.[24]

NOTES

1. Richard Wright, "Blueprint for Negro Writing," *New Challenge* 2 (Fall 1937): 62–63.

2. Herman Melville, *Moby-Dick*, ed. Charles Fiedelson, Jr. (Indianapolis: Bobbs-Merrill, 1964), 23.

3. Ralph Ellison, "Richard Wright's Blues," *Antioch Review* 5 (June 1945): 208.

4. Richard Wright, *12 Million Black Voices* (New York: Viking, 1941), 41. Subsequent references to this book are given in parentheses.

5. In an attempt to teach Jim that English is not the only language spoken on earth, Huck says:

"S'pose a man was to come to you and say Polly-voo-franzy— what would you think?"

"I wouldn't think nuffin; I'd take en bust him over de head—dat is, if he warn't white. I wouldn't 'low no nigger to call me dat."

"Shucks, it ain't calling you anything. It's only saying, do you know how to talk French?"

"Well, den, why couldn't he say it?"

"Why, he is a-saying it. That's a Frenchman's *way* of saying it."

See *Adventures of Huckleberry Finn* (Boston: Houghton Mifflin, 1962), 79.

6. Richard Wright, *Black Boy* (New York: Harper & Row, 1945), 151. Subsequent references to this book are given in parentheses.

7. Addison Gayle, *Richard Wright: Ordeal of a Native Son* (Garden City, N.Y.: Anchor Press/Doubleday, 1980), 173–74. According to Gayle, Senator Bilbo of Mississippi condemned *Black Boy* on the floor of the U.S. Senate on 7 June 1954: it is "the dirtiest, filthiest, lousiest, most obscene piece of writing that I have ever seen in print . . . it is so filthy and dirty . . . it comes from a Negro, and you cannot expect any better from a person of his type" (173).

8. "Fire and Cloud," Wright's earlier short story, also deals with the corruption of the black leadership in southern cities.

9. Richard Wright, *Lawd Today* (New York: Walker, 1963), 160. Later references to this novel are given in parentheses.

10. Irving Howe, "Black Boys and Native Sons," *A World More Attractive* (New York: Horizon, 1963), 109.

11. I agree with Edward Margolies, who says: "Yet Silas's redemption is at best a private affair—and the Negro's plight is no better as a result of his own determination to fight his oppressors with their own weapons. He is hopelessly outnumbered."

See Edward Margolies, *The Art of Richard Wright* (Carbondale: Southern Illinios University Press, 1969), 67.

12. Richard Wright, *The Outsider* (New York: Harper & Row, 1953), 129. Subsequent references to this novel are given in parentheses.

13. Richard Wright, "How 'Bigger' Was Born," in *Native Son* (New York: Harper & Row, 1940), xii.

14. Horace Cayton, a sociologist and Wright's close friend and associate, observes that for a black man "punishment in the actual environment is ever present; violent, psychological and physical, leaps out at him from every side." See Horace Cayton, "Discrimination—America: Frightened Children of Frightened Parents," *Twice-a-Year* 12–13 (Spring/Summer/Fall/Winter 1945): 264.

15. The competition the black man faces in the city creates a tension quite different in nature from the tension in the segregated South. One of Jake's friends in *Lawd Today* says: "The only difference between the North and the South is, them guys down there'll kill you, and those up here'll let you starve to death" (156).

16. Richard Wright, *American Hunger* (New York: Harper & Row, 1977), 1–2. Subsequent references to this book are given in parentheses.

17. Besides liberals such as the Hoffmans, the Jewish delicatessen owner, undergound gangsters also treated black people with equality and compassion, as Wright notes in *12 Million Black Voices*: "through the years our loyalty to these gangster-politicians remains staunch because they are almost the only ones who hold out their hand to help us, whatever their motives. . . . The most paradoxical gift ever tendered to us black folk in the city is aid from the underworld, from the gangster, from the political thief" (121–22).

18. Jake Jackson among Wright's characters is often the object of disparaging remarks by critics, but there are some notable exceptions. Granville Hicks affectionately defended *Lawd Today*, calling it less powerful than *Native Son* and *Black Boy*, but uniquely interesting. What interested Hicks is that although Wright was an avowed Communist at the time he wrote the novel, he did not make a Communist out of Jake Jackson. Jake even despised communism, Hicks points out, and refused to become a victim of the capitalist system, either. Jake was delineated as uneducated, frustrated, and "erring but alive" (37–38). Lewis Leary, regarding Jake as a caricature of the white world, calls him "incongruously, enduringly alive." See Lewis Leary, "*Lawd Today*: Notes on Richard Wright's First/Last Novel," *CLA Journal* 15 (June 1972): 420.

19. Blyden Jackson, "Richard Wright: Black Boy from America's Black Belt and Urban Ghettos," *CLA Journal* 12 (June 1969): 301.

20. While Wright dismisses Christianity as useless for black people's freedom and independence, he values the black church in the city because it enhances their community life. In *12 Million Black Voices*, he observes: "Despite our new worldliness, despite our rhythms, our colorful speech, and our songs, we keep our churches alive. . . . Our churches are centers of social and community life, for we have virtually no other mode of communion and we are usually forbidden to worship God in the temples of the Bosses of the Buildings. The church is the door through which we first walked into Western civilization" (130–31).

21. Margaret Walker, a fellow black novelist who knew Wright well, writes: "Wright's philosophy was that fundamentally all men are potentially evil. . . . Human nature and human society are determinants and, being what he is, man is merely a pawn caught between the worlds of necessity and freedom. . . . All that he has to use in his defense and direction of his existence are (1) his reason and (2) his will." See Margaret Walker, "Richard Wright," *New Letters* 38 (Winter 1971): 198–99.

22. Charles I. Glicksberg, in "Existentialism in *The Outsider*," *Four Quarters* 7 (January 1958): 17–26, and in "The God of Fiction," *Colorado Quarterly* 7 (Autumn 1956): 207–20, saw parallels between Wright and Camus in the treatment of their existential heroes. Michel Fabre, Wright's biographer, specifically indicates that Wright's composition of *The Outsider* "was influenced in subtle ways by his reading of *The Stranger* in August 1947. He read the book in the American edition at a very slow pace, 'weighing each sentence,' admiring 'its damn good narrative prose,' and remarked:

> It is a neat job but devoid of passion. He makes his point with dispatch and his prose is solid and good. In America a book like this would not attract much attention for it would be said that he lacks feeling. He does however draw his character very well. What is of course really interesting in this book is the use of fiction to express a philosophical point of view. That he does with ease. I now want to read his other stuff."

See Michel Fabre, "Richard Wright, French Existentialism, and *The Outsider*," in *Critical Essays on Richard Wright*, ed. Yoshinobu Hakutani (Boston: G. K. Hall, 1982), 191.

23. Edward Margolies in his comparison of Damon and Meursault, the hero of *The Stranger*, points out the similarities between the two characters. See Edward Margolies, *The Art of Richard Wright*, 135.

24. Quoted from Wright's unpublished journal, 7 September 1947, in which he wrote: "Sartre is quite of my opinion regarding the possibility of human action today, that it is up to the individual to do what he can to uphold the concept of what it means to be human" (Fabre 186).

4

"No Street Numbers in Accra": Richard Wright's African Cities

JACK B. MOORE

Two strong images of African life are projected in Richard Wright's *Black Power*[1] before he begins explaining why he wanted to travel to his ancestors' homeland, and both refer to an older, non-urban Africa. He dedicates his book "TO THE UNKNOWN AFRICAN . . . who, alone in the forests of West Africa, created a vision of life so simple as to be terrifying, yet a vision that was irreducibly human." The anthropological validity of Wright's thinking that earlier African life vision is "simple" is questionable, but his picture of the "primal" African existing far outside the city is clear.

Next, he quotes an excerpt from Countee Cullen's famous poem "Heritage," in which the black American search for identity transports "One three centuries removed / From the scenes his fathers loved" back to a land remembered as jungle, a terrain of the mind that possessed a "Jungle star" and "jungle track" when it was a kind of paradise where "birds of Eden sang." The place seems like a version of the pastoral replete with a "Spicy grove" and "cinnamon tree": Africa before the white man, before colonial empires, before the age of technology. Although Africa contained vast and great cities before whites seized political control of the continent, Wright does not mention these yet. The Africa that captivates his dreams is peopled with "Strong bronzed men, or regal black / Women" who are jungle people, free people. His own progress to manhood, humanity, and artistry directed him away from small towns and agricultural regions to big cities like Chicago, New York, and Paris. Trying to find out "am I African?" (10) he would soon voyage to Accra, the Gold Coast's (or Ghana's) biggest city, no forest or jungle of Edenic flocks and sweet redolence. And that posed problems for Richard Wright.

At the start of *Black Power*, Wright describes himself sitting at lunch in the city of his choice, Paris, on a quiet, pleasant day. He is sipping coffee and staring "at the gray walls of the University of Paris that loomed beyond" his window when Dorothy Padmore asks him why doesn't he go to Africa? His answer, "*Africa?*" is italicized indi-cating his shock. "But that's four thousand miles away!" he protests. He describes himself feeling "on the defensive, feeling poised on the verge of the unknown." The intensity of his response is caused partly by the disparity between the city where he is placed—Paris, here presented as a city of calm and beauty, Paris in the spring (it is Easter Sunday and "footfalls from the tranquil Paris street below echoed upward")—and the terra incognito that frightens him even as it lures him to it, "as something strange and disturbing stirred slowly in the depths of me" (9). Africa is the land of mystery, "fabulous and remote: heat, jungle, rain" (10). Paris is one of the most culturally distin-guished cities of Western civilization, a symbol of great art, tradition-ally a city treasured as a center of learning (suggested by the great and ancient school whose walls Wright says "loomed" near). Great distance separates this Paris in Wright's mind from the cities of the Gold Coast: "Cape Coast, Elmina, Accra, Kumasi" which are for him not even cities but only "strange place names" he thinks of after "conjuring up" the jungle (12). Yet the story he will tell in *Black Power* is a narrative of a trip to the city, the African city.

First Wright had to travel through two English cities which, like Paris, represent something of the Western world that had been his home. London and Liverpool illustrate the unpleasantness, the cruelty and exploitiveness that hopefully he would not find duplicated in the Gold Coast. London is cold so that in his boat-train Wright "huddled in his macintosh" and longed for the heavy coat he had packed in his trunk. His discomfort in London partly results from the cold, partly from viewing the depressing landscape outside his train window which he says "was as bleak as any described by D. H. Lawrence or Arnold Bennett or George Moore" (13). London is a counter image to his imagined picture of the warm Gold Coast which, according to the *Encyclopedia Britannica* he consulted, "was vivid, replete with dangerous reptiles, gold, and diamonds . . . and teemed with mineral and agricultural wealth" (12), another image of African land outside the cities.

Liverpool "was the city that had been the center and focal point of the slave trade; it was here that most of the slavers had been organized, fitted out, financed and dispatched with high hopes on their infamous but lucrative voyages" (13). Liverpool had sent ships to Africa and then across the Atlantic between 1783 and 1793, carrying more than 300,000 slaves "whose sterling value has been estimated as being over fifteen million pounds" (17). Although the city looked "calm" and "innocent" now, Wright knew its "foundations . . . were built of human flesh and blood." Although skies were sunny on the June day, Wright was cold as he had been in London. English cities offered "massive and solidly built buildings" (18), visible signs of a technologically advanced civilization, but they still chilled Wright who knew the slave trade had helped build them and that "Until 1783 the whole of English society, the monarchy, church, state, and press backed and defended this trade in slaves." Even after the trade was legally abolished (if not completely stopped), the cities were main-tained by the imposition of colonial rule throughout West Africa, creating "a vast geographical prison whose inmates were presumably sentenced for all time to suffer the exploitation of their human, agricul-tural, and mineral resources" (17). And now that prison was being destroyed. No wonder Wright was excited, and apprehensive.

It is hard to know what Wright really expected to find in the Gold Coast once he actually arrived there, given that what he imagines about it depicts a pastoral Africa long past (if it ever existed) that had been replaced by an abolitionist's nightmare. The colonial West African prison he describes resembles the notorious image Stanley Elkins put forth in slavery that compared slavery to something like a concentration camp many of whose inmates learned to shuffle and grin like Sambos in order to survive, a depressingly deterministic con-cept. Just before he disembarks from his ship he tells a West African judge, "I don't expect to find anything there that's completely new," but that seems more bravado than prediction. He had by this time already seen plenty that was new in his first Gold Coast city that under its "blanket of blue mist . . . seethed with activity" even early in the morning. The "forest of derricks, cranes, sheds, machines" (33) he observes seem to mirror Wordsworth's description of London in the morning in his sonnet "Composed upon Westminster Bridge," with its "Ships, towers, domes, theatres, and temples" open to the sky. But all industrial devices Wright saw in Takoradi were operated by black men. The vision appears to corroborate a hope he had stated earlier when he conjectured what would be the consequences of colo-nialism's death since "machines had a nigger-loving way of letting even black hands operate them." Perhaps free Africans could benefit from the industrialization that for so long had fueled the growth of the West. "Africans were talking boldly of hydroelectric plants and the making of aluminum" (19).

But Wright's pleasure at seeing the activity of so many black work-ers, at being guided by Mr. Ansah who owned a lumber business employing two hundred (black) men who cut, dressed, drew, and shipped timber "to all parts of the world," at not being in the minority for once, is short lived. He is embarrassed in a modern store staffed by Africans when he is asked what part of Africa he came from and he answers he does not know, because "you fellows who sold us and the white men who bought us didn't keep any records" (35). Here Wright is wounded by something in his past and Africa's and now the city suddenly does not excite him nearly so much, nor give him cause for pleased wonder. He is glad to return to the docks, because the city's heat and humidity make him feel as though his "flesh was melting from [his] bones." He boards a government bus and rides at first "slowly through streets clogged with black life" (36). The word "clogged" suggests his feelings of gummy torpor. He could have selected many other far more positive terms—described streets vibrant or rich with black life. Even the more neutral word "crowded" would have been less despairing than "clogged," but would not have so accurately depicted the city's impact on him.

Then within a few minutes Wright leaves and learns that "African cities are small and one is in the 'bush'—the jungle—before one knows it." This is not a source of delight for him. There is in *Black Power* no expressed reverence for village life, although individual villagers please him. The "mud huts ... [n]aked black children.... Black women, naked to the waist," and finally the "rich red" soil "like that of Georgia or Mississippi" momentarily delude him "into thinking I was back in the American South." Wright seems overwhelmed but definitely not dazzled by the "kaleidoscope of sea, jungle, nudity, mud huts, and crowded market places" that cause a deep conflict within him, a "protest ... against the ... strangeness of a completely different order of life" (36). At this early moment of emotional crisis (and Wright will experience many others as he seeks black power), he has "the foolish feeling that I had but to turn my head and I'd see the ordered, clothed streets of Paris" (37). The nudity Wright objects to here seems not simply a comment on African sexuality (though he does not appear in *Black Power* to have greatly understood that) but on African lack of civilization—in the Western sense founded upon successful and power-laden use of advanced technology. The order he apparently yearns for is the proper and potent arrangement of that technology, embodied in the high civilization of Paris. When Wright left Takoradi he discovered himself soon in the bush, but what he does not acknowledge (and this will cause him greater confusion throughout his stay in the Gold Coast) is that the African city as he experiences it contains within its confines elements of the traditional life he associates with his concept of the bush or village. He observes this but he does not comprehend it.

Wright's life in the chief city of the Gold Coast, Accra, provides a greater source of disappointment than Takoradi. He recognizes little of this African city's colorful vitality but instead slogs through it daily in increasing despair. His life in Accra makes even bolder the hope he projects sporadically throughout his sojourn in the country, and almost heroic his hortatory letter to Nkrumah at his trip's end calling for a democratic revolution independent of the West (including Russia) but fought for by "The People" (351).

Accra was the Gold Coast's capital city when Wright arrived there; it sprawled flatly out from the ocean without a good port and contained about 350,000 inhabitants, most of whom were relatively poor by western standards and packed into what were originally three smaller towns once known as British, Dutch, and Danish Accra: essentially the Jamestown, Usshertown [sic], and Christiansborg sections of the more modern city. Like many of the chief West African cities during the time of Wright's visit (1953), Accra differed physically from many European cities (and the American cities Wright knew best such as New York, Chicago, perhaps Memphis) in lacking tall buildings, large enclosed spaces (like big theaters or sports arenas) and probably most importantly, extensive, mechanized industrial sectors and middle-class suburban areas. The city's sprawl was low and flat, comprised of few-storied offices and stores downtown; acres and acres of small, shed-like houses and small, rather basically constructed apartment buildings; a large, low-lying open market area and several smaller markets; and on the outskirts of the city, small pockets of wider, fine homes neatly landscaped, often owned or lived in by expatriates.

Wright's text of *Black Power* underscores the confusion he felt incessantly in Accra and the Gold Coast by not containing some coherent, broad, familiarizing vista of the city. Wright never draws back and studies its greater topographic details; he never orients the reader or himself to its generalized contours. Thus, he is never led to consider or discuss some of the African city's imminent problems, such as underemployment in an area of concentrated, accelerating population with a minuscule industrial base. I do not point this out to suggest his lack of astuteness. He was perceptive about some of Ghana's future political issues: how would a democracy evolve in a land where the will of the people had been rigidly suppressed for generations; how could that deterministic pressure be removed? How could tribal ways fit into a participatory democracy? I wish merely to describe his skill in creating (or reporting on) a personage in his text who is honestly confused by what he sees in the city but who strives to surmount his confusion to establish some link to a land he wishes to admire but is ill prepared to understand in its complexity.

Physically, Accra devastates Wright, thus diminishing the original, excited resolve he felt contemplating his trip back, and increasing his anxiety. Accra increases his doubts about Africa's chances in the new world he thought it was entering. His first morning in the city after a night's sleep in a "beautiful bungalow . . . built expressly by the British authorities for the creature comforts of the new African minis' ters" (47), he takes a taxi and plunges directly into Accra. "There were no sidewalks; one walked at the edge of a drainage ditch made of concrete in which urine ran. A stench pervaded the sunlit air" (48). He described the market (ordinarily one of the African city's most fascinating attractions) selling bits of products, with "carts piled with cheap mirrors . . . and cheaply framed photos of Hollywood movie stars" and concludes "Was it a lack of capital that made the Africans sell like this on the streets?" (49).

On this first day and frequently throughout his time in Accra, "The sun was killing" (49). His hopes for some communion with Kwame Nkrumah start caving in while the city's heat makes him feel more strongly his discomfort in the city. In the text immediately following his claim that "the Africans had been so trained to a cryptic servility that they made you act a role that you loathed, live a part that sick' ened you," he notes depressingly that "At midday when the tropic sun weighs upon your head, making you feel giddy, you discover that there are no parks in Accra, no water fountains, no shade trees, no public benches upon which one can rest from a weary walk. There are no public cafes or restaurants in which one can buy a cup of tea or coffee" (178). He does not add, nor does he have to, ". . . as there are in Paris." He finds an absence of structure in the city, which at times resembles an expressionistic landscape contorted to erase direc' tion and order. "There are no mail deliveries. You went to the post office each morning for your letters" (111). Worse, "Houses have no street numbers in Accra" (176).

He observes two funerals in Accra but no baptisms or marriages. At one funeral he sees men and women dancing and keeps asking "why?" (125–26) and at the other he watches a parade of city people with a boy carried on a palaquin and "men in red firing muskets" and as they pass he stands "feeling foolish and helpless in the hot sun," concluding "I had understood nothing, nothing" (130). Always the artist, Wright turns Accra into the embodiment of his futility. Like a man with a mouth filled with bad teeth who probes his tongue at his most exposed nerve, he moves from his cool bungalow into one of the worst sections of Accra surrounding the decrepit "Seaview" (actu'

ally "Sea View") hotel where he will reside as he waits for a call from
Nkrumah. Although the hotel is adjacent to the ocean, "No breezes
blew here to freshen the air. My skin was always oily and wet and
tiny mosquitoes bit deeply into my arms and ankles." The toilets howl
when flushed, the air is constantly humid, "there were flies, greasy
food, splattered walls." He grows accustomed, he says, to "the early
morning stench of home-made soap . . . the vapors of excrement drifting into the hotel from the open drainage ditches outside."

From his balcony he can look down and see "Africa in all its squalor,
vitality and fantastic disorder." Although he seems to enjoy watching
the fishermen at work nearby, squalor and disorder seem more apparent than vitality in the streets around the Sea View where he finds
"but a few trees," no grass, and "no flowers" (80–82) in the "maze"
or surrounding region. Even the city's wealthy black bourgeoisie who
lived at the city's fringes on paved streets in large, fine houses "enclosed by high concrete walls the tops of which held barbed wire
and jagged shards of glass to keep out intruders" had no flowers or
landscaping around their homes, according to Wright. Their houses
were widely separated and their yards "usually overgrown with weeds
or . . . bare or littered with rubbish" (179). Predictably, his depression
increases. At one point he complains, "My money is melting under
this tropic sun faster than I am soaking up the reality about me," but
his narrative demonstrates that the city is draining him also of the
ability to understand what the Africans "are thinking and feeling"
(136–37). And what surrounds him is not necessarily reality.

Because *Black Power* is ostensibly nonfiction, it is easy to consider
its descriptions of physical facts and conditions mere reporting, descriptions of a sort presumably any informed observer might make.
Elsewhere I have dealt with the benefits proceeding from an examination of the book as a novel with a central character, an outsider who
explores territory strange to him and is disconcerted by it. Even journalistic reporting, however, contains themes and motifs that need
analysis to see what patterns they fit into. Anyone writing about
West Africa might mention the heat, though it is interesting how
many of the best novels of traditional African life outside the cities
do not describe it as an overpowering force. Certainly the "Africa my
Africa" of so many nostalgic African poems is not a stupefyingly hot
land. But heat pervades Wright's memory of Accra, along with decay
to an extent which suggests that he is not simply delivering a weather
report but using these conditions symbolically as a novelist would to
describe the climate for progress in the city that is about to become
the capitol of a new land of the free—if its citizens can free themselves
of the various kinds of torpor that colonialism and tribalism have

imposed upon them. Wright seems to turn the heat into an unnatural force, though of course it is quite natural to the region, a power mortifying (in the sense of bringing to decay) the land, perverting natural life cycles: "I was told that vegetables grew so swiftly in this hot and red earth that they were not really nourishing! Lettuce re-fused" (as though it had a life and will of its own) "to form a head here. . . . Other vegetables turned into soft, pulpy masses" (206–7). It is almost as though Wright were describing that foul heat that carried with it evil, turning love into lust, that the Elizabethan playwrights and poets wrote about. Only in the Gold Coast does it operate upon other animals in the kingdom. "The heat makes insect life breed pro-lifically: mosquitoes, ants, lizards, and myriads of other creatures swarm in the air and underfoot. A lump of sugar left in a saucer will draw ants in an hour even to the second floor of a stone building" (207). The heat acts like bad magic.

Queerly, as the heat drives life forward too fast or engenders a prolixity among bugs that is treated as malfunctional to man, together with the damp it tears down man's paraphernalia of civilized exis-tence. One morning like many others in Accra, Wright awakes more tired than "When I had gone to sleep. I was gripped by an enervation that seemed to clog the pores of my skin. I was about to pull on my shoes when I discovered, to my horror, that my clothes were getting mildewed, that my shoes were beginning to turn a yellowish green color. I scraped at it; it was mold" (160). As Wright declines, he finds the city world around him rotting. In his hotel room he picks up his nail file and is shocked that it is red. Like objects in a horror film, everything in his toilet kit is "a deep, dark red. I rubbed my fingers across the metal and a soft mound or wet rust rolled up. . . . What could last here?" He wonders what would happen if the Gold Coast were isolated from the West for ten years (123). True, the Old Slave Market in Christianborg is crumbling, its walls rotting and columns broken into rubble (180), but that is made to seem not a symbol of the old life's death, but of the constant decay of matter in the city where Ghana's new life will soon be constructed and centered.

Wright also visited the Gold Coast's second largest city, Kumasi, less than half as populous as Accra at the time of his trip there. Although fewer than two hundred road miles inland northwest from the seacoast city, Kumasi seems to belong to a different world. "A brooding African city. . . . You get the feeling that the white man is far away. . . . This is the heart of historic Negrodom" (272). The ter-rain leading from Accra to Kumasi prepared Wright for a different city. The route departing from Accra after a short time spirals up a palisade from which it is possible to look down almost level with rain clouds at the flat lands leading back to the capital. The road then seems to ride the crest of this high plateau winding through some small villages before slowly curving down and then heading directly to Kumasi. Wright's taxi tunneled through heavily wooded forests dense with great, tall cotton trees whose thick, grey trunks looked hard as iron. These trees seem driven like dynamo shafts into the ground the sun's rays rarely reach. Their roots drip down from branches big as trees themselves about twenty feet up from the earth. Whole jungles of thick vines and creepers and green ferns festoon down from the lower limbs that are still much too high to scale, hairy tendrils crawling with bugs and animated by flapping insects and butterflies. The sight is striking, and it is possible to feel swallowed up by these forests, especially if one drives through them in the dusk or dark. The day I drove this route I followed for a long time a wobbling Volkswagen "Bug" whose bowlegged wheels shivered under its tottering and crumpled body. When I could finally pass its arrhyth-mic and unpredictable veering, I noticed a sign on its side saying "Safety First Driving School." About a fourth of the way to Kumasi just beyond Korforidua I saw a sign with three vultures squatting on it directing visitors to the "President Nixon Business College." I felt Wright would have appreciated these incidents.

Wright is ambivalent toward Kumasi, from which "perhaps millions of slaves were marched down to the coast and sold to white traders" but where centuries later "Negroes stood stalwart against the British in war after war" (272) culminating in the ferocious siege of British troops huddled in the fort at Kumasi after their commander boldly demanded the Ashanti Golden Stool, symbol of Ashanti nationhood. Wright respects the old Ashanti kingdom for defending itself, though unsuccessfully at the time, from British political domination. Yet in the history lesson the city provides him with an opportunity to deliver, he deplores also the region's complicity in the slave trade. Thus in local history he finds both examples of the African search for freedom from European outsiders and its acceptance of an internal system of oligar-chic power he abhors. He even finds a form of slavery alive in the present Asantehene Queen Mother's court. From his hotel window he can see below him the streets of Kumasi "alive" but the family he observes seems still to live in the old, traditional (non-twentieth cen-tury urban) fashion: their front yard is a "combination of bathroom, kitchen, dining room, and living room." The mother is "nude to the waist," another woman fans "a charcoal fire," a "tall, black girl" pounds corn in a wood vat (274).

Suddenly Wright is "enervated from the heat and dampness again." In Kumasi "There is little or no sun. . . . Weather broods over the city; always it feels like rain, looks like rain, smells like rain" but only "a fine drizzle falls" (279). Wright feels that from the sky the city must be invisible. The people of Kumasi are as much a puzzle to him as had been the people of Accra. Kumasi is more black than Accra had been, but no more reassuring to his search for the foundations of African political freedom. The life of the Asantehene's court makes him suspicious and sometimes angry, and he cannot figure out "why do most of the people spit all the time?" (283). He tries to spit as he claims the Ashanti do, and only dribbles saliva down his shirt.

The Ashanti kingdom radiating around Kumasi is rich in black history of defiance which Wright is careful to recount, but now its chiefdom appears superstitious and conniving to him. His description of the city underscores what must have been his disappointment in finding no sense of brotherhood, no communion, with the Akan nation. Where he early describes the city as "vital" (272), before long he is complaining that the foul rainy "Weather dominated everything, created the mood of living . . . tinted the feelings with somberness, with an unappeasable melancholy." He looks out his window and claims "there is no sky" (283), and when it is not raining the sky is simply cloudy and he sees "huge black vultures wheeling" in it "all day long" (272). The hotel at which he resides is "dank and musty." It is an "African hotel" which by now connotes that it is inefficient and unpleasant. Kumasi's wealthy West Africans can live otherwise, he discovers, when a young local man points out to him a "big white house . . . that looked like a hospital surrounded by a high cement wall" (301). He is told the owner of the house has grown rich from political corruption. Elsewhere he sees a new housing development for more ordinary citizens, "neat, new wooden houses" in a "plot overgrown with all weeds." But no one lives in this surrealistically depicted sub-section of Kumasi because the homes "cost too much. Africans can't buy or rent them." They stand finely built, "solid," empty (300).

Open markets that sell a variety of goods—food and drink, house-hold equipment, clothes and textiles, livestock—dot the neighbor-hoods of most West African cities, and each city contains a central open market. These markets are (or were when Wright visited Ku-masi) a focus of African city life. No matter what your station in life, if you were African you gathered at some time in the market. The central market was the Times Square of African city life. What Wright experienced when he finally visited Kumasi's central market, in his phrase, "decided to descend into the maelstrom" (defined by dictionaries as a dangerous "whirlpool of extraordinary size or vio-lence"), reflects his state of mind much of the time he was in the Gold

Coast and his perhaps unconscious but natural tendency to denigrate the African city in comparison to his idealized European city. "It was a vast masterpiece of disorder . . . filled with men and women and children and vultures and mud and stagnant water and flies and filth and foul odors." Immediately he thinks Paris's large *"Le Marche aux Puches"* (its famous Flea Market) "and *Les Halles* would be lost here." Paris had been lovely and peaceful, civilized; the market at Kumasi represents for Wright "that indescribable African confusion" where he hears "a babble of voices" and sees "men and women and children, in all . . . degrees of nudity" (294) (the streets of Paris had been "ordered, clothed" [37]).

Perhaps because he in effect is writing a travel narrative, it is easy to forget how solipsistic Wright's description is here. What he calls a "babble" is actually many people speaking in their own languages that he cannot understand. The "babble" is in his mind, not on their tongues. Much of the disorder and confusion he perceives in the market is similarly in his mind. Market life is rather rigidly codified and operates according to rules of customary regulation. When I retraced Wright's steps and traveled to Kumasi, of course I visited the market. My notes as it happens do not stress disorder or confusion. "The market is like a bowl radiating roads and railroad tracks from its center. When I looked into the base of the bowl from half-way up its sides and blurred my eyes I could see black masses swirling smoothly, like the flow of protoplasm you see in films of magnified amoebae— black amoebae." I mention my notes here definitely not to prove my view of the market superior to Wright's—I am not so foolhardy—but simply to indicate the difference in my perception which might have many causes (e.g., my own background, the fact that I had lived a while in Africa before I had journeyed to Kumasi, the fact that I had previously read Wright's account). I did experience temporary disorder in the market when the shoppers and vendors became agitated as a short, naked man whose body was lathered with sweat and speckled with blood that dripped from his torn eye suddenly appeared running and crashed into several stalls trying to escape "the mob" (my notes) pursuing him. I held my two-year-old daughter in my arms and dashed behind a car when the man glowered at me. Some people in the crowd laughed and a woman standing next to me holding a bolt of cloth giggled. Then the man dashed at a policeman and the policeman ran from him and the crowd laughed even more loudly. I did not. The very black man still dripping deep red blood like sweat as he ran, disappeared down an alley. The crowd buzzed for a short time, then shopping resumed as usual. The market, it seemed to me then, had assimilated this incident. That was my tinctured perception at the time.

Leaving Kumasi and heading north in his rented taxi, Wright enters a "forest jungle . . . not as thick as it had been about Kumasi; the air was less heavy and I felt almost normal for the first time in many days. The heat was there . . . but a horizon opened out to all sides" so that the jungle did not make him feel "hemmed-in" (297). In a small village he attends another funeral and asks the Information Service member who has accompanied him "Just how many" human sacrifices "are needed" now "when a member of the royal family dies?" and he is told "That depends upon who dies" (298). Back in Kumasi, Wright reports that he cannot see the sun but he can feel its heat through a white mist. "Scores of vultures wheel silently over the city" (299). He has seen in it no more cause for hope than in Accra.

Richard Wright was primarily a creative writer, and Black Power is at least as much a creative as reportorial work. It demonstrates how creative a supposedly reportorial work can be. His African cities are as much constructs of his creation, of his mind, as they are real places on real maps, or more to the point, on real territory. His Accra and Kumasi exist in the shadows of his Paris, and probably his New York and Chicago, too—and certainly his London and Liverpool. Accra and Kumasi are symbolic cities prefiguring Aky Kewi Armah's Accra in his post-Nkrumah novel The Beautyful Ones Are Not Yet Born that also focuses on (now) Ghana's political hopes for the near future, and perhaps Africa's as well. Physically and symbolically, Accra is remarkably alike in both narratives though Armah's city desperately awaits rain as Wright's does not. Otherwise, Armah's Accra is even more insistently depressing than Wright's, and possibly filthier, filled with excrement, urine, mucous, rot, rust, spit, foul odors, sweat, grease, and encrusted filth. There cannot be a page of the novel without some ugly description of what makes up the city, of what the book's obsessed protagonist focuses on in the city. In his work office, "Sometimes it was possible to taste very clearly the salt that had been eating the walls and the paint on them, if one cared to run one's hand down the dripping surfaces and taste the sticky mess. . . . Everybody seemed to sweat a lot, not from the exertion of their jobs, but from some kind of inner struggle that was always going on" (20). Even the money smells like corruption, "a very old smell, very strong, and so very rotten that the stench itself came with a curious, satisfying pleasure" (3). "Oozing freely," an "oil-like liquid" drips from a sleeping man's mouth and becomes "entangled . . . in the fingers of the man's left hand" (5). The polish of a much-used bannister "was supposed" to "catch the rot. But of course in the end it was the rot which imprisoned everything in its effortless embrace" (12). A once "gleam-ing white" garbage receptacle now "covered over thickly with the juice of every imaginable kind of waste matter" (7) contains the boldly printed message KEEP YOUR COUNTRY CLEAN BY KEEPING YOUR CITY CLEAN. But Armah's Accra is foul and its inhabitants nearly all as filled with the decay as its streets and buildings. His novel concludes with possibly one man's salvation during "Passion Week," but political hope for Ghana's future seems gleamless, bleak in the presence of such moral and physical disintegration. The sign on a poda-poda delivers his psychosocial-political message: "The Beautyful Ones Are Not Yet Born." Still, when Armah's unnamed, detribalized, deracinated protagonist, an exile in his own homeland, decides to return home to an "aching emptiness" that "would be all that the remainder of his own life could offer him" (160), he seems to have performed an act of moral heroism. He had just aided the escape of a corrupt friend during a coup ("for the nation itself there would only be a change of embezzlers and a change of the hunters and hunted" [160]) by disappearing with him down the toilet hole of a latrine, repeating and parodying the legendary hero's journey underground to knowledge. Later, at sea, he jumps from the boat which is sailing his friend away and swims in an innertube back to the beach where he finally lies cold but vaguely free. Perhaps his brief break from passivity, his determination to follow his will and perform an action instead of passively submitting to the forces of rot that appear to control life in his Accra, will enable him to stand against the history of defeat he has experienced in the city. Even so, no ulti-mate victory is certain: "He walked very slowly, going home" (180).

The Accra Wright constructed or created or saw is not as bleak as Armah's nor is his conclusion to *Black Power* as tentative. Both books are in the naturalistic tradition and demonstrate the difficulty or im-possibility of overcoming deterministic environmental and social forces that trap individuals and entire societies. In this hostile scheme the city is a power that seems to drag humanity down with it through its own disorder and decay. It also is a symbol of the disintegration and corruption of its inhabitants, of their irrationality and sometimes their craziness even while it is the locus of their dreams.

Wright's art is tricky in *Black Power,* whether he knew it or not. Travel literature traditionally presents a "true" picture of strange sights but has for a long time—maybe from the beginning—blurred the distinction between fact and fiction: remember John Smith's *A True Relation,* his *Generall Historie,* or Melville's *Typee,* other travel books about westerners visiting exotic technologically undeveloped lands. The blur is perhaps more self-consciously achieved in modern travel books such as those by Paul Theroux, V. S. Naipaul, and John Krich. In many ways, *Black Power* is part of this tradition thought of as recent and so well represented in Paul Fussell's *The Norton Book of Travel* (New York: W. W. Norton, 1987). *Black Power* purports to be and is about the Gold Coast on the eve of its independence from Great Britain, but it also is a highly subjective account of an exile's journey to the land of his long gone ancestors, a quest of the self in search of itself. The central landscape of this quest is not the fabled jungles of African and black American legend, but cities of Africa today which are also cities of Wright's imagination: the two may be but are not necessarily the same. Neither Accra nor Kumasi is really ready for a successful revolution, and for Wright that is what African independence demands. As cities of the mind, neither is a place Wright can call home. They threaten to envelop him, drain him, drug him, erode his self. As a device to achieve objectivity, which can be seen as another way of asserting the self, he relates chunks of Gold Coast history, but with this he mixes myth and what he considers superstition, which only further erases the distinctions between fact and fiction. The cities which he portrays as places of disorder and confusion reflect or are projections of the disorder and confusion he experiences in his own quest (an American, an African, descendent of Du Bois's double Negro, an exile fresh from Paris). He fills his book with dialogue which should lend a travel book or reporter's account verisimilitude, but which here also makes his story seem like fiction. He uses what Mikhail Bakhtin called "polyphony" to communicate his "hidden message,"[2] different voices he, the constant stranger, hears along his way, that orchestrate his ambiguous journey during the Gold Coast's solidly historical event.

At the conclusion of his journey and his book, Wright sets down a letter of advice to Kwame Nkrumah, perhaps because he has lost personal contact with him completely. He concludes, despite all the evidence he has delivered seemingly to the contrary, that he "felt an odd kind of at-homeness, a solidarity" in the Gold Coast that has nothing to do with race. The link he feels is psychological or emo-tional, forged "from the quality of deep hope and suffering embedded in the lives of your people" (342). Wright has suffered, yet he hopes. This letter also reverses the drift of *Black Power* in its hortatory opti-mism, its strength and confidence of statement, in advising Nkrumah how to achieve the revolution necessary to restore Africa the Gold Coast (and Africa) to greatness in the modern world. Wright's force-ful charge seems doubly ironic. Throughout his text he has questioned the ability of Gold Coast leaders to command this kind of revolution and the capacity of their constituency to follow their guidance.

Furthermore, though he concurs with the "*African* path" Nkrumah has followed so far (350), his text consistently questions primary components of that way—tribal structures and African religions, for example.

By turns patronizing, naive, and wise, Wright's words to Nkrumah fit best into the scheme of *Black Power* as a revelation of Wright's own human condition. A victim of racial and class oppression, he fought with the hardness and discipline he calls for in the Africans, to escape the deterministic traps of recurrent victimization. He attempted to chart his own path to freedom by not slavishly following the Western or Russian way. In exhorting Africans to become "MILITARIZED! . . . NOT FOR DESPOTISM BUT TO FREE MINDS FROM MUMBO-JUMBO" (347), he is confessing what he tried to achieve in his own life as a writer. The "hope and faith!" (354) he terminates his quest with were virtues necessary for him to maintain his struggle to determine his own identity and fate against the controlling forces he knew opposed him or any human. His letter demonstrates he knew Africans shared his needs in their dubious political battle.

In his double quest, which becomes a journey beyond reason, Wright achieves self-definition not through the cities he departs from in Europe or discovers in Africa, but by not succumbing to them. Perhaps only fables of his construction, like African riddles, they may illuminate reality when deciphered.

NOTES

1. I quote from the following texts in my essay: *Black Power*, by Richard Wright (London: Dennis Dobson, 1954), and *The Beautyful Ones Are Not Yet Born*, by Aky Kewi Armah (New York: Collier Books, 1969). Page numbers are cited in the text. Once again, I am pleased to thank the American Philosophical Society for enabling me to retrace Wright's steps in Ghana. All ellipses are mine.

2. I am indebted to Casey Blanton for discussing with me travel literature and Bakhtin's theories relating to the genre.

5

Stadtluft macht frei!: African-American Writers and Berlin (1892–1932)

EBERHARD BRÜNING

Right from their very beginnings, American cultural life in general and American literature in particular have been both nationalistic/provincial and international/cosmopolitan, "New World"-oriented as well as European-minded. Because of this historic dualism, a considerable amount of ambiguity—affection and condescension—has developed over the past centuries and influenced views on both sides of the Atlantic.

American writers and intellectuals past and present have always revealed a lively interest in Europe to which they usually refer as the "old country" or the "Old World." As one observer has noted, "From the time of the early settlements onwards, the authors of the 'New World' always regarded Europe and her nations as the correlate to the new continent and its people."[1]

When, during the early decades of the nineteenth century, young writers, artists, and scholars of the United States flocked to the "old country" eager to widen their intellectual horizon and, in W. E. B. Du Bois's words, "to obtain the best results of European scholarship and culture"[2] which they thought indispensable for their individual and their nation's education and further cultural emancipation, Germany became a much preferred and sought-for country. But, strangely enough, neither the promising young scholars of the "New World" nor the already prominent American writers of that time found the Prussian capital interesting or famous enough for a visit or a stay of longer duration.

Although Cogswell, Ticknor, Bancroft, Everett, and Gildersleeve, household names in early nineteenth-century American culture, all visited Berlin during or after their studies in Germany, as did Bismarck's roommate Motley, the University of Göttingen usually was the first place American students and young scholars hurried to for extending their knowledge or taking an academic degree. At Göttingen, English was spoken and understood to a much greater extent than in Berlin, where even renowned professors had great difficulty in pronouncing an English name correctly. Besides that, the whole layout of this medieval-looking Göttingen and its social and scholarly life were greatly to the liking of these transatlantic visitors.

When in 1858 the young law student Henry Adams took up residence in Berlin for the first time, he experienced this city as "a nightmare . . . in the remote Prussian wilderness . . . a poor, keen-witted, provincial town, simple, dirty, uncivilized, and in most respects disgusting."[3] His observations on Berlin, as laid down in *The Education of Henry Adams* (1907), in a way set the pace for some time to come for almost all subsequent emotional and rational approaches to that city by American authors. Generalizing his impressions, Adams points out: "A student at twenty takes easily to anything, even to Berlin . . . but a week's experience left him dazed and dull . . . Berlin astonished him . . . Life was primitive beyond what an American boy could have imagined. Overridden by military methods and bureaucratic pettiness, Prussia was only beginning to free her hands from internal bonds. Apart from discipline, activity scarcely existed . . . German manners, even at Court, were sometimes brutal, and German thoroughness at school was apt to be routine."[4] But there is also a certain ambiguity in Adams's attitude toward the German people which again is very characteristic and proved to be paradigmatic. The uneasiness Berlin induced had nothing to do with American chauvinistic anti-German feelings, since as Adams confessed, "he loved, or thought he loved the people, but the Germany he loved was the eighteenth-century which the Germans were ashamed of, and were destroying as fast as they could . . . Military Germany was his abhorrence. What he liked was the simple character; the good-natured sentiment; the musical and metaphysical abstraction; the blundering incapacity of the German for practical affairs."[5]

It is quite interesting to note that American writers of some standing who traveled in Germany during the decades before the foundation of the "German Reich" under the dominance of Prussia did not consider it worthwhile to include Berlin in their itinerary. While the Germanophile Longfellow preferred Göttingen, Heidelberg, and Boppard during his four extended visits to German, such distinguished men of letters as Washington Irving and James Fenimore Cooper selected Dresden as their favorite place for a longer stay and were quite enthusiastic about its architecture, parks, bridges, and art collections. Even during the second half of the nineteenth century, and in spite of a more realistic view of the once romanticized small residences of the many kingdoms and dukedoms of Germany, none among such globetrotting American literati as James Russell Lowell, William Dean Howells, Bret Harte, Henry James, or Stephen Crane touched upon the Prussian capital.

But there is one important exception—a noteworthy and outstandingly singular case: Mark Twain. This famous "Innocent Abroad" enjoyed a rather pompous but not too expensive lifestyle during his stay in Berlin from 1891–1893. Through the windows of his eight-room suite at the Hotel Royal, he watched the German Emperor parading "Unter den Linden" and was flattered by being addressed as "the grand old man of American letters," or by being mistaken for Theodor Mommsen, Berlin's most famous scholar, who resembled him somewhat in appearance. He even suppressed his often convincingly demonstrated democratic and anti-imperialist principles, when he eagerly accepted the invitation of the General von Versen to dine and converse with Kaiser Wilhelm II at the former's house. Twain's literary essay on Berlin, which, however, does not contain this event, bears the title The German Chicago (1892). It opens with a statement that strikes the keynote of all later Berlin descriptions: "I feel lost in Berlin." A few lines further down we read: "The city itself has no tradition and no history It is a new city; the newest I have ever seen. Chicago would seem venerable beside it . . . The main mass of the city looks as if it had been built last week . . . Berlin is the European Chicago."[6]

It certainly is no coincidence that the Chicago author George Ade shared Twain's sentiments after having seen Berlin in 1908. "Berlin," he said after his return to the United States, "is Chicago—only washed, starched and ironed."[7] Twain's well-known humorous and ironic style, as well as his sharp satire, abound in all the following passages:

> Berlin is a surprise in a great many ways—in a multitude of ways, to speak strongly and be exact. It seems to me the most governed city in the world, but one must admit that it also seems to be the best governed. Method and system are observable on every hand—in great things, in little things, in all details, of whatever size . . . It has a rule for everything, and puts the rule in force . . . The calm, quiet, courteous, cussed persistence of the police is the most admirable thing I have encountered on this side . . . Everything is orderly . . . and the police do not like crowds and disorder here. If there were an earthquake in Berlin the police would take charge of it and conduct it in that sort of orderly way that would make you think it was a prayer-meeting.[8]

Without doubt, Twain's observations and explanations get to the heart of the matter. Although they sound quite humorous and witty in general, one nevertheless can sense the uneasiness and dichotomy in all his emotional and rational response to this city and its inhabit-ants. On the one hand, there is a certain amount of admiration for their efficiency, discipline, and orderliness, and on the other, there is this never vanishing feeling of discomfort about being too much or-dered around and spied upon, because he believes that the state offi-cials' prying into the private concerns of Berliners or visitors might severely curtail personal freedom and individual lifestyle. Twain's im-age of Berlin, the literary spotlight he throws on some basic traits of the Prussian society and manners as well as on the German character and mentality in general, has proved very durable and is echoed in many other publications not only by Twain's contemporaries but also by writers who visited Berlin in the years between the world wars.

The aforementioned American writers and intellectuals, of course, were all white Americans and representatives of the dominant white culture of the United States. The question arises: How did black American authors respond to Berlin—that is, those promising and race conscious young men who had succeeded in traveling to Europe despite all the handicaps and restrictions imposed on them at home? Did they react to this urban center in the same way as their white contemporaries or were there any differences?

During the period under consideration, less than a handful of black American authors/intellectuals of some standing either passed through Berlin or stayed there for some time. Almost at the time when America's then most famous and popular author experienced Berlin and gathered the material for his literary essay, *The German Chicago*, another American—still a young man but later an internationally known scholar and author—became a keen observer of the daily life and the intellectual scene of this ambitious upstart amongst European capitals. In the fall of 1892 the African-American, William Edward Burghardt Du Bois, registered at the University of Berlin in order to broaden and enrich his knowledge of history, sociology, philosophy, and economics. To this former Harvard student and "exotic" new-comer, Berlin's academic hall glistened with that "ethereal sheen which, to the fresh American, envelopes everything European,"[9] but by Christmas time the sheen had worn off, and the young scholar settled down to his ambitious program of studies in the social sciences. He was particularly fascinated by such controversial learned celebri-ties as the philosopher Wilhelm Dilthey and the sociologist Max Weber or the nationalistic and chauvinistic historian Heinrich von Treitschke and the more socially and democratically oriented economist Gustav Schmoller. The latter, for whose Seminary of Political Economy he had prepared a scientific thesis on *The Large- and Small-Scale Management of Agriculture in the Southern United States, 1840–1890*, was greatly impressed by Du Bois's careful and comprehensive work. Schmoller, together with his colleague Adolph Wagner, strongly recommended the young American to pass the doctor's examination. "This work would have been sufficient," Schmoller wrote on the letter of recommendation, "but the Faculty refused to admit him to the oral examination, because according to their rules only those persons can be admitted to examination who have studied 6 semesters in German universities."[10] Unfortunately Du Bois's funds were depleted and he could think of no way to remain at Berlin University in order to fulfill this requirement. To Du Bois's deep regret the Slater Trustees at Cambridge, who had granted him a loan and a scholarship twice, did not renew his award a third time and asked him to return to the United States and offer himself as a candidate at Harvard since, at the president of the John F. Slater Fund put it, "I think that the Harvard degree would be, in all respects, as advantageous to you as that of Berlin."[11]

During his two years' stay in Berlin, Du Bois developed a strange, ambiguous attitude toward the cultural and socio-political situation in Germany at the turn of the century. Although his empirical observations and rational thinking drew him to the left and made him a sympathizer of the Social Democratic Movement ("I frequently attended their meetings"),[12] he otherwise felt much attracted by the Germans' passionate patriotism and the pageantry which he found absolutely thrilling. "The march of soldiers," he wrote in his *Autobiography* (1968), "the saluting of magnificent uniforms, the martial music and rhythm of movement stirred my senses. Then there was that new, young Emperor . . . Ever and again he came riding ahead of his white and golden troops on prancing chargers through the great Brandenburg gate, up the Linden . . . I even trimmed my beard and mustache to a fashion like his and still follow it."[13]

This German patriotism was a great surprise to him as he compared it with the patriotism of his own country, particularly in New England, which he described as "cool" and "intellectual." Du Bois again visited Berlin in 1936 when he stopped in Germany during his trip around the world. At that time "the streets of Berlin rang with the sound of heavy boots; Hitler's raucous voice shouted over the radio; people were afraid to talk. He did not tarry," remembered his wife, Shirley Graham, in her *Memoir of W. E. B. Du Bois*.[14]

Then, reflecting on Du Bois's third visit to Berlin in 1959, when

the faculty of economics of the Humboldt University bestowed on
him the honorary degree of Doctor of Economics, she continued:

> When we were alone, W. E. B. stood silent at the wide window, looking
> down into the street. After a while, he sighed and said, "There's nothing
> out there I remember. I suppose this section of the city was completely
> destroyed." After a short silence, he commented, "The streets are well
> paved—so straight, so clean—but there are very few people moving about;
> scarcely any traffic . . . In the early evening, when we set out on our drive,
> the streets presented a different aspect. Wide, two-laned Karl Marx Allee,
> the main thoroughfare, was lined with shops and business buildings. Cou-
> ples strolled along the broad sidewalks, and children were about. We
> turned into another wide avenue—clearly an old street, for it was lined
> with trees, now bare in the autumn chill, some of them twisted and bent.
> Du Bois touched my arm. "Now I remember. This is Unter den Linden."
> And in another minute he exclaimed, "There's my university! Look, Shir-
> ley, there it is!"[15]

Berlin plays only a minor role in Du Bois's literary writings. But
there is an interesting chapter in the third volume of his trilogy of
novels on the life and education of an African-American intellectual
from 1870 to about 1950, in which the hero travels in Germany and
settles in Berlin for awhile in the middle of the 1930s. We do not
learn very much about the city itself in this book, whose title is *Worlds
of Color* (1961). The protagonist, whose name is Mansart, "began to
see Berlin as a great and efficient modern city. But it was tense, filled
with meetings and its streets thundered with glaring radio propa-
ganda."[16] However, there is one episode of the novel which is of
special importance to our topic. Mansart pays a visit to "Siemens-
Stadt," a city within a city, the center of the electrical industry of
Germany before World War II. Here he is particularly startled by the
training program of the corporation's apprentices, carefully selected
boys highly motivated to become skilled workers and to enter a life
of work for Siemens. Mansart comes to the conclusion that the chief
aim of the managers' efforts

> was to produce a human product of the most careful and precise nature,
> to be used in the productive processes of this mighty industry. Industry
> here was dealing with men as it would deal with cotton: studying them,
> experimenting with them. Knowing exactly what it wanted men for, it
> proceeded with painstaking care, endless experiment and expert training
> to deliver a finished product which was unsurpassed in the world for
> efficient, delicate, precise and regular workmanship . . . With a skilled
> working class, educated for a specific life work, it was evident to Germany
> that democratic control of the state could not be entrusted to them. Indus-

try in Germany was to be controlled by a closely knit hierarchy for support of a wealthy class to whom the bulk of income and of power went.[17]

Berlin as urban center and focal point of German virtues and vices! Again, this doubleness and contradictoriness. Twain and Du Bois became deeply embarrassed and emotionally upset in their response to the German people, their character and their achievements, which attracted and repelled them at the same time. They admired Germany as what Du Bois called "a great country of science and education, of ideals, with music and art."[18] But they were suspicious of and irritated by the orderliness, carefulness, efficiency, cleanliness, discipline, and precision "made in Germany," in the idolatry of which they quite rightly sensed dangerous instruments to suppress all individuality and subordinate man to a soulless state machinery or to powerful industrial corporations run and organized by military principles. For Twain and Du Bois, then, such principles were followed to master all activities and to stifle every free and independent impulse.

Although this obvious consensus seems to be quite remarkable, there exist, nevertheless, a number of fundamental differences in Twain and Du Bois's approach to and image of Berlin, which derive from differences in age, race, and temperament. For Twain, an already outstanding writer and distinguished representative of the cultural and social establishment of the United States, Berlin was more or less just another interesting place of the "Old World." Berlin allowed him an elegant but not too expensive lifestyle so that he could easily mix with people of high society as well as with people of the middle classes, unconditionally accepted by them as a white man of letters in a white man's world. Du Bois, however, had arrived at the German capital as a young scholar with little money to spend, and had eagerly intended to study and learn as much as possible at this renowned place of learning. Being an African-American with a life-long experience of what it meant to be a black man with scholarly ambitions in a country like his, he was completely unsure whether he could associate unrestrictedly with his fellow students and the common people, without fear of discrimination because of his skin color. Thus, a new dimension is added to Du Bois's approach to this city. Different criteria became instrumental for molding his view of Berlin, the criteria which are characteristic for him and for all African-American intellectuals who arrived after him until the early 1930s and which would hardly be understood by or were of any relevance to any of his white contemporaries.

The city's architecture and structural layout or the bureaucratic regimentations and restrictions exercised by the Prussian officialdom, which caused so much irritation and abhorrence to almost every white American writer since Henry Adams, were not Du Bois's main con-cern. His view of Berlin and lasting impressions of the city were predominantly determined by what one could call "the human factor" closely bound up in "the color problem." In this respect, Germany and Berlin meant a totally new experience to Du Bois, something of a "culture shock" in a highly positive sense. This experience left its everlasting marks on him and somehow changed his whole view of life and his outlook toward the world in general. "Du Bois's early memories of Germany," to quote Shirley Graham again, "dating back to 1892, were among the brightest of his life. Going there as a graduate student from Harvard University, he said, 'For the first time I was just a human being. I was accepted or ignored on the basis of my own worth."[19] Looking backward to these happy years, he emphasizes this particular aspect in his *Autobiography* in the following way:

> I met men and women as I had never met them before. Slowly they became, not white folks, but folks. The unity beneath all life clutched me. I was not less fanatically a Negro, but "Negro" meant a greater, broader sense of humanity and world fellowship. I felt myself standing, not against the world, but simply against American narrowness and color prejudice, with the greater, finer world at my back. In Germany in 1892, I found myself on the outside of the American world, looking in. With me were white folk—students, acquaintances, teachers—who viewed the scene with me. They did not always pause to regard me as a curiosity, or something sub-human; I was just a man of the somewhat privileged student rank, with whom they were glad to meet and talk over the world; particularly, the part of the world whence I came.[20]

These reminiscences correspond with his sentiments expressed in two letters of 1893. "To the American Negro," Du Bois addressed himself to the trustees of the John F. Slater Fund, "even more than to the white, is the contact with European culture of inestimable value in giving him a broad view of men and affairs, and enabling him to view the problems of his race in their true perspective ... I have also put myself to considerable pains to ascertain just the sort of reception a Negro receives in Germany socially, both in public and in private, with curious and instructive results."[21]

It would certainly be of some interest to know how another promis-ing young scholar and later prominent African-American educator and author, Alain Locke, had felt when he immersed himself in grad-uate study of philosophy at the University of Berlin in 1910–11. Un-fortunately, we are left in the dark about the Berlin experience of this animator of the "Harlem Renaissance" with whom Du Bois more than once differed in opinion.

About a decade later we get at least a glimpse of it provided by the black American writer Claude McKay, who also had his problems in getting along with Locke. When McKay met Locke for the first time in Berlin in 1923, the university professor took the poet and famous author of *If We Must Die* for a promenade in the Tiergarten. McKay points out in his autobiography, *A Long Way from Home* (1937):

And walking down the row with the statues of the Prussian kings supported by the famous philosophers and poets and composers on either side, he remarked to me that he thought those statues the finest ideal and expression of the plastic arts in the world. The remark was amusing, for it was just a short while before that I had walked through the same row with George Grosz, who had described the statues as "the sugar-candy art of Germany." When I showed Dr. Locke George Grosz's book of drawings, *Ecce Homo,* he recoiled from their brutal realism. (Dr. Locke is a Philadelphia blue-black blood, a Rhodes scholar and graduate of Oxford University, and I have heard him described as the most refined Negro in America.) So it was interesting now to discover that Dr. Locke had become the leading Negro authority on African Negro sculpture. I felt that there was so much more affinity between the art of George Grosz and African sculpture than between the Tiergarten insipid idealization of Nordic kings and artists and the transcending realism of the African artists.[22]

There is, however, one literary item, small but very telling, of the pre–World War I period which fittingly relates to Du Bois's "new sense of manhood" he felt after he had spent two years at the University of Berlin. In James Weldon Johnson's autobiographical narration, *The Autobiography of an Ex-coloured Man,* first published anonymously in 1912, the protagonist, a black pianist who has traveled widely in Europe, asserts that his stay in Berlin has proved an essential turning point in his personal life and professional career. He has eventually found himself and won new insights into his talent and future as a musician as well as into his ethnic position. This process of self-awareness was more or less triggered by his encounter with Berlin musicians who immediately accepted him and worked with him without any racial prejudice. They also made him understand the very richness of black music in the United States. The narrator sums up:

In Berlin, I especially enjoyed the orchestral concerts, and I attended a large number of them. I formed the acquaintance of a good many musicians, several of whom spoke of my playing in high terms. It was in Berlin that my inspiration was renewed . . . The desire to begin work grew stronger each day. I could think of nothing else. I made up my mind to go back into the very heart of the South, to live among the people, and drink in my inspiration firsthand. I gloated over the immense amount of material I

had to work with, not only modern rag-time, but also the old slave songs —
material which no one had yet touched.[23]

Although World War I and the post-war era had profoundly
changed many aspects of social and cultural life at home and abroad
and had added new accents to German-American relations as well, the
attitude of American writers, white or black, toward Berlin basically
remained the same as before the war. It cannot be denied that the
studies they offered contained useful observations; nevertheless, they
often used a close-up lens where a wide-angle was needed. By now
some of the city's contours appeared even more edgy, irritating, and
provocative, and daily life in it almost resembled a surrealistic film
scenario. American writers and artists began to see Berlin "through
the eyes of George Grosz," as John Dos Passos put it in his "informal
memoir," *The Best Times.*[24]

It soon became obvious that this former Prussian residence and
imperial capital of Germany, which had expanded too rapidly into a
modern metropolis, presented itself more as a strange, mysterious,
and incomprehensible place, where American writers, journalists, and
scholars could not feel at home. Neither the city's inner or outward
structure nor its social and cultural atmosphere and lifestyle seemed
to favor or stimulate literary creativity—not even during the so-called
"Golden Twenties" when Berlin acquired the reputation of being "the
American city of Europe,"[25] totally "Manhattanized,"[26] as well as of
being the world's most lively, eccentric, and advanced center for modern culture and art.

Berlin, nevertheless, was often visited by Americans in the time of
the Weimar Republic. There has been no other place in the world
where living was so cheap during those years. Especially in the early
twenties the almighty dollar with its astronomical rate of exchange
became a sort of "miracle currency" with which one could make a
fortune almost overnight, buy exquisite pieces of fine art, or publish
highly elitist avant-garde periodicals. Although many Americans
profited by this peculiar situation, there were a number of artists and
writers, mostly of the younger generation of "expatriates," who felt
disturbed by the city's cult of mammonism and moral deterioration
which reduced cultural values to the cash-nexus. This was another
reason why the majority of American authors who hurried to Europe
during the twenties to get acquainted with the various "isms" and to
absorb the mushrooming modern and avant-garde trends of writing
and thinking preferred to stay in France and made Paris "A Movable Feast."

Among the impressive number of American writers, including Sinclair Lewis, Theodore Dreiser, John Dos Passos, Ernest Hemingway, Malcolm Cowley, Michael Gold, Elmer Rice, Paul Bowles, Katherine Ann Porter, Lillian Hellman, and Thomas Wolfe, who had stayed in Berlin during the twenties and early thirties, were two African-American writers of national and international reputation: Claude McKay and Langston Hughes. Both were only transient guests who—like many of their white contemporaries—had stopped at the German metropolis, and their views of the city were no less ambivalent and contradictory than those of W. E. B. Du Bois and James Weldon Johnson.

McKay and Hughes were real "city men" who felt at home in big cities. "I rejoiced in the lavishness of the engineering exploits and the architectural splendors of New York," McKay says in A Long Way from Home.[27] And on the first page of the book's chapter "Berlin and Paris," we read this surprising sentence, "Berlin was by a long way brisker and brighter than London,"[28] which conspicuously corresponds with James Weldon Johnson's statement, "I found Berlin more to my taste than London, and occasionally I had to admit that in some things it was superior to Paris."[29] Although Hughes felt depressed by the gray slums that ringed the downtown area of Berlin, he, nevertheless, enjoyed the "beautiful buildings and wide avenues in its center."[30] What a contrast to the utterances and views of white American writers, artists, and journalists who reacted so negatively after having cast a first glance at Berlin. Berlin's architecture, monuments, streets, and squares provoked their disapproval at first sight. They thought them more than strange and felt so much irritated by them that they could hardly hold down their abhorrence and sarcasm. Berlin architecture seemed to Henry Adams "a particular sort of gloom never attained elsewhere,"[31] and George Cabot Lodge wrote in a letter to his mother in 1897: "This place is gray, gray, gray."[32] Theodore Dreiser complained in A Traveler at Forty (1913), "The public monuments of Berlin, and particularly their sculptural adornments are for the most part a crime against humanity."[33] "Our hearts sank at the Berlin we saw then," Matthew Josephson asserted in his memoir, Life among the Surrealists (1962), remembering his and his wife's first impression of this city in 1922:

> This sprawling metropolis of recent growth had never known the elegance of old Paris, nor did it have the sympathetic homeliness of London. In the late war it had seen hard days; its buildings, most of which had ugly stucco façades, had their paint peeling off. Even the Germans, comparing Berlin with their older, more beautiful cities, sometimes thought of it, in the terms of the artist George Grosz, as "a stone-grey corpse." It was in its own way stridently and offensively "modern," with big electric signs,

gaudy shops for people of fashion, and dreary slums that were interchange-
able with those of Liverpool or Chicago—in short, Everyman's City of
modern times.[34]

All the public buildings of Berlin's inner city, so carefully arranged,
so pompous, so very correct, made Christopher Isherwood feel depressed or provoked an overflow of satire, which becomes most outspo-
ken in his characterization of the cathedral, whose architecture
betrays "a flash of that hysteria which flickers always behind every
grave, gray Prussian façade."[35]

As for McKay and Hughes's more positive opinion of Berlin as an
urban center, the root cause of it apparently was the problem of color
with all its emotional and psychic implications. Historic discrimination certainly helped to create a greater sensibility to human and
social essentials of modern city life. "Color-consciousness . . . ,"
McKay wrote in his memoirs, "was something with which my white
fellow-expatriates could sympathize but which they could not altogether understand. For they were not black like me."[36] Ever since Du
Bois's first encounter with Berlin's everyday life and the man in the
street, black visitors from the "New World" had voiced their satisfaction of having been treated much better and with altogether more
consideration in Germany than in America and England. "Personally,
I had not sensed any feeling against me as a Negro in the fall of 1923,"
McKay declared in A Long Way from Home, and continued: "Often
when I stepped into a café there were friendly greetings—'Schwartz'
Mohr'—and free drinks . . . Well, everywhere in hotels, cafés, dancing
halls, restaurants and trains, on the river boats and in the streets, I
met with no feeling of hostility. In spite of the French black troops
on the Rhine I was treated even better in Berlin in 1923 than in
1922."[37] Ten years later one notes still the same impression and the
same reaction by Langston Hughes, who in his I Wonder As I Wander:
An Autobiographical Journey (1956), recalled his short stay in the
German capital in June 1932 as follows: "In Berlin, Negroes were
received at hotels without question, so we settled down to await visas
[for the Soviet Union—E. B.]. We ate in any restaurant we could
afford. In the German capital, I could not help remember my recent
experiences in the South with restaurants that served whites only,
and autocamps all across America that refused to rent me a cabin in
which to sleep."[38]

Despite all this, Berlin's lifestyle during the Weimar Republic has
always been viewed in America with both approval and dismay. Although African-American visitors almost unanimously praised the
Berliners' indifference to their color of skin, the general atmosphere,

the highly controversial and sophisticated social and cultural scene of this metropolis were not in the least to their liking. The inflationary situation with its mad speculation in dollars during the early twenties, the obvious poverty of the overwhelming part of the population, the growing demoralization, corruption, and brutalization of public life with its frank, unveiled, vulgar display of vice and every thinkable sexual perversity, which had made post-war Berlin into the modern Sodom and Gomorrah or "the most decadent city in Europe," as Christopher Isherwood put it,[39] produced something of a culture shock to both white and black American writers. Here their opinions converge again, and we register the same naive reaction under the influence of typical Puritan morality and sexual prudery. American writers, artists, and journalists responded to Berlin's libertinism and avant-garde lifestyle of the twenties and early thirties in a most ambivalent, basically schizophrenic way. On the one hand, they were conventionally shocked and deeply hurt in their Puritan/Victorian beliefs in sin and morality, and on the other, overwhelmed by an untamed curiosity and unashamed desire for the satisfaction of all their secret dreams and suppressed lustfulness. For quite a number of them the Berlin of the Weimar Republic assumed a strangely irrational function: it became a combined heaven of beatitude and hell of guiltiness. As to African-Americans, their naivete, shock, and disgust seemed to have been even greater than those of their white contemporaries.

"There was something sullen and bitter, hostile and resentful in the atmosphere of Berlin," McKay generalized his impressions of 1923.

And I believe Berlin expressed the resentful spirit of all Germany. There were *Wandervögel* everywhere like a plague of flies. They had lost their romantic flavor. More imitation than real *Wandervögel*, with their knapsacks slung over their shoulders, casually taking to the streets as nature lovers take to the woods, and they gave one a strange impression of Berlin as a futuristic forest. I do not know of anything that has rendered so perfectly the atmosphere, temper and tempo of the Berlin of that period than George Grosz's *Ecce Homo*. For me that book of drawings is a rare and iconoclastic monument of this closing era even as Rabelais is of the Renaissance.[40]

About ten years later, Hughes comes to the exact same conclusion. Going more into detail, he observes in his personal narrative of travel and adventure around the world:

in spite of racial freedom, Berlin seemed to me a wretched city . . . Our hotel was near one of the big railroad stations. There I put a coin into what I thought was a candy-bar machine, but a package of prophylactics

came out instead. The streets nearby teemed with prostitutes, pimps, pan-
derers and vendors of dirty pictures. Some of the young men in our group
got acquainted for the first time with what Americans in the pre-Kinsey
era termed "perversion." Unusual sex pleasures from beautiful girls were
openly offered in no uncertain phraseology on every corner and at pathetically low prices . . . The pathos and poverty of Berlin's low-priced market
in bodies depressed me. As a seaman I had been in many ports and had
spent a year in Paris working on Rue Pigalle, but I had not seen anywhere
people so desperate as these walkers of the night streets in Berlin.[41]

With France and Paris it had always been quite different. To
Americans who wanted to escape the moral restrictions of Main
Street to get rid of their puritanical frustrations and inhibitions and
to have some fun, the fabulous "city of lights" on the Seine symbolized
a "devine section of eternity," as E. E. Cummings put it,[42] and appeared as a place where one, according to Elmer Rice, "immediately
felt at home."[43] In Paris the frivolity, the "loose life," and the freedom
of sexual pursuits did not hurt one's aesthetic feelings, since they
presented themselves with delicacy, subtlety, playfulness, and hand-
someness. Even, as Cummings says, "the whores are very beautiful
with their diseased greenness."[44] So Paris meant Bohemia, a stimulating atmosphere and alluring charm—a more elaborate Greenwich
Village!

Berlin was much too direct, too violent, too vulgar, too extreme,
too blatant. The whole life of the town seemed "as though there were
almost no privacy behind doors," as Stephen Spender described it.[45]
Isherwood, pondering over this phenomenon, finally came to this conclusion: "Wasn't Berlin's famous 'decadence' largely a commercial
'line' which the Berliners had instinctively developed in their competition with Paris? Paris had long since cornered the straight girl-market,
so what was left for Berlin to offer its visitors but a masquerade of
perversion?"[46]

It was only a couple of years after his first visit to Berlin that
Hughes published a collection of short stories under the title The
Ways of White Folks (1934). It contains the moving story "Home,"
which is about a white lynching mob's brutal murder of an ill and
homesick black musician who had studied music and played jazz in
various European cities and returned home to a village in Missouri
where he wanted to see his mother again before he was to die. In a
short flashback he recalls the time when he had played with his orchestra in the nightclubs of Berlin. "Behind the apparent solidity of that
great city," the narrator summarizes Roy Williams's experience, "behind doors where tourists never passed, hunger and pain were beyond
understanding. And the police were beating people who protested, or

stole, or begged. Yet in the cabaret where Roy played, crowds of folks still spent good gold. They laughed and danced every night and didn't give a damn about the children sleeping in doorways outside, or the men who built houses of packing boxes, or the women who walked the streets to pick up trade. It was in Berlin that the sadness weighed most heavily on Roy."[47]

It stands to reason that black American writers usually gained a much deeper insight into and won a greater understanding of the basic contradictions and problems of the city's social and cultural reality. They came to know Berlin much more intimately than their white colleagues who often behaved like "the rich uncles from America" touring and exploring exotic territory, always in good custody of the English speaking hotels Adlon, Eden, Esplanade, or Bristol. "Folks catch hell in Europe," Hughes's protagonist muses in "Home" on what he had seen in Vienna and Berlin.[48] And right he was!

After the Nazis took over power in Germany in 1933, Berlin eventually had to be regarded as the archetypal enemy city, the very symbol of evil, and "Hitler's degenerate Berlin," as Elizabeth Nowell called it.[49] Particularly to antifascist-minded authors, the city had finally turned into a "damnation jail," in Katherine Ann Porter's words,[50] or just "an awful place to be," as Lillian Hellman wrote.[51] How fundamentally things had changed in respect to Berlin's once praised "racial freedom" or "color indifference" since Hughes's stopover in 1932 became conspicuously evident when only two years later the world-famous African-American actor and singer, Paul Robeson, passed through Berlin en route to Moscow. While waiting on the platform of Bahnhof Friedrichstrasse for the train, Robeson was confronted by a phalanx of young Nazi brown shirts. "A near disaster was averted as Paul Robeson braced himself to take on the small army, to the death, only to be spirited away by his companions. From that point on Robeson was definitely anti-fascist."[52]

The fact remains, however, that for African-American writers, Europe and her capital cities have usually been symbols of a "better life," especially as an alternative to the restrictions and narrowness of the rural South. Thus Paris became the "city of refuge" for Richard Wright after World War II.[53] And James Baldwin confessed in 1972: "My flight . . . *away* from America . . . had been dictated by my hope that I could find myself a place where I would be treated more humanely than my society had treated me at home, where my risks would be more personal, and my fate less austerely sealed. And Paris had done this for me: by leaving me completely alone."[54]

Dreams of a new and better life, and of freedom, have typically been a motive for African-Americans' moving into and about in Europe's great cities. This formed a pattern of thinking and behavior. It also expresses a hope for a better future which, historically, has made the city attractive—a fact that calls an old slogan to our mind when way back in the Middle Ages peasants flocked to the expanding cities in order to escape feudal bondage: "Stadtluft macht frei!" ("city air provides freedom!").[55]

Notes

1. Waldemar Zacharasiewicz, "National Stereotypes in Literature in the English Language: A Review of Research," in *Real: The Yearbook of Research in English and American Literature*, ed. Herbert Grabes, Hans-Jürgen Diller, and Hans Bungert, 1 (1982): 97.

2. W. E. B. Du Bois, Letter to the Educational Committee of the Honorable Trustees of the John F. Slater Fund, Berlin, 10 March 1893, *The Correspondence of W. E. B. Du Bois*, vol. 1, Selections, 1877–1934, ed. Herbert Aptheker (Amherst: University of Massachusetts Press, 1973), 25.

3. *The Education of Henry Adams, An Autobiography*, with a new introduction by D. W. Brogan (Boston: Houghton Mifflin, 1961), 76f.

4. Ibid., 77f.

5. Ibid., 83.

6. Mark Twain, *The German Chicago*, in *Literary Essays by Mark Twain*, 24 (New York: Harper & Brothers, 1918), 244.

7. Cf. Henry F. Urban, *Die Entdeckung Berlins* (Berlin: August Scherl Verlag, 1912), 3.

8. Twain, *The German Chicago*, 246ff.

9. W. E. B. Du Bois, "Harvard in Berlin," diary fragment, November–December 1892. Cf. Francis L. Broderick, *W. E. B. Du Bois: Negro Leader in a Time of Crisis* (Stanford: Stanford University Press, 1959), 27.

10. Ibid., *The Correspondence of Du Bois*, 28.

11. Ibid., 29.

12. *The Autobiography of W. E. B. Du Bois: A Soliloquy on Viewing My Life from the Last Decade of Its First Century* (New York: International Publishers, 1968), 168. See also W. D. Kindermann, "Preussische Lehrjahre eines schwarzamerikanischen Autors: W. E. B. Du Bois," in *Welcome to Berlin: Das Image Berlins in der englisch-sprachigen Welt von 1700 bis heute*, ed. Jörg Helbig (Berlin: Stapp Verlag, 1987), 63–69.

13. *The Autobiography of Du Bois*, 169.

14. Shirley Graham Du Bois, *His Day Is Marching On: A Memoir of W. E. B. Du Bois* (Philadelphia & New York: Lippincott, 1971), 254.

15. Ibid., 255.

16. W. E. B. Du Bois, *Worlds of Color* (New York: Mainstream Publishers, 1961), 53.

17. Ibid., 58.

18. Ibid., 61.

19. Shirley Graham Du Bois, *His Day*, 253.

20. *The Autobiography of Du Bois*, 157.

21. *The Correspondence of Du Bois*, 22f.

22. Claude McKay, *A Long Way from Home* (New York: Lee Furman, 1937), 312f.

23. James Weldon Johnson, *The Autobiography of an Ex-coloured Man* (New York & London: Knopf, 1927), 140ff.

24. John Dos Passos, *The Best Times: An Informal Memoir* (New York: Andre Deutsch, 1968), 174.

25. Lion Feuchtwanger, *Centum Opuscula* (Rudolstadt: Greifenverlag, 1956), 416.

26. Ed Falkowski, "Berlin in Crimson," *New Masses* (March 1930): 10.

27. McKay, *A Long Way from Home*, 244.

28. Ibid., 237.

29. Johnson, *The Autobiography*, 140.

30. Langston Hughes, *I Wonder As I Wander: An Autobiographical Journey* (New York & Toronto: Rinehart, 1956), 71.

31. *The Education of Henry Adams*, 76.

32. Henry Adams, "The Life of George Cabot Lodge," in *The Shock of Recognition*, ed. Edmund Wilson (New York: Farrar, Straus & Cudahy, 1955), 773.

33. Theodore Dreiser, *A Traveler at Forty* (New York: Century, 1913), 466f.

34. Matthew Josephson, *Life among the Surrealists: A Memoir* (New York: Holt, Rinehart & Winston, 1962), 192.

35. Christopher Isherwood, *Goodbye to Berlin* (London: Triad/Panther, 1985), 186f.

36. McKay, *A Long Way from Home*, 245.

37. Ibid., 239.

38. Hughes, *I Wonder As I Wander*, 71.

39. Christopher Isherwood, *Christopher and His Kind 1929-1939* (London: Eyre Methuen, 1977), 29.

40. McKay, *A Long Way from Home*, 239f.

41. Hughes, *I Wonder As I Wander*, 71.

42. See Richard S. Kennedy, *Dreams in the Mirror: A Biography of E. E. Cummings* (New York: Liveright, 1980), 140.

43. Elmer Rice, *Minority Report: An Autobiography* (New York: Simon & Schuster, 1963), 211.

44. Kennedy, *Dreams*, 141.

45. Stephen Spender, *World Within World* (London: Hamilton, 1953), 111.

46. Isherwood, *Christopher and His Kind*, 29.

47. Langston Hughes, *The Ways of White Folks* (New York: Knopf, 1934), 33f.

48. Ibid., 33f.

49. Elizabeth Nowell, *Thomas Wolfe: A Biography* (Garden City, N.Y.: Doubleday, 1960), 271.

50. Katherine Ann Porter, *The Leaning Tower and Other Stories* (New York: Harcourt, Brace, 1944), 199.

51. Lillian Hellman, *The Searching Wind* (New York: Viking, 1944), 59ff.

52. Joseph Hanzel, *Paul Robeson: Biography of a Proud Man* (Los Angeles: Holloway, 1980), 148f.

53. James Baldwin, *Nobody Knows My Name* (New York: Dell, 1963), 149.

54. James Baldwin, *No Name in the Street* (London: Michael Joseph, 1972), 42.

55. Cf. Ernst Werner, "Stadtluft macht frei. Frühscholastik und bürgerliche Emanzipation in der ersten Hälfte des 12. Jahrhunderts," *Sitzungsberichte der Sächsischen Akademie der Wissenschaften zu Leipzig, Philologisch-historische Klasse* 118, no. 5 (Berlin: Akademie-Verlag, 1976).

6

Richard Wright's Paris

MICHEL FABRE

AMONG abundant notes recording ideas for "Celebration," a novelistic series he was planning in the mid 1950s, Richard Wright jotted down that he should try to capture the relaxed talk that went on among American blacks in a Paris café. Their carefree mind, he believed, made them play on words with loud laughs, the fun deriving from contest in rhymes, or from jokes that came out of the mood and ambiance of the talk. This is a good indication of what Paris stood for in his writings; that is, not only a beautiful history-laden city, but a place where a black man's mind could be carefree enough to give utterance to his spontaneous joy and verbal creativity. When applied to Wright himself, this image was encapsulated in a sentence in his 1945 journal: "Paris is the place where one can find one's soul." I have already dealt with his French experience, which was largely limited to Paris, several times: in a biography, *The Unfinished Quest of Richard Wright* (New York: William Morrow, 1973), in three essays dealing with Wright's association with French existentialist and French-speaking Africans, about his exile and image of France (essays collected in *The World of Richard Wright,* University Press of Mississippi, 1985), and in *La Rive Noire* (Paris: Lieu Commun, 1985), published by the University of Illinois Press in 1990 as *From Harlem to the Seine.* Therefore, here I concentrate on the use and image of Paris in his creative writing.

Admittedly, few of Wright's published works deal with Paris when measured against those of other black American writers then living in France. Among a handful of essays, "There Is Always Another Café" is mostly a vignette on the Monaco Bar, his favorite Latin Quarter haunt before the Tournon became *the* place. A May 1946 article in *Samedi-Soir* and a couple of letters to Dorothy Norman in the 1948 *Art and Action* volume deal respectively with his first reactions to the GI-filled city and the state of affairs in post-war France.

This is little in comparison with more than a score of brilliant essays written by James Baldwin, which bear on Americans, black and white, who find their cultural and racial identity in Paris. Only one short story by Wright, "Man, God Ain't like That," is set in Paris, with a police inspector as one of the characters, but it really deals with an African boy's unexpected reactions to the kind of "civiliza-tion" which well-meaning but naive Westerners attempt to impose upon him. In no way can this story be compared to Baldwin's "This Morning, This Evening, So Soon," for instance, whose theme impor-tantly depends upon its Parisian setting. As for Wright's novels, only in *The Outsider* does one find references to the capital of France. Interestingly, they appear in quotations from the travel diary of the major female protagonist in the novel, Eva Blount, the wife of an uncongenial communist organizer—a sensitive soul who juts down her first impressions of the City of Light:

June 10th

I am at last in Paris, city of my dreams! What a wedding gift from Gil! Poor dear, he's so busy with Party work to show me the beauty of this wonderful Paris. . . . But I do manage to see it for myself. The art exhibits, the artists' studios, the sense of leisure, the love of beauty—will I ever be myself again after all this?

Notre Dame! Rising nobly in the warm summer night like a floodlit dream—The tourist bus is crawling away, taking from me this vision of beauty, remote, fragile, infused with the mood of eternity. At the next stop I got off and walked back to Notre Dame; I could not keep to the schedule of a tourist bus! I sat on a bench and gazed at Notre Dame till almost dawn. How quiet the city is. A lonely, shabby man is pushing a handcart through the city streets. Lines, space, harmony, softened by dark mists . . . Dusk of dawn kissing the pavements with tenderness . . . I doubt if Gil would understand feelings like these, yet they mean so much to me, to my heart. Mine is the glory of those angels against the background of that pearly, infinite sky.

June 15th

It all began that afternoon when I went to see a Left Bank art exhibit. I stayed behind and got to talking to some of the younger artists, both American and French, all of whom were complete strangers to me. One young man, an American expatriate, obviously a Trotskyite, began a vio-lent tirade against the Party, charging that membership in the Party was death to artists.

June 21st

I've just come from an American movie where I saw mothers with their young children. It was a horrible gangster film with a tense, melodramatic atmosphere. How can mothers take their children into such places?

June 24th

I am afraid my loneliness and melancholy are making me morbid. . . . In the Paris Métro, I saw something that made me sad. In front of me, on one seat, sat a young mother, middle-class, her face well made-up and glowing with motherly pride; she was holding a little girl about two years old on her knees. And that sweet little baby girl, all dressed up in delicate, lacy things took a liking to a pale little boy of about nine or thereabouts. He was filthy, badly dressed; he seemed too mature for his age; he sat next to a huge, vulgar, toothless, harsh-voiced woman—no doubt his mother. Both the little children were at once keen on each other, but the big mother kept telling her son to stop looking and smiling at the baby. The little girl's hands tried to take hold of those of the boy and the boy was enjoying it. The young mother did not like it but she was too well bred to want to hurt the little boy's feelings . . . finally the young mother pried the tiny, playful, rosy little fingers out of the boy's dirty hands. The baby cried and I wanted to cry too.[1]

No need to say these impressions more or less echo Wright's own, whether repeatedly expressed in his 1947 journal and in letters to American friends, or reported by Douglas Schneider, who thus described the Wrights' first day in the city:

We drove from Saint-Lazare to the Arc de Triomphe, down the Champs-Elysées filled with sun; we drove round the Place de la concorde and along the Rue de rivoli, then across the Gardens of the Tuileries, a gorgeous mosaic of sparkling geraniums and goldflowers. Then along the quais, past Notre-Dame, and up Boulevard Saint Michel. Richard Wright was sitting in front by my side. Very talkative at the beginning, he had become more and more silent but I could hear him whisper, "What beauty, my God, what beauty!" As we were driving around the square in front of Notre-Dame, he turned towards me and said: "Can you imagine what this means to me? I never knew a city could be so beautiful. This is something I shall never forget."[2]

While Wright repeatedly asserted that Paris was a place where one's skin color did not matter, he also praised the city's quietude and gentleness, and this led him to entertain high hopes for France as a leader in the post-war reconstruction of humanistic values and ideals in Western Europe. He could well react as a tourist from a technologically advanced country who found Parisian plumbing and sanitation facilities and driving habits damn "primitive"; he could find the French "earthy" and unashamedly sensual—which both titillated and estranged his rather puritanical sensibilities—in the attitudes to food and sex. He could well be irritated by the lack of efficiency and drive, the lack of interest in success which seemed to prevail in a country where shops were closed for two hours at noontime. He nourished great expectations for Paris as the place where an appeal to the humanity in man would be made in a materialistic age, a new definition created of what Malraux called "the human condition."

Considering how easily Wright could lend his own feelings about Paris to Eva Blount, one may be surprised that he made so little use of the city in his works. His fellow black Americans appear to have dealt with Paris at much greater length in fiction than he did. Baldwin took Paris as the only background to his second novel, *Giovanni's Room*, not to mention the numerous idyllic French episodes found throughout his subsequent fiction, from *Another Country* to *Just Above My Head*. William Gardner Smith's *The Stone Face* also was set in Paris and dealt in depth with French reactions to blacks from several countries and racism vis-à-vis North Africans. And, not to speak of Chester Himes's autobiographies, his novel *A Case of Rape*, set in the Latin Quarter, also treats of French racial prejudice. One must consider, however, that Wright's unpublished novel, "Island of Hallucination," which was to be completed around 1958, should be taken into account because it was all-important in his fictional depiction of Paris.

Indeed, the whole story told in "Island of Hallucination" is set in Paris, with the exception of the initial scenes which occur in a transatlantic plane and at Shannon airport. Interestingly, when the protagonist escapes from the racist nightmare of Mississippi and flees to France with six thousand dollars in cash, he initially does not harbor any precise expectations concerning Paris. His buddies, now stationed with the NATO forces in Europe, have only written him that it was a swinging city where friendly girls were plentiful and black boys not unwelcome. At the end of *The Long Dream*, the initial volume in the Fishbelly trilogy and then the only one published, Zeke's letter to Fish reads:

> ". . . you ought to come to France. . . . Get out of jail and come over here and take a long rest from all of that white folks mess. France ain't no heaven, but folks don't kill you for crazy things. These white folks just more like human beings than them crackers back there in Mississippi." . . .
> That letter made up his mind. It was to France he would go, to Paris. The moment he was free he would be off.[3]

In reality, Rex Fishbelly Tucker's first initiation to Paris is a hard confrontation. Two French characters, the congenial lawyer Jacques Duval and the luscious singer Nicole Rivet, whom Fish meets separately during his air trip, both express joy at returning to the pleasant atmosphere of the city and they display a striking, easygoing friendliness toward the young black American. But their congenial, unprejudiced manners are simply part of a confidence game which the two accomplices play on the newcomer. Under pretense of helping him get an apartment, they make off with a third of his fortune. As a result, the black American's first favorable impressions of Paris are immediately counterbalanced by negative thoughts. While waiting for Jacques to return with information about Nicole's whereabouts, he sits in a café and notes physical and cultural differences: in Paris, the knobs are in the center of the doors; the waiters ladle you your change out of bulging pockets; hot milk is used in coffee instead of cream; mostly the women seem relaxed and not ashamed of being females. Watching a pretty woman with a big diamond ring sop up the salad dressing in her plate and lick her fingers, he likes the earthiness of these people as well as their politeness to him. But Jacques never shows up and Fish realizes he has been cheated. The couple have used sex and racial balm as a bait and sympathy as the come-on; on his guard against racial taunts only, he was so hungry for human attention that he fell an easy prey to a guise of kindness.

Mulling over this, Fish later stands upon a bridge, looking blankly into the dark, indifferent waters of the Seine. At the end of book one, in the manner of Honoré de Balzac's Rastignac ready to go to the conquest of Paris, he confronts the city, swearing with iron resolve never to be such a fool again. Again, at the close of chapter 14, he reiterates his defiance, shaking his clenched fist at the sleeping metropolis, for, by then, he has found his revenge: he is going to impregnate French girls until the French people are paid back in a fashion they'll never forget.

In fact, because of his initial misadventure, Fishbelly is too wrapped up in his own obsessions to be aware of even the architectural beauty of Paris, although he spends his first evening walking through the city. Later, however, it strikes him now and again. As he walks past closed bootstalls along the embankments toward the seventh arrondissement at night, he suddenly notices on his left a squat structure whose Grecian pillars remind him of his history book pictures and on whose upper facade he can read "Chambre des Députés." Beyond the stone bridge, there swims a sea of lights. It is the Place de la Concorde, which he crosses, going down an avenue toward a dreamlike church bathed in floodlights; he later walks past movie houses and huge neon-lit cafés until he finds himself in darker side streets where prostitutes ply their trade. A Parisian will recognize the Madeleine area and the Grands boulevards. There Fishbelly comes across Anita, a prostitute with whom he spends tumultuous hours. He emerges with his suitcase, walking like a blind man in the dark streets, not caring whither he goes, unaware even of the name of the city. Returning to the Left Bank after vainly checking for a message from his pals at the Gare des Invalides air terminal, he slouches back through the Latin Quarter until he comes across orgiastic jazz music streaming from the lighted windows of café La Pergola. There he feels more at home, as he is in a black district. While an ornate juke box plays "Send for Me," a bespectacled youngster, who prides himself upon writing for *Real Jazz,* asks him point blank whether he knows who played trumpet for Earl Hines in 1924 at the Sunset Cafe in Chicago. Fish cannot answer, and to his amazement, the youngster tells him that jazz is his *culture,* a term he had never heard anybody in America apply to black music. For him, jazz is relaxation, but the French study it as art. It becomes evident by now that Wright exposes his black American protagonist to a series of culture shocks in order to emphasize his inability to understand the new scene he must function in.

The protagonist's approach to Paris is as blundering as that of any uninitiated tourist. But a few friendly French people help; Madame Couteau, the owner of the Prinspol Hotel where he is staying, sends him to a nearby café where some English is spoken and he lives on coffee and sandwiches for a few days. He even ventures to the Right Bank again, finding himself watching an American movie on the Champs-Elysées. Gradually, he can relax in cafes with whites of all nationalities sitting next to him. He is elated by the number of Africans, Chinese, Indonesians, and colored people who swarm the streets. He can watch Africans escorting blondes on their arms and think of doing the same.

At this juncture there occurs the first of the "Five Episodes" from the novel, which were published in the anthology *Soon, One Morning,* edited by Herbert Hill. Fastidiously dressed up, Fishbelly sports a colorful set of clothes and a gray felt hat with a pecked orange-and-black band adorned with a red feather. In high spirits, he saunters down to the Place de la Sorbonne and comes across a student demonstration against American forces in France under the command of General Ridgeway. The police stand by with truncheons ready. The demonstrators are greatly amused when, catching sight of Fishbelly's hat, they change their slogan from "Ridgeway, Go home" to "Quel chapeau americain" (what an American hat!), and start running wildly after him. They are only after his outlandish hat but Fish does not see the fun of it, so present in the mind are the Mississippi lynching mobs. A last minute rescue by Madame Couteau at the hotel door does not save him from abandoning his hat to the cheering mob.

The next episode in the novel, which was also published, deals with a scene at Imbert's Restaurant. It begins like a vignette of typical Parisian life:

> Entering Imbert's restaurant on rue Casimir Delavigne, he found every table taken and he took his place inside the door in a short queue to wait his turn. The restaurant was a family business operated by jolly, bustling, rotund Madame Imbert and her pretty daughter who served the tables. Monsieur Imbert, who could be seen manipulating pots and pans on a sizzling stove through a window-like rear wall, was a beefy, red-headed man wearing a white chef's cap and apron. Knowing his ignorance of the language, the Imberts were always kind to Fishbelly and made him feel at home.[4]

But the scene has quite a different aim than providing a glimpse of a cheap Paris eating place. When Fishbelly sits at the table which an old woman has just vacated reluctantly, he discovers that what she was vainly looking for was her set of false teeth. He runs after her in the street to return it to her, and she thanks him by slapping him angrily, so great is her shame. Here, the narrator stresses the similarities between the woman's shame because of her toothless mouth and the shame of the black man linked to the color of his skin.

Soon, the newcomer becomes acquainted with other members of the black American colony. He meets J. Carter Brown, alias Mechanical, a strange-looking, psychologically complex creature who makes a living by spying on the group for the CIA. He is taken to café Tournon, which indeed was very much part of the Left Bank setting in the mid 1950s. When people crossed the Rue de Vaugirard behind the Luxembourg Palace, they could not fail to notice a throng of young people, all the shades from white to black, seated on brightly colored cane and aluminum chairs under a bright yellow awning; there, loud conversation and boisterous laughter mingled with the blue smoke of cigarettes. But the novel focuses more extensively on dialogue and characterization than on description in order to illuminate the political and sentimental intrigues and rivalries afoot among the black expatriates and their associates or bedmates, most Scandinavian or English girls and French students.

Among these, Fish meets Yvette Lafon, the communist daughter of a well-off senator and, attracted to her though not really in love, he can now enjoy April in Paris, looking at tender green leaves or the liquid gold of the afternoon sun splashing against the gray, age-old buildings. To seduce Yvette, he takes his cue from the stereotypes of the American visiting Paris like a pilgrim—a thing he now claims he has wanted to do all his life after reading and hearing about the city. When the young woman tries to dispel the romantic myth, telling him that there is another Paris—one of hunger and destitution and suffering under the smiling boulevards—Fish characteristically sends politics to hell and prays to have his dream for at least one day. They roam the streets together. From the Tuileries Gardens, beyond the swirling traffic on Place de la Concorde, they catch a glimpse of the long vista leading up to the Arc de Triomphe and they walk up the Champs-Elysées, strolling under jutting branches of blooming chestnut trees, past spouting fountains and beds of flowers. This time the ambiance and even the physical appearance of the city are harmoniously tinged by the protagonist's feelings of desire and elation. He claims he is in love with Yvette's Paris, with its streets, the people sitting, drinking, and reading. More, he is curious about France, about what it represents for Yvette whom he clearly casts into the role of his initiator to French culture. Surprisingly, the young communist's vision is expressed in terms which are not reminiscent of French revolutionary ideals but rather of what the Statue of Liberty symbolizes: not only is France seen as stern, though compassionate, with the fires of justice burning in her eyes, but she holds a flaming torch and, nearly in the words of Emma Lazarus, outdoes America in offering shelter, light, and comradeship to the ignorant and homeless of the world. France is ready to provide for all, regardless of creed and race. Also, her sacred mission consists in keeping alive on earth the sense of grandeur, glory, and destiny in man. Admittedly, this is only an idealistic girl's point of view and humanistic gospel, but she takes it seriously. And the reader is invited to do so, as Fishbelly himself claims he now finds in Yvette an embodiment of France.

After having café crème upon the terrace at Fouquet's, the swankiest place on the Champs-Elysées, the couple later recross the Seine in order to have dinner at the Méditerrannée, on Place de l'Odeon, at Yvette's suggestion. This is a plush restaurant with a uniformed doorman and stiffly resplendent maitre d'hotel in black and white. It introduces the reader to the Paris of gourmets. After drinking apéritif, the couple enjoy "homard aux aromates" with cold, dry white wine and "tounedos sauce béarnaise" with red. As a result, after this luscious symphony of lobster, steak in perfumed cream, crisp bread, and generous wines, the delights of haute cuisine leave Fish elated, while Yvette is somewhat tipsy even before they return to Club Monseigneur, the most expensive boite in the city where he gallantly treats Yvette to champagne brut, drinking a toast to freedom. That night, Yvette, still

a virgin, yields to Fishbelly who, were he not bent on avenging himself
upon the French, might fall in love with her as much as she has done
with him.

In brief, the familiar image of Paris as a city of architectural beauty,
the cradle of refined culture and generous ideals, the provider of fine
food and entertainment gradually displaces the image of an indifferent
metropolis where crooks can take advantage of the black American's
thirst for love. Repeatedly, Yvette remarks that Fish can't relax and
simply be happy in Paris. There is so much beauty in the city and he
hardly notices the changing weather. The nights, the colors, the
sounds are all so wonderful and he remains involved in considerations
about the racial problem.

The narrator seems to imply that some of the gifts Paris has to
offer are wasted on such a complex-ridden, uncultured protagonist as
Fishbelly. Like a stereotypical American he is uninterested in French
history, or in history per se, which he only conceives as "something
that happened." Yvette tells him about kings and popes and courtly
life, yet he is mostly fascinated by the bloody massacres of the Revolution while his favorite hero is not Joan of Arc, but Fouché, Napoleon's
chief of the secret police.

Nevertheless, he is curious about Yvette's childhood during World
War II. This enables Wright to add a dimension to the image of
French life which Paris represents. The city now consists, so to speak,
of layers and accretions of time, of memories, of eras which may be
bygone but still shape the present. Thus Yvette tells about her life in
the city during the early years of the war, with so little heat and food
that the children stayed in bed half the day to save energy; she tells
about their growing lettuce in window boxes and tomatoes in the
bathtub which they had dragged on to the balcony. She talks about
eating black market rabbits which might well have been cats; she
reminisces about her warming herself by burning in the stove butter
pilfered from her father's stock in the cellar without his missing any,
so enormous were his hoardings of it. And her worst memory was of
a German air raid, with a direct hit which nearly trapped her in the
shelter from which she only emerged to see a man cut off a dead
woman's finger with his pocket knife in order to steal her diamond
ring.

But Paris also is evoked as a city very much alive in the present,
laboring under ideological pressure and the claims of allegiance made
by the competing blocks during the Cold War, even sometimes torn
by brutal strife. Another unpublished episode from the novel recounts
a second anti-American demonstration, this time violently repressed
by the police, with an uncanny sense of place. On rue de Vaugirard,

Fishbelly looks at walls scrawled with stenciled slogans: RIDGEWAY, GO HOME! A BAS L'IMPERIALISME! A BAS L'AMERIQUE! VIVE LE PARTI COMMUNISTE! which he has seen daily since his arrival. Turning into rue de Médicis, he sees, flanking the Jardin du Luxembourg, a throng of blue-caped, steel-helmeted *gardes mobiles* with bayoneted rifles at the ready. He walks down rue Corneille aiming for the shelter of his hotel. Once again his way is barred as he sees, through the columns of the Théâtre Français, that the Place de l'Odéon is jammed with students flaunting banners and chanting: "RIDGEWAY, GO HOME! RIDGEWAY, GO HOME!" While hundreds of people watch from the windows of the buildings forming the place, still more guards rush at a dead run out of rue Casimir Delavigne. His heart in his mouth, Fishbelly whirls into rue de Conde and manages to take refuge in a barbershop as the owner is frantically pulling down the grillwork over this glass window. He can watch the guard push the mob back with rifle butts and nightsticks under a hail of cobblestones. Shattering glass explodes, blood glistens on the pavement, and Fish can even catch a glimpse of Mechanical acting as a police indicator before tear-gas grenades burst like white blossoms and he doubles up, vomiting.

So, Paris also is a violent, dangerous city where the forces of law and order are ruthless, as Fish discovers when he finds that Yvette, wounded by the police, has dragged herself to his hotel room. Paris is the white man's territory, as Ned Harrison, a friendly and wise black American lawyer reveals to the greenhorn. Worse, it is the center of the Cold War, since UNESCO, NATO, and SHAPE have headquarters there or nearby. The city may well be described as a crossroads of politics, culture, ideologies, and entertainment. It seems to be free, but the French police and international spies are watching. French people think they are at liberty to act wild but they are really under surveillance.

For everybody's enlightenment, Ned, who clearly derives much from Wright himself, contrasts the old, civilized ideals of the French, who are sentimental and cynical at the same time, with the newness of America, but he has no illusions about the degree of liberty one can really enjoy there. He even thinks the French are among the bosses of spies like Mechanical. Having lived in France since the end of the war, he is persuaded that the French love black Americans and want them in Paris. But it is necessary to speak the language and understand the culture in which one lives. Fishbelly's mentor launches into a brief explanation of French culture: it was created and has been maintained out of the Catholic belief in a mission, that of civilizing the globe, characterized as a world of heathens, among whom blacks are the most visible. If tribal Africans are a real challenge to French culture, black Americans are already broken in and civilized, which is why the French like them so much.

The language barrier must disappear, at least in part, for Paris to be understood. Gradually, though his French is very crude, Fishbelly manages a boulevard variety of it. His manners help, too; always well-dressed and polite, he tips generously and is popular with many Parisians who call him "a good guy." Yet his ignorance of the language plays tricks upon him. In a brief episode, linguistic inadequacy is the basis of comedy as well as difficulties. Fish is drinking his beer in a cafe when he hears a swarthy customer seated next to him shout to the waiter, "Un noir bien chaud" (literally a "A very hot black"). This means "a sizzling hot black coffee," but Fish understands it to mean "Here's a black (man) in great danger." Later, when "Enlevez le noir" is shouted from the pantry, he understands it again to mean "Take away the black (man)," instead of "Here's your black (coffee)." Because Yvette's brother, angry at Fish because he is her sweetheart, is said to be after him, Fish rushes to the door and dashes off into the street to escape being snatched away. When he hears a shout "Voilà le noir" ("Here's our black man"), he glances back and sees Yvette's brother and his friends brandishing walking sticks. His previous, uncalled-for agitation due to linguistic misunderstanding has signaled him to their attention, and they chase him until he disappears into a basement.

Topographically, apart from the Concorde and Champs-Elysées area, Wright's Paris in this novel hardly stretches beyond the Latin Quarter. On one occasion, Fish and Mechanical take a taxi to the red light district of Pigalle. Beyond Place Blanche, they alight at the door of the Cigale, a popular jazz club, and come across the Nigerian friend of Anita, the whore who has just taken a client into her hotel. The novel, however, does not indulge in vignettes of low-down life in "gay Paree." The description of the joint is spare; a five-man Negro orchestra makes the music roar for an international audience mostly composed of black and white GIs in civilian clothes. Contagious blues music, bursting bosoms, nude shoulders, and rouged lips fill the place, whose atmosphere is dense with cigarette smoke. The setting is only briefly sketched toward an explanation of the techniques of selling women to soldiers.

At the end of the book, the very center of Paris becomes the scene for tragedy as Mechanical, at the close of a series of suspenseful hesitations and moves, jumps from the towers of Notre Dame in front of countless spectators. The episode recalls the melodramatic sequence in which Quasimodo, the grotesque hunchback, barricades himself into the cathedral and faces the angry populace in Victor Hugo's *Notre Dame of Paris*.

The spy has been exposed and, in what should be construed as a desperate attempt to create a link with men rather than to escape punishment, he has climbed the steps to the towers and now threatens to jump while the police plead with him. Fish and Ned drive to Place St Michel, only to see a background of velvety darkness against which the gargoyle-laden facade shines in the rain under the spotlights. Along the minuscule and narrow rue du Chat-qui-pêche, they rush to the scene. The paved square in front of Notre Dame is filled with a crowd interspersed with opened umbrellas while the characteristic "Paaam-pooong" of the French police sirens and the whistles of the traffic cops are heard all around and roving spotlights cut through the night in an atmosphere of ominous excitement reminiscent of the rooftop chase in *Native Son*.

French voices are heard, commenting on the occurrence: That man is mad! Does he really want to kill himself? Is it a stunt for an adver-tisement? Is it a joke? Doing this on top of a church is blasphemous! However, quite unable to understand Mechanical's reasons, the Pari-sians remain a sort of choir in the tragedy which is indeed a sort of self-inflicted black crucifixion. Some of the French are actors, however: a priest argues with the desperate man, whose hands and legs clutch the tip of a gargoyle while his body swings free, in order to catch his attention, while others throw a rope net over him. But Mechanical draws his knife and slices across the wet strands which he twists to hang himself; his limp body spins at the end of a rope until a priest cuts it loose, not to let such blasphemy last, and it plummets down and crashes on the pavement below. Again, rain and night, and the revolving beacon of the Eiffel Tower circling a golden blade through the Paris darkness—like the beacon of Memphis airport in "Bright and Morning Star"—such details hark back to similar scenes in Wright's earlier fiction, notably to the death of Aunt Sue, or the capture of Bigger Thomas. The novelist's visual, nearly visionary imagination decidedly found an apt setting to recast again a climaxing melodramatic episode.

The publication of "Island of Hallucination" would reveal that Wright's use of Paris and its changing image favorably compares with the use William Gardner Smith made of it in *The Stone Face* (with the very important difference that Wright does not deal with the plight of the Arabs in Paris while Smith illuminates it all along and denounces French racism). It goes far beyond what Chester Himes makes of the city in *A Case of Rape* but remains somewhat slight in comparison with James Baldwin's treatment of the theme. All four novelists deal primarily with black American expatriates, but Wright's novel, more than any other, focuses on the debates, intrigues, and rivalries which agitated the group at the café Tournon; these are exposed and analyzed in detail, sometimes to the detriment of his depiction of French life.

It is tempting to infer, and indeed possible to document, that many of the events in the novel actually happened and that the city which Fishbelly explores is patterned after Wright's own images and discoveries of Parisian life. As indicated at the opening of this essay, I have dealt elsewhere with Wright's own experiences in, and reactions to, the French capital. Without going into redundant detail, a few salient points can be emphasized among Wright's own expectations and impressions as they shaped his image of Paris.

First, Wright went to Paris not as a greenhorn but as a full-fledged, widely recognized writer in search of the "movable feast" celebrated by Hemingway and very much as a black successor to the Lost Generation, whose high priestess, Gertrude Stein, represented in his eyes an American literary star who beckoned him to Paris, as is shown by their correspondence of the mid 1940s.

He also went to Paris as an American intellectual of the left-wing persuasion, attracted by the philosophy of existentialism as represented by Sartre, Camus, and De Beauvoir. He believed they could provide answers to the societal questions which plagued the chaotic, postwar world and which the United States was incapable of even formulating. He was also confident that so-called "old" Europe could find a way of rejecting both the materialism of capitalist America and the totalitarianism of Stalinist Soviet Union. He came looking for an expression of the humanism which the Enlightenment had given the West in order to adapt it to the needs of the world.

Lastly, and as important, he left the United States because racism made it difficult for him to live there, just like his having been a Communist made his return risky, if not impossible, during the McCarthy witch hunts.

On the one hand, these circumstances must be borne in mind when one evaluates Wright's image of Paris as a racial haven, a cultural hotbed, and the capital of humanism. On the other hand, one must take into account what Wright actually did find in Paris, which changed his assumptions about it: the increasingly felt presence of a non-European immigrant population; and the continuous importance of political intrigues, pressures, and strife between right and left as well as between East and West, which riddled even the black expatriate colony; the difficulty of getting into French life, which was compounded by Wright's somewhat inadequate knowledge of the language; but also the congenial welcome and reactions of many people, which persuaded him that they were not racists as far as black Americans were concerned.

Finally, unlike his fictional protagonist, Fishbelly, Wright went to France with his family and did not experience solitude in Paris. Yet, when he emphasized the rootlessness of the black American expatriate among the friendly Parisians, there seems to be an autobiographical hint, like the one found in Baldwin's essays about his first years abroad and discovery of his identity in Paris. Wright did not project the image of "fair France" found, for instance, in certain poems by Countee Cullen, nor did he condemn France national chauvinism as flamboyantly as Claude McKay had done in *Banjo*. In his eyes, Paris represented French culture, and he could admire it and, with time, enjoy the beauty of age-old monuments without being awed by them; yet, he could not, as a black man, accept the notion of the country's "civilizing mission" which had furthered and backed colonial conquest. As a result, somewhat like Fishbelly, he lived *in* Paris but he was not really *of* it. His acquaintance with the city and knowledge of French society were sufficient to make him realize that he would never know them completely. Rather humbly, he was satisfied with celebrating the better aspects of Parisian life and the glories of French culture while limiting his use of Paris as a setting to what he was most conversant with—the circles and groups, mostly American and black, with whom he associated in the Latin Quarter cafés around rue Monsieur le Prince; that is, his "alien" home outside of his homeland.

Notes

1. Richard Wright, *The Outsider* (New York: Harper, 1953), 206–10.
2. Letter to Michel Fabre, 12 December 1964.
3. Richard Wright, *The Long Dream* (New York: Harper & Row, 1958), 398.
4. Herbert Hill, ed., *Soon, One Morning* (New York: Knopf, 1962), 245.

7

Selves of the City, Selves of the South: The City in the Fiction of William Attaway and Willard Motley

JOHN CONDER

OF his two novels, William Attaway's first, *Let Me Breathe Thunder,* is not at all race conscious, whereas *Blood on the Forge* has a strong racial consciousness at its very center. Something milder must be said of the Nick Romano series, the two novels by Willard Motley relevant to this essay:[1] *Knock on Any Door* and *Let No Man Write My Epitaph.* The first of the series can hardly be considered race conscious in any serious way, centering as it does on Nick Romano, an Italian-American in Chicago. But the second work in the series does *become* race conscious because an interracial action in one of its subplots concludes the novel. Of course this second novel hardly has race at its center, focusing as it does on three white characters: Nellie Watkins; her illegitimate son, Nick Romano, Jr., whose father is now deceased; and Louie, the brother of the deceased Nick Romano. The interracial action nonetheless involves one of the novel's three central characters (Louie, who falls in love with black Chicago waitress Judy), and thus it is linked to the broader action of the work. Its development in the last fifth of the novel, and its continuation even into the novel's concluding pages, gives it a place of special prominence.

The work of each novelist ends on a note of hope related to the city as an environment. In *Blood on the Forge,* former southern black sharecropper Big Mat dies in industrial violence in a Pennsylvania mill town; his two surviving brothers do not return to their home in Kentucky but instead depart for Pittsburgh, a city described as a place offering a possibly viable future for the battle-scarred brothers, Melody and Chinatown Mott. In *Knock on Any Door,* the execution of Nick Romano is an appropriate ending to a novel notable throughout for its unrelieved gloom. In the sequel, *Let No Man Write My Epitaph,* the environment of Chicago is a knife cutting two ways for Nick Romano Jr., the son of the executed Nick. Although he becomes a dope addict, Chicago has provided him with sufficient psychological childhood nutriments to make it possible to speculate, at the end, that he will remain permanently unaddicted, that he will become an artist, that he will overcome the doubts of the liberal socialite Holloways and marry their daughter, Barbara, in due time. And although both black and white Chicago frown on interracial relationships, Judy, who at the end deliberates whether to retain her relationship with Louie, may indeed return to him and marry him. Motley treats this matter, too, in such a way as to make this speculation possible.

Not in the South, but in the northern city Attaway offers hope for his black people; and, at the last, after the unmitigated horrors of *Knock on Any Door* and the mitigated ones of *Let No Man Write My Epitaph,* Motley offers Chicago as a symbol of hope for black and white people alike. But this parallel is not sufficient to describe the true relationship between the works of these writers. Attaway's novel and those by Motley supplement each other. Their respective novels depict a historical reality. Attaway's novel focuses on the movement of southern blacks to the industrial North. There he shows that racial conflict, a reality in the South, is but a mask concealing the underlying reality of class conflict in the North, a battle engendered there by economic forces spawned by industrialization. Attaway concludes his novel with his black people departing for Pittsburgh. Despite the presence in his novel of a mystique of the land that serves as a force giving identity to southern blacks, Attaway does not permit his black characters to return home. He offers no guarantees, but he does suggest that if they are to have a future which they can regard without fear and trembling, it must be found in the northern city.

Motley's novel *Knock on Any Door* can be thought of as picking up where Attaway's left off. Chicago is Motley's substitute for Pittsburgh, and his novels portray a city life which black people from the South will inevitably confront when they settle in northern cities. *Let No Man Write My Epitaph,* the second novel in the Nick Romano series, shows that the city retains a modified form of the race conflict depicted in Attaway's South. The shock of the Romano family when Louie brings Judy home to dinner and the hostility of black people to Louie when Judy brings him to a black bar—these are cases in point. Motley's first view of the city may be that it is primarily a destructive environment, and he later shows that race poses serious problems; but he finally suggests that the city will be the only environment for solving racial problems. How else could anyone explain Motley's ending on a note of hope for the future of Judy and Louie in Chicago?

I understand the reasons for hesitating before reading Motley's novels as an extension of Attaway's. In the context of both Nick Romano novels, the Louie-Judy relationship seems but a minor coda, less than ten percent of the total volume of these two works. Black author Motley focuses mainly on white Italian-Americans, a point that brings us to the second reason to hesitate before reading these authors' works in tandem. Whatever problems Italian-Americans encountered in the city, Italian ethnicity made them Italian problems, not black ones. Finally, a third cause for hesitation emerges: if Attaway had written a city novel about black (or white) people, his vision of their problems would probably be different from Motley's because they are, after all, two different writers.

I believe there is a brief and reasonable answer to these objections, and it is found in Blanche Gelfant's view of the distinctiveness of the twentieth-century American city novel. Techniques may vary from author to author as each strives to capture the city as antagonist, but these differing techniques nonetheless emphasize certain shared themes, the self-alienation of the central character being one of them. In *Knock on Any Door*, Gelfant finds that Motley "in order to stress the sociological thesis . . . has reduced character, situation, and setting to skeletal essentials."[2] Much the same can be said of *Let No Man Write My Epitaph*, even if the novel is a bit more complicated by the fact that Nick Jr. absorbs some positive influences from an environment that transforms him (we hope not permanently) into a dope addict.

I disagree with Gelfant that style, structure, and characterization are so lean as to constitute a defect in *Knock on Any Door*. But have it as you will, one point still remains true: these novels by Motley represent the paradigm of all city novels in which a self is destroyed or damaged by its environment. Motley's novels convey these essential features of the city novel which no writer would likely avoid, no matter what victimized group were the center of attention. Motley's Italian-Americans are *generic* city victims. Their problems are the generic problems of the city's victimized poor. To create this sense of the generic seems to have been Motley's intention, since the title, *Knock on Any Door*, means that we will find the counterpart of a Nick Romano behind any slum door. Had Attaway written his own city novel, our experience with this kind of novel suggests that his idiosyncratic vision would nonetheless have adopted something like the themes of Motley's work. This view is fortified by the fact that Attaway pivots his novel about an identity problem suffered by his black characters after they arrive in the industrial North but *before* they leave for a northern city. But more of this identity problem later.

Attaway's and Motley's novels are compatible not only on a thematic level but also on a formal one. Read sequentially, the novels unfold before the reader a variety of naturalistic visions, and it is their *variety* that is crucial here. The character of each vision forces us to see with great clarity that the movement of black people from the South to the North is a highly qualified benefit to them. In leaving the South, they leave positive as well as negative elements behind. When they arrive in the North, they encounter an environment destructive of themselves. The North offers hope only in a distant future. Adding to the poignancy is the fact that these naturalistic visions produce an accurate historical overview of the great black migration alluded to earlier.

Our history lesson begins in the first section of *Blood on the Forge*, which establishes an important mystique of the land which emerges in comments like Big Mat's statement: "Muck ground git big every year jest like a woman oughta," or "Muck ground jest a woman," or more personally "Maybe muck ground my woman."[3] The parallel between the fecundity of the muck land (that tiny portion of the land which the Mott brothers rent and which is still fruitful) and of human life is reinforced again when Big Mat reflects: "It was a good thing to break the land for seeding and watch the land get big. Field, animal or man—the seed should be sunk in the spring for a good crop" (31). These parallels between the human and nonhuman worlds create a relationship between the two worlds very much like the one prevailing in Steinbeck's *Grapes of Wrath*.[4] Like Steinbeck's novel, Attaway's book suggests with great power that human beings are a part of nature. For Attaway, a sexual force running through each world links the two worlds, and this view leads to another: that nearness to the land is a great good because it is a source of personal identity and freedom. This latter perception manifests itself when Mat, feeling sick because he is depersonalized in the industrial North, reflects, "These would be good days for sick men to feel the earth" (200). This same second view is supported by the narrative statement: "The fire and flow of metal seemed an eternal act which had grown beyond men's control. It was not to be compared to crops that one man nursed to growth and ate at his own table" (212).

Of course, in the novel's first section the land is nearly infertile. As Mat puts it, "Wind and rain comin' outen the heavens ever' season, takin' the good dirt down to the bottoms" (17). "The land done got tired. All the land got tired, 'ceptin the muck in the bottoms" (44). Hence the parallel between the land and the human world emphasizes unproductiveness: the barrenness of the land and the inability of Mat's wife Hattie to bear children (pregnant a seventh time, she has had six miscarriages) symbolize the fact that the black family unit has no future in the South. To be sure, Mat sees Hattie's inability to carry to term as a curse God placed on him for being an illegitimate child. But if this sharecropper is cursed, he is cursed by white southern landowners who make unreasonable demands for payments of debts which Mat has been driven to incur. These demands converge with false allurements from northern industrialists who want cheap black labor to break white labor unions, and the convergence impels Mat to make this the occasion to leave land and wife behind and, with his brothers, to seek out the possibilities for a better life in the North.

In the Pennsylvania steel mill town where Mat and his brothers work, they encounter Smothers, a black man who has been seriously injured in the steel mills, crying out: *"It's a sin to melt up the ground"* (178) and "the ground got feelin'" (62). The novel's first naturalistic vision depends on the fact that "the ground got feelin'." Because it does, man, as part of it, can absorb that sense of kinship to gain a sense of personal wholeness and autonomy in a world where he is no alien. Because the land was not always infertile, this was Mat's essential experience before he left the South. Once he leaves, he and his brothers enter another naturalistic world, one which has lost all contact with nature, a purely social world whose patterns are inexorably formed by the prevailing economic conditions.

This new naturalistic world, however, is not the destiny of Mat and his brothers alone. Attaway makes it quite clear that it heralds a new phase in history, a phase which inescapably will embrace all the South, black and white alike. Mat speaks for more than himself when, before he departs for the North, he says:

> Ain't nothin' make me leave the land if it is good land. . . . Take more 'n jest trouble to run me off the hills. . . . The old folks make crop here afore we was born. . . . Now the land done got tired. . . . It do somethin' to a man when the corn come up like tired old gents.
>
> Somehow it seem like I know why the land git tired. And it jest seem like it come time to git off. The land has jest give up, and I guess it's good for things to come out like this. Now us got to give up too. (43–44)

The larger part of the novel traces the consequences of people having to "give up." They enter a phase in history where economic determinism dominates, and this determinism becomes the major element of the novel's other naturalistic vision. The first naturalistic phase depicted men with free will who were close to and, in fact, part of nature. The deterministic phase is far more frustrating than the earlier naturalistic phase, precisely because the second phase does *not* deny free will. It divorces humans from closeness to the land and makes them part of an economically determined society. Although they still possess free will, that society limits so drastically the options of individuals that certain consequences follow with statistical certainty. Better to have no free will in such a world than a freedom whose exercise is meaningless.

The triumph of economic determinism produces three consequences. The first is that an exploitative economic structure results in class warfare because it appeals to human greed. To resist exploitation, ethnic whites try to form unions which put them at odds with the capitalists who exploit them; and the capitalists respond by luring southern blacks north in an effort to break the unions. They believe the black people are so used to exploitation that they will work for lower wages outside a union context.

The second consequence is that these southern blacks inevitably, even if temporarily, lose their individual identity in such a structure because changed conditions make it impossible for them to express their true selves in unfamiliar surroundings. The point is made by a white ethnic, Zanski, to black Melody: "Feller from long way off die like plant put on rock. Plant grow if it get ground like place it came from" (98). At the novel's end, the blindness of Chinatown makes him a "twin" to another blind black person, a soldier, thus showing the loss of identity in two plants put on alien rock.

This loss of individual identity is emphasized in the person of Big Mat in a way that points to self-alienation for all those who have lost contact with the land. Despite his hatred of white Southerners, Mat retains his identity in the South because he had a sense of control over the land when it was fertile and because he had a sense of community with his wife, despite the fact that she is unable to carry a child to term successfully. The land acts as a vital substitute for his failure to become a father, and that is one meaning of his statement, "Muck land jest a woman." His relationship to his wife and to the land are thus inextricably intertwined, for in a sense he is married to both. These relationships constitute his identity. Once he loses these, he loses his identity; and because his identity restrained his hatred of white people, he loses that restraint and becomes a mass of dehumanized hatred, a strikebreaker described in these terms: "He had always been the man to slaughter animals, and now these people became merely frightened animals" (253). After he slays one white man, he himself is slain by another, but in a sense he has already died because he has been stripped of his individualizing selfhood.

It is easy to see a third consequence of economic determinism, the race warfare which seems prophesized in the sheriff's estimate of the events leading to Big Mat's death. Deputized by that sheriff to put down a strike, Big Mat is animated by hatred of white people to fulfill his mission, a fact interpreted by the sheriff in this way: "That's the thing 'bout nigger deputies—they're fightin' the race war 'stead of a labor strike" (275). But Attaway's novel sees the warfare in other terms. It is sympathetic to the class-warfare interpretation of the plight of everyone in the North, black people included; and in sending his remaining Mott brothers to Pittsburgh, Attaway sends them in quest of a new identity, a black urban identity, now that they have lost their old one. Although Melody thinks for a moment that he and Chinatown might return to Kentucky, "he did not think about that very hard. *He was beginning to feel the truth: they would never go home. Now they would go to Pittsburgh*" (276, emphasis provided).

Attaway knows that his black people have no future in the South and so must remain in the North, but clearly he is ambivalent about their fate in the city:

> Many Negroes had gone to Pittsburgh before them; many were castoffs of the mills. They had settled in the bottoms of that city, making a running sore at those lowest points. But a man had told Melody where to live: the Strip, a place where rent was nearly free and guys who knew how to make out would show them the ropes. That was good. (276)

The quotation has a dual meaning, of course: in Pittsburgh there is danger, but there also is hope. The very ambiguity of the statement raises the question, what *will* happen to these black people once they get to Pittsburgh? To answer that question, call Pittsburgh, Chicago. Let migrant turn into *immigrant*. Think of Nick Romano as a *generic* victim. What happens to *him* in the city?

The naturalistic vision that supplies the answer is not a pretty one, though Willard Motley is not so skeptical about city life as Dos Passos. Unlike Dos Passos's moneyed class, Motley's elite group, the Grant Holloways among them, escape the self-effacement of the city to gain authentic selfhood. This difference between Motley and Dos Passos suggests that Motley will also find some hope for the underprivileged to gain self-realization in the city, and that hope blossoms as a hope in *Let No Man Write My Epitaph*. But that is to get ahead of our story which, in *Knock on Any Door*, is a grim tale indeed, and made all the uglier by the defining ingredient of its naturalistic vision: pessimistic environmental determinism. If the Grant Holloways flourish, the Nick Romanos are destined by their environment to die. The Nick

Romanos possess will, to be sure, but their true selves are not in charge of it because a self which is a social product has usurped the position of authentic self.

One can see how neatly Attaway's novel, which shows the loss of identity in black people in industrialized northern areas, joins with Motley's view of the northern city. If, for Attaway, southern blacks lose their identity in the industrial wastelands of the North, Motley's naturalism does not permit them to regain it once they move to the city. Instead, the city will develop for them a social identity alien to their own true beings. The determinism of *Knock on Any Door* shows the development of that self, and its development is unavoidable, an inexorable product of social conditions.

This view of the self as social product seems to be behind Aunt Rosa's words to Nick: "There's nothing wrong with people, Nick. There's something good in everybody. . . , People don't do no wrong. Not when they're left alone."[5] Now that "something good in every-body" happens to be that unique core of individuality which is man's true self, the self that represents his true nature, and it is this self which is thwarted in its development by the imposition of society's self on it. This view is supported by the lawyer's words: "There was never any happiness in this boy's life nor was there even any tinge of happiness unless it was when he was serving God at the altar. . . . Let's get out of the fog and the rain of contradictory evidence . . . When and where do we put the finger on him—on the *real* Nick Romano?" (450).

The lawyer is speaking to a jury at a trial charging Nick with slaying a brutal policeman. He argues that the murder is the climactic action of a life in which Romano began as an altar boy, then was subjected to repeated brutalities at the hands of the legal authorities (and others), and finally became a criminal. And the action of the novel dramatizes the lawyer's words that Nick is "the victim of his environ-ment" (419) through the use of a dual-self theory which shows the social conditions in the city "stripped his altar boy garments from him," as the lawyer puts it (451), and imposed an alien self on Nick which takes charge of his will.

The broad outlines of the novel show that behind its dual self-conception lies determinism. The work opens with Nick's altar-boy self basking in an admiring relation with Father O'Neil, and this altar-boy self remains with Nick to the end, though it is never permitted development beyond the age of twelve. But even after he has devel-oped the self of criminal, the altar-boy self suppressed by the socially imposed criminal self surfaces three times to take control of his will. He returns money stolen from reporter Grant Holloway during a trip to Wisconsin on which Holloway takes him because Holloway wishes to get him away from his criminal Chicago surroundings. The surfacing of that self, its repossession of the will, is comprehensible. He identifies Grant with Father O'Neil, who nurtured the altar-boy self. It surfaces again when he marries Emma. Again, the action is comprehensible. The altar-boy self, which itself was brutalized, sympathizes with the girl who was brutalized by her family. Finally, it erupts at the climactic moment of the trial when Nick confesses that he killed the brutal cop, Riley.

Significantly, Nick does not crack when he handles the gun he used to kill Riley. This had been the major worry of his lawyer in deciding to put Nick on the stand to testify in his own defense. The criminal self has too much will power for that to happen. Only when the prosecutor asks, "Isn't it true that your wife killed herself because of you?" does he confess to the murder by asserting, "I'm glad I killed him! I'd do it all over again!" (437–38). The conscience of the altar-boy self converges with the knowledge that that same self possesses. It experiences deep remorse that his criminal self led him into sexual dalliances and criminal activities that impelled his wife to suicide, and it openly affirms that rightness of the criminal self's murdering a brutal policeman, the symbol of that society which denied the altar boy his right to develop.

Meanwhile the major action of the book is devoted to its deterministic content, to showing the conditions which created the new self of criminal. Two major lines of action illustrate the dramatization of this deterministic point of view. The first is represented by that change in economic circumstance, brought on by the Depression, which forces the Romano family to move from a middle-class neighborhood to a lower class one filled with what are called "young toughs." Moved to another school filled with tougher kids, Nick gets an unexpected beating from a priest, and the shock waves generated by the beating loosen the hold of the altar-boy self by beginning the creation of a new self through a relationship with a sympathetic delinquent (Tony by name)—a relationship which climaxes in these words: "To Nick this relationship took the place of the closeness he had felt to Father O'Neil, the comradeship he had enjoyed with his brother before they moved, the sympathy Ma had never given him, and the understanding Pa had withheld" (17).

That a new self is aborning becomes clear during Nick's reform school days, whose brutal injustices issue in the view that "each affront to one of the inmates is an affront to you" (72). The final step in the process of the creation of a new self is represented by words which describe his relations to the criminals on West Madison and

Halstead streets where Nick Romano spends most of the rest of his life: "Nick, Butch and Juan walked along West Madison each a sepa-rate and individual, unalike yet alike, set of hardboiled mannerisms; each a small fleck of undeveloped malehood swaggering, big-footed, square-shouldered, down the street" (152). From there on in, condi-tions develop the undeveloped malehood into a criminal selfhood that smothers the altar boy whenever the altar boy tries to speak. Little wonder that before Nick's execution, the narrative reads; "There was little left of him to kill, little left to die" (499).

In the cities conditions may reign supreme to the detriment of hu-mans who cannot escape their harsh environment. Certainly Motley stresses this side of life in Knock on Any Door, and the conclusion of Blood on the Forge makes it difficult to think that the surviving Mott brothers will not encounter hard times in the city, just as Motley's characters do in his first Nick Romano novel. But it is Motley's distinc-tion to recognize that if conditions make victims of us all, the condi-tions for victimization appear in rural areas as well as cities. It is also his distinction to recognize that a kind of actuarial table predicting future happiness would show that the odds for achieving self-realization are on the side of cities, not rural areas. On both points he is in a tradition of American writers stemming from Sherwood Anderson. Motley shows his allegiance to this tradition in Let No Man Write My Epitaph, and he shows it mainly in the person of Nellie Watkins, once a lover of Nick Romano and mother of his ille-gitimate son, Nick Jr.

To strengthen the connections between his two novels, in Let No Man Write My Epitaph Motley has Nellie Watkins recall the trial of Nick Romano that concludes Knock on Any Door and, as if to cement the union between the two works, Motley embodies this flashback in virtually the same words used to dramatize a portion of the trial in the earlier novel. After binding Let No Man Write My Epitaph to its companion work, Motley prepares us, slowly but surely, for a changed view of the city by giving Nellie a broader personal history than she had in the earlier work, Knock on Any Door. That personal history includes life in rural areas. In Let No Man Write My Epitaph, we discover that as a child, Nellie was left by her mother in an Iowa detention home which also doubles as a home for unwanted children. There Nellie learned that in order to get enough to eat, it was wise to manipulate the system so that she could work in the kitchen. Food was not in greater supply on the Missouri farm where she is taken in by her Uncle Clarence and Aunt Martha. The aunt complains per-petually of the child's appetite. She would have done better to remain alert to her husband's sexual appetite, since Uncle Clarence has sex with Nellie before her stay with the couple comes to an end. There is a bit more to Nellie's background than what I have just mentioned. Aunt Martha ships Nellie off to Detroit cousins who so maltreat her that Nellie flees to Chicago, her only hope for a better life. But it is Nellie's rural background that I want to stress.

Nellie's experiences with rural life before she arrives in Chicago are a crucial part of the novel. The relationship that she imagines between her life in the detention home and her life in Missouri symbolized all of her experiences before her arrival in Chicago. Of her life on the farm, she reflects: "This was no different from the world inside [the detention home]."[6] If rural life is no different from a prison, then by way of repeated imagery Motley makes it clear that despite the dangers of Chicago life, Chicago is no more dangerous than the rural world. Hence he portrays the hazards awaiting Nellie on her entrance into Chicago by using images that merge the awesome city with the rural world: for Nellie, "The blue-black animal was always there, lying in the tall grass of skyscrapers" (37). "The tall, skyscraper night-grass hemmed them in" (41). The conditions for victimization appear both in city and country by virtue of the logic of this image, and Nellie's experiences in both places validate that logic.

But if conditions make victims of us all, some of us are luckier victims than others, and, as I mentioned earlier, the odds for self-realization are on the side of Chicago, not rural Missouri. This appears to be the main message emerging from the second Nick Romano novel, *Let No Man Write My Epitaph*. The same dreary Chicago scene dominates, and the reader is never allowed to forget that unfortunate people are inescapably a part of their environment: "*If you don't know Chicago you don't know yourself*" (183). In this milieu appears Nick Romano's illegitimate son, Nick Jr. Yet one point becomes increasingly clear. Nick's father may be dead, and circumstances are far from happy, but from lowly causes may spring noble effects. Despite Nick's troubles, conditions emerge to give him that sense of "wholesome" family which also can allow readers to see hope for this child's future.

The lowly causes are mainly people who, by and large, are themselves victims of their environment. One can begin with Nick's biological mother, Nellie. She may become a drug addict, but she has enough of the mother about her to conceal this fact for several years from her son, who remains innocent sufficiently long to think that she simply drinks too much. Even when she does suffer from a simple alcohol hangover, however, she remembers to leave her son with a coloring book before she goes out on the street to get another drink to wash her hangover away. She has an authentic sense of the need for education if her son is to flourish in this Chicago mud puddle, and she manages to transform the alcoholic (former) Judge Sullivan into a father figure for her son. He teaches her to speak well so that she can pass on that gift to her son. The judge knows the relationship between Christmas and wholesome family values and, together with three other figures who are shadier than he, purchases an electric train for Nick Jr. to play with beside a Christmas tree on Christmas Day. The father-figure and the mother thus impress the sense of family onto Nick by awakening him to the joys of Christendom's ideal family. And even the reprobates Norman, Phil, and Max reinforce Nick's sense of family by thinking of themselves as Nick's "uncles" and by behaving like uncles to him as they strive to protect him from the dangers of that very environment of which they are a part. Grant Holloway, once sympathetic to the original Nick Romano, comes across Nick's son as Grant investigates the drug problem in Chicago. He, too, can act as a sufficiently strong father to give Nick Jr. the stability to love a woman, Grant's daughter Barbara. Nick even gets a sense of the Church when he is baptized; more important, through the baptism he gains another father-figure in Juan, who was associated with Nick Sr. in the first volume and who, in this second volume, becomes Nick's godfather. Even the former Romano family, or what functioning ones are left, impart to Nick some sense of family; notably, Aunt Rosa, who visits him and identifies relationship to him, although she is of greatest help to Louie, brother of the original Nick and uncle of Nick Jr.

This "family" of the second Nick Romano may be less than ideal, but it is a supportive group, and hence Nick can grow up as at least a partly stable individual, with hope that he will, at the last, keep away from drugs for a full year so that he can, perhaps, himself become a family man by marrying Barbara. His uncle, Louie, has already become a role model, at least from the reader's perspective. If Louie can establish the ties that bind with a black woman, he will display a personal strength unprecedented in the men of the Romano family. To defy the strictures against intermarriage mandated by the "healthy" part of society is surely a sign of strength. And if Nick fulfills the condition that he himself set—to remain free of drugs for a year before seeing, possibly marrying, Barbara—he will himself have shown a capacity for transcendence: for transcending, that is, the diseased part of the society that infected him. But the real interest of the final pages of Motley's concluding novel in the Nick Romano series is that Motley comes to make it virtually impossible to distinguish the "healthy" part of society from the "diseased" part. Drugs alone seem to separate the two worlds, but if drugs are a sign of disease, so too is the racism characterizing society's "healthy" sector. If transcendence does become a reality, who then can tell whose transcendence will be the greater, Nick's or Louie's? And who can deny that in this new phase in history, transcendence must take place in the city, if it is to take place any-where at all?

Notes

1. The thematic weakness of *We Fished All Night* (1951) makes it inappropriate for discussion. The Mexican setting of *Let Noon Be Fair* (1966) disqualifies it. For a balanced discussion of the earlier novel's thematic weaknesses and technical strengths, see Robert E. Fleming, *Willard Motley* (Boston: Twayne, 1978), 74–88.

2. *The American City Novel* (Norman: University of Oklahoma Press, 1954), 249. For a discussion of "personal dissociation" as the major theme among many, see 21–26, quoted phrase 21.

3. William Attaway, *Blood on the Forge* (Chatham, N.J.: Chatham Bookseller, 1969), 27. This edition is a reissue of the original edition published by Doubleday, Doran & Co. 1941. Subsequent quotations are from the Chatham edition and page numbers appear parenthetically.

4. For a development of this point, see my *Naturalism in American Fiction: The Classic Phase* (Lexington: University Press of Kentucky, 1984), 154–58.

5. Willard Motley, *Knock on Any Door* (New York & London: Appleton-Century, 1947), 478. Subsequent quotations are from this edition and page numbers appear parenthetically.

6. Willard Motley, *Let No Man Write My Epitaph* (New York: Random House, 1958), 22. Subsequent quotations are from this edition and page numbers appear parenthetically.

8

The City as Psychological Frontier in Ralph Ellison's *Invisible Man* and Charles Johnson's *Faith and the Good Thing*

ROBERT BUTLER

In her recent study of the American heroine, Blanche Gelfant argues that the city often becomes for women characters a modern equivalent of the West because it offers them the sort of free space necessary for achieving a "new life":

> In a city throbbing with dreams and desires, the heroine learns to identify her own needs, and living among strangers she has the privacy to cultivate personal desires usually condemned by family and friends as "selfishness". . . . Enjoying physical and social space in the city, the heroine moves about freely and experiences movement as freedom. For her, the territory ahead—the essence of freedom in male myths of the West—lies around the corner, a few streets away, in another neighborhood where nobody knows her and where she alone will say who she is.[1]

Something very similar to this occurs often in African-American literature which, unlike the fiction found in main tradition of American literature, typically views pastoral places as humanly restrictive and urban space as a frontier offering human renewal. What Gelfant calls the "physical and social space" of the American city frequently provides modern black heroes and heroines with the new "territory" containing the opportunity of expanded possibilities leading to new lives. In African-American letters the northern city has often held the prominence which the West has had in mainstream American literature as a symbolic space stimulating human development, so it is not surprising that many important black writers envision the city as a liberating frontier. Ralph Ellison's *Invisible Man* and Charles Johnson's *Faith and the Good Thing* are two particularly vivid illustra-

tions of this since both novels are centered in journeys wherein the
central characters achieve radically new lives by moving from stagnant
rural existences to urban worlds characterized by greatly increased
freedom, independence, and growth.

The hero of *Invisible Man,* for example, rejects pastoral settings
such as the small town and the bucolic campus, moving to New York
which he comes to experience as a psychological frontier. The American West, described by Frederick Jackson Turner as "the meeting
point between slavery and civilization,"[2] is reborn again in Ellison's
underground, a "border area" which mediates between "the jungle of
Harlem" (5) and the decadent Manhattan of Emerson's Calamus Club
and Jack's intricate political games.[3] Although his underground, like
the West, has been "shut off and forgotten during the nineteenth
century" (5), he can reopen it through a prodigious act of will and
imagination. A vital source of power and light, it converts him from
an impotent robot into a fully conscious being able to direct his life
in his own way. Ellison's underground, then, is a revealing contrast
to the underworlds portrayed in Wright's "The Man Who Lived
Underground" and Baraka's *Dutchman.* Whereas Wright's and Baraka's victimized protagonists are murdered in tomb-like settings beneath the streets, Ellison's hero sees his ingenious subterranean
"home" (5) as a place of "hibernation" (11) providing him with the
kind of new life which traditional American heroes have found in
the West.

In biographical observations Ellison stresses the importance of the
frontier in the development of his own American consciousness. In
Shadow and Act, for example, he describes his Oklahoma boyhood as
very different from Richard Wright's southern background because
Oklahoma at that time was a "border" state having no tradition of
chattel slavery and thus it put him in contact with the liberating
values of the frontier life—independence, freedom, and a "boy's dream
of possibility."[4] In *Going to the Territory* he once again stresses the
positive aspects of the Oklahoma he grew up in as "a territory of hope"
which was in "a relatively unformed frontier stage." Furthermore, he
describes New York City as a new kind of psychic frontier which he
explores by assuming the "American role of pioneer." Emphasizing the
fact that he came to New York because he wanted "room to discover
who I was," he makes the city a kind of West because it opens up the
psychological "space" necessary for self-discovery and development.[5]

The underground is for Ellison, therefore, an urban equivalent of
what the frontier was for Thoreau, a brilliant metaphor of the limitless
possibilities of the self. Just as Thoreau exhorted his readers to become
"the Lewis and Clark . . . of your own streams and oceans; explore

your own higher latitudes,"[6] Ellison artfully interiorizes the Western myth by suggesting that selfhood may be attained by descending into our *lower* latitudes, the underground of the self which is "space, unbroken" (428), a "dimensionless room" (429) reflective of the self's "infinite possibilities" (435). Converting the territories ahead into the territories *inside* his head, Ellison's hero becomes a true citizen of his own "city . . . of dreams" (122).

Before he can become a citizen of such a liberating city however, Ellison's hero must undergo a paradoxical journey from an apparently innocent rural setting, which is in fact corrupt, to an apparently deadly urban world, which turns out to be life-giving. The small town in which the hero grows up, ironically given the pastoral name of "Greenwood," is revealed in the Battle Royal episode as a place intent on blinding him with illusions about American life and trapping him in a debilitating role of a segregated society. The college he attends appears to be a kind of "Eden" but is in reality a "flower studded wasteland" (29). The hero's experiences in both of these seemingly idyllic settings arouse his hopes of finding a place for himself in the American dream but actually reduce him to the level of a robot controlled by people who use him for their own purposes.

His movement to New York City, however, suggests a way out of these traps. After he has been "expelled" (91) from his false Eden and "cast into the darkness" (105), he moves North to a larger and potentially freer existence. As Ellison himself has observed of his hero in *Shadow and Act,* "He leaves the South and goes North; this, as you will notice in reading Negro folktales, is always the road to freedom— the movement upward. You have the same thing when he leaves his underground cave for the open."[7] This is the Dreiserian "city of dreams," a "world of possibility" (122) which the hero beholds in wonder as he steps off a Greyhound bus and contemplates Harlem for the very first time. As he reveals late in the novel, New York is for him a fluid, open space with "all boundaries down," a new frontier where "you could actually make yourself anew" (377).

What the hero must discover, however, is that the city which he beholds in such wonder is not a simple place containing one meaning but is in fact a tangle of painful but fruitful contradictions. Like himself and American reality in general, the city is complexly double. He eventually discovers his own duality when he realizes that "there were two of me" (281), a public self enslaved by society's expectation that he climb the ladder of outward "success" and a private self which is deformed by this "black rite of Horatio Alger" (87). In the same way, he comes to see New York as two mutually opposed cities. On the one hand, New York is the city classically portrayed in Horatio

Alger novels, an urban world enticing him with external rewards such as money, power, and status. On the other hand, it is an existential city which offers an enriched consciousness leading to freedom and genuine selfhood.

His movements in these cities take two distinct forms. The Algerian city invites him to move "upward" in American life toward various forms of outward success. But as the Battle Royal and his early experiences in New York clearly indicate, this upward movement exacts a terrible price, because it forces him to move away from the self toward various false roles eroding his identity. His movements in the existential city, however, are consistently *downward*, moving away from outward success and toward a greater degree of personal freedom, independence, and self awareness. Rushing toward the center of Harlem late in the novel, he describes this movement as a race to the self: "I ran through the night, ran within myself" (403).

But, for much of the novel, the hero is engaged in a fruitless "footrace against" (287) himself as he moves blindly through an Algerian city mapped out by others intent on using him. He is sent to New York by Bledsoe ostensibly to redeem himself after the fiasco at the Golden Day. His letters of recommendation to various important people in the city apparently will put him touch with the "sponsors" who in the Alger myth always open the doors of success for the hardworking young boy desirous of "rising" in life.[8] The hero temporarily takes up residence in Men's House, a place which has traditionally housed black men who have left the South to pursue the American Dream in the North. But when he finds out from Emerson's son that his letters will not lead him to sponsors interested in helping him to "rise" in life, but, on the contrary, will put him on a wild-goose chase toward a "horizon" which "recedes ever brightly and distantly from the hopeful traveler" (145), he rejects everything which Men's House stands for and resolves to make his own way in the city.

Ironically, however, he uses another recommendation, the one provided by Emerson's son, and this brings him to Liberty Paint, which is described as a "small city" (149). What he encounters there is another version of the Alger myth which now promises upward mobility by becoming part of a complex industrial society. Here again, the city seems to offer freedom from a restrictive southern past but in fact provides him with another version of that past. Working for Kimbro, whom his fellow workers characterize as a "slave driver" (151) and whom he sees as "a Northern redneck, a Yankee cracker" (152), he becomes part of an urban plantation which reduces him to the level of a sharecropper at best and a slave at worst. The hero is exactly right when he thinks that "there were unseen lines which ran from

North to South" (128). Attaining one's freedom is not a simple matter of physically moving to a northern city because the urban North has been contaminated by the same racism and brutality which character-izes the pastoral regions of the deep South.

Even in his acts of conscious rebellion against the Alger myth the hero ironically repeats the experience of slavery in the northern city. Signing up with the Brotherhood because it promises him "the highest possible rewards" (268), and a liberating role to play, he ultimately discovers that he is trapped in the same way that he was trapped in the Battle Royal. Here again he is carefully monitored by whites who want to make him "the new Booker T. Washington" (231), a person who will channel black political energy into forms which are accept-able to whites. And just as his involvements in the Battle Royal result in self-destructive violence for himself and others, his involvement in the Brotherhood culminates in the Harlem riot which the Brotherhood engineers, a mad explosion which the hero ultimately describes as "not suicide but murder" (417). Put another way, his Brotherhood experiences lead him to yet another dead-end, confinement in a Dan-tean "city of the dead" (324), a Hell brought on by his own blindness and desire for power and status.

What he needs to enter the existential city of possibility is the kind of consciousness necessary to correctly *read* his urban experiences so that he can map his own way through the city and thus discover the city as a reflector and liberator of the self. In the Vet's words, he has "to learn to look beneath the surface" (118). This ultimately brings him literally into an existential underworld which frees him by com-pletely inverting the values of the Horatio Alger myth, sending him *down* to the liberating regions of the self instead of *up* towards the material goals which have in fact enslaved him all his life.

Getting to the urban underworld, however, is no easy process be-cause he has always been trained to see success in Algerian terms as upward movement and freedom in Booker T. Washington's terms as rising from a condition of servitude. He begins the process of liberation leading to the "underground" of the self by spontaneously wandering through the hidden parts of the city, slowly becoming more aware of it as an emblem of the hidden parts of himself. Penetrating a city which he informally maps for himself, he gradually discovers the secret recesses of his own nature.

This process begins shortly after the Hospital sequence where he takes the subway to Harlem and then passes out on the streets. Stunned by the explosions at Liberty Paint and the electroshock ther-apy at the Hospital, the hero is freed from the Algerian "plan" for success imposed on him at the Battle Royal and reinforced in all subsequent episodes. Significantly, he moves to Harlem which is a kind of underground, a "city within a city" (122). His free movements in Harlem repeatedly result in increased self awareness as he discovers the falsity of an American Dream which promises freedom for all but creates an immense ghetto depriving enormous masses of their political, social, and economic rights. Developing the habit, while living with Mary Rambo, of reading books from the library during the day and "wander[ing] the streets until late at night" (197), the hero begins the slow process of reading the city and the self. Deciphering the codes contained in books and the urban landscape, he finally begins to interpret the secrets that have been deeply buried within himself for most of his life.

The first example of this occurs approximately half way through the novel when, hurrying through the streets one day, he comes upon a vendor selling yams. This key episode endows him with "an intense feeling of freedom" (201) because it awakens in him a renewed respect for folk traditions and their ability to "nourish" him more than the Alger myth which prompts him to reject soul food for a standard breakfast of toast, juice, and coffee. This scene contrasts sharply with a prior episode on the city streets when the hero meets the man calling himself Peter Wheatstraw. Whereas in this scene the hero was not able—and probably unwilling—to decipher the folk codes which are such a key part of his identity, here he understands what the street vendor is talking about and identifies strongly with the rich ethnic past which the sweet yams evoke. The earlier street scene with Wheatstraw resulted in his rejecting his racial traditions, thinking "they're a hell of a people" (135), but this scene in Harlem culminates in his thinking with pride "What a group of people we were" (200).

Shortly after this he moves into "a side street" (202) where his perceptions are developed further as he witnesses an old black couple being evicted from their apartment. The vaguely felt nostalgia induced by eating the yams becomes a much more disturbing feeling of anger and betrayal when he sees all of the couple's possessions thrown out on the street, reduced to what he will later describe as "junk whirled eighty-seven years in a cyclone" (211). Again, the urban scene speaks to him in a vital way:

> I turned aside and looked at the clutter of household objects which the two men continued to pile on the walk. And as the crowd pushed me I looked down to see looking out of an oval frame a portrait of the old couple when young, seeing the sad, stiff dignity of the faces there; feeling strange memories awakening that began an echoing in my head like that of a hysterical voice stuttering in a dark street. (205)

Here the outer cityscape becomes a compelling metaphor of the hero's self, which is tied to a cultural and racial past for which he finally takes responsibility. As he observes the dispossession of the old couple, he realizes that he too has been dispossessed of the same American Dream promised to them. The outward street thus becomes the "dark street" of his mind, filled with a critically important new sign of selfhood, the "hysterical voice" so long repressed since the Battle Royal but which now cries out for full articulation.

Throughout the remainder of the novel the hero continues to move into the self as he freely explores the existential city. He thus slowly becomes aware of the wisdom of Wheatstraw's statement that Harlem may be a "bear's den" but "it's the best place for you and me" (123). Wandering the streets after he has witnessed Clifton's death, he thinks "It was as though in this short block I was forced to walk past everyone I had ever known" (335). More importantly, he becomes increasingly sensitive to two voices which he had previously been trained to ignore—the voice of the city and the voice arising from the deepest levels of his consciousness. From his very first moments in Harlem he has been aware that these two voices are somehow related:

> I had always thought of my life as being confined in the South. And now as I struggled through the lives of people a new world of possibility sug-gested itself to me faintly, like a small voice that was barely audible in the roar of city sounds. I moved wide-eyed, trying to take in the bombardment of impressions. (122)

Just as the roar of the city awakens his sensations so that he sees and hears in an intensified way, it also releases in him a "small voice" of possibility which was muffled in the Battle Royal episode and com-pletely silenced in his interview with Bledsoe. The vital sounds of the city, so unlike the deadly silence of the campus, begin a true process of education for the hero because it draws from him the exis-tential "voice" which is at the core of his self.

As the novel progresses, the hero's small voice amplifies as his con-sciousness of the city becomes more comprehensive and enriched. After delivering a Brotherhood speech, he thinks "I threw my voice hard down against the traffic sounds" (278). While speaking at Clif-ton's funeral he imagines the crowd looking at "the pattern of my voice on the air" (343). By the end of the novel, he has developed a voice which is as richly complex and sophisticated as the city itself. Moreover, he has switched from an oral to a written voice, moving from the status of orator to novelist. This is a crucial change, for it makes him less dependent upon the needs of his immediate audience and better able to sound his own depths. The role of writer also grants his voice a greater degree of permanency and universality, enabling him to reach the "lower frequencies" (439) which speak to all people of all times.

Invisible Man, therefore, stops modeling himself on Norton, Bledsoe, the Founder, the others who deceived him with the Horatio Alger myth. He ultimately sees himself as a latter day Frederick Douglass, the man who liberated himself by moving from the rural South to the urban North and who transformed himself by becoming the master of his own voice. For he comes to regard Douglass as the man who "talked his way from slavery" (285) and created his own name, thus signifying the fact that he was a truly self-made man, one who become humanly successful, not by accumulating wealth and status but by fully actualizing the self. In this way he rejects a superficial Algerian plan for success and celebrates a more essential American Dream, an existential version of Emersonian self-reliance.

He is careful to remind us, however, that his descent into self does not result in an egotistical rejection of his racial roots or social responsibilities. As the Prologue makes clear, his descent into self is made possible only by encountering the full complexity of his racial past which contains both the pain of slavery and the transcendence afforded by black artists such as Louis Armstrong who have made "poetry" (6) out of their racial experience, thus converting a condition of oppression into "a beam of lyrical sound" (6). Moreover, his descent into the innermost reaches of the self paradoxically empowers him finally to return to the above-ground city where he is determined to play out a "socially responsible role" (439). He lays great stress in the Epilogue that "the old fascination with playing a role returns and I'm drawn upward again" (437). Several important social roles do indeed await him in the above ground world; for example, he does in fact become a writer who reveals the truth about his society, and he could become involved in political activity very different from that prescribed by either Jack or Ras. Now that he has effectively studied "the lesson of [his] own life" (432), he could also become, like his grandfather, a teacher in the broadest sense of the word. These roles are fruitful because they enrich the self while allowing the hero to connect himself to a larger social world which is urban in character. In this way, each of these new roles is quite different from the old roles which nearly turned him into a robot because they arise from his own enriched, deepened, consciousness rather than the "plans" other people have devised for him. He therefore tells us that his "hibernation" (433) in the urban underground is nearly over and that he goes above ground every night to seek out "the next phase" (435) of his life.

Although he is not yet able (or willing) to define precisely the exact nature of the roles he will play for fear of being limited by them, the two anecdotes he relates about his above ground experiences offer ample proof that he is not "jiving" (439) when he speaks of acting effectively in the city. Both of these stories, the fight which he describes in the Prologue and the conversation with Norton which he dramatizes in the Epilogue, establish the hero as fundamentally different from the victimized country bumpkin he was in his preunderground days. Whereas he formerly lacked the consciousness necessary to direct his life and was therefore easily manipulated by others, he is now in full control of himself and is beginning to master his social environment.

Aware in the Prologue that his white attacker is a sad victim of a racist world which blinds his eyes and blunts his heart, Invisible Man can transform violence into awareness, laughing with "sincere compassion" (4) at a man who was mugged by an invisible man. He thus saves himself from the self-defeating violence which has threatened him in nearly every major episode in the novel, from the Battle Royal to the Harlem Riot. He also extends the same kind of richly human "mixed feelings" (436) toward Norton when he sees him pathetically lost on the subway and asking for directions to Centre Street, the locus of political power and government in New York City. Whereas he had earlier made Norton an Algerian sponsor and begged him for direction in life, he now gives subtly ironic directions to Norton who is too hurried and self-deluded to become aware of their meaning: "Take any train; they all go to the Golden D—" (437).

No longer riding on the hard rails of other people's expectations which lead to madness, the hero can reject the Algerian city which still dominates Norton's life. Abandoning Norton's city of delusions once and for all, Invisible Man returns temporarily to his urban underground, a psychological frontier giving him a new life. He thus becomes more fully aware that he has ultimately found a truer "center" to his existence—the urbane consciousness which will allow him to transcend existentially the "fate" imagined for him by the Nortons of the world.

*   *   *   *   *   *

Charles Johnson, who in *Being and Race* has described *Invisible Man* as "something of the modern Ur-text for black fiction," a book which "provided artistic direction for black writing of the 1970's,"[9] is clearly one of the many contemporary black fictionists who are strongly influenced by Ellison's techniques and vision. This is particularly apparent in Johnson's portrayal of urban and rural life in America. For example, Rutherford Calhoun, the hero of *Middle Passage,* shares invisible man's dislike for rural existence and lustily celebrates the city, characterizing the Illinois farm on which he was enslaved as "hateful, dull" and describing the "black underworld" of New Orleans as an exciting new social space which enables him to assume a satisfying picaresque life. For these reasons, he boldly declares "New Orleans wasn't home. It was Heaven."[10]

Johnson's first novel, *Faith and the Good Thing,* likewise, is in close agreement with Ellison's sharp criticism of the pastoral ideal and his largely affirmative reading of urban experience. Faith Cross, like invisible man, is born into a segregated rural society which severely limits her and comes to achieve a new set of possibilities in a northern city which she first perceives as a kind of Hell but eventually regards as a frontier helping her to achieve the sort of protean identity which invisible man develops. The city for Johnson, therefore, is very similar to the complexly double world which Ellison defined in *Invisible Man;* for those who lack sufficient consciousness it can be a trap, but for those who develop existential awareness, it is a reflector of the uncharted reaches of the self.

Johnson's novel, like *Invisible Man,* opens in the rural South which is associated with stasis and death. It is a rigidly segregated society predicated upon a "divinely established order"[11] that restricts blacks to lives as second class citizens. Faith's father, Todd Cross, gets trapped in a sharecropper's life which amounts to little more than "imprisonment" (69) and, when he rebels against white expectations, he is lynched. His corpse, significantly, is described as "stiff as a board" (7), reduced to the inert condition of "stone or slime" (46). Faith's mother, who accepts the codes of the South, is always described in terms of a deadly stasis. She insists that nobody ask questions of her for fear that this might lead her to challenge the hierarchical assumptions of southern life and thus dissolve her secure but enervated existence. Her static life is suggested by her "silent kitchen" (12), characterized by its calendar whose pages have not been changed for months and its "meticulous housekeeping" which ensures that nothing, including herself, is ever "misplaced" (5). Mrs. Cross's spare moments are spent on the front porch in a rocking chair, mindlessly "smoking and squeezing from the pores of her waxy nose things she called worms" (16).

Faith instinctively recoils from Lavidia's corpse-like existence and after her mother's death she leaves home. She also rejects the fundamentalist religion of the South as a force which also tries to immobilize her spirit and encourage her to accept passively the restrictive roles allotted to blacks in southern society. Rev. Alexander Magnus, the "spirit man" (9) preaching at revival meetings, horrifies Faith with his Jonathan Edwardsian vision of God as a "perfect being" who treats mankind as squirming spiders helplessly suspended over a "smoking fire" (9). When Rev. Brown later tries to intimidate her into a profession of faith, she feels "trapped in a room of mirrors" (12) and mechanically tells him what he wants to hear, in much the same way as invisible man tells whites at the Battle Royal what they want to hear.

Returning to her house after her mother's funeral, Faith rejects the static life which the house symbolizes and instinctively runs away, seeking the new space which she needs for growth. While in the act of running, she momentarily glimpses back at the house, seeing it as a kind of grave which "appeared to descend into the soft ground" (16). Thus fleeing a world that she fears will bury her, she moves to two new spaces which at first frighten but eventually help to liberate her. After walking for hours, she arrives at the Swamp Woman's shanty, a liminal world at "the edge of the swamp" (16) which is an indeterminate space free of the conventional values and static roles of southern society. Now liberated from a restrictive past and at the boundary of the miraculous and unfamiliar, she is encouraged by the Swamp Woman (an exact opposite of her mother) to envision her life as an ongoing quest for selfhood rather than a materialistic pursuit of comfort and status. She therefore urges Faith to leave the South and "go to Chicago" (27) in search of a new life. For Chicago is to Faith what New York is to invisible man, a radically new space offering fresh possibilities. While this new space is at time terrifying and submits Faith to considerable suffering, such pain results in the sort of human growth which invisible man experiences in the city.

Like Ellison, Johnson initially describes urban reality in a very suggestive, impressionistic way to stress its qualities as a protean world, a psychological frontier inviting human growth. When Faith steps off the train she sees the city as the same kind of kaleidoscopic blur of apparently random motion and disconnected images which initially assault the senses of Ellison's hero. Just as invisible man is dazzled by the "roaring traffic," fast-moving crowds and "roar of city sounds" which bombard his senses and open his mind to "a new world of possibility" (122), Faith is at first stunned by the "shrill whistle" (49) of the train as it enters Chicago and then is struck by the "fast-moving crowd" (49), "thudding car tires and blast of horns" (50) of Chicago's traffic. Unlike the South which numbs her with stasis, Chicago quickens her pulse with accelerated movement and change, "the endless, mad flux of things" (81). Like invisible man, she sometimes imagines the urban environment as a kind of hell but eventually experiences the city in a more affirmative way as a purgatory which cleanses her spirit and stimulates her growth.[12] Even though she initially senses the city as "a burial place which had invaded her, shaped her wholly" (78), she comes to realize that her immersion into urban life plays a crucial role in her salvation. For the harsh realities and constant change of urban life force her out of the passivity which southern life has imposed upon her and prod her into significant growth. Both she and invisible man, therefore, can be compared to Odysseus, Dante, and other epic heroes whose descents into underworlds enlarged their consciousness. And like Dante who is helped by Virgil to move through Hell toward Purgatory, they are assisted by mentors who keep them from being overwhelmed by the chaos they encounter. Just as Ellison's hero is nursed by Mary Rambo after undergoing traumatic experiences in the Liberty Paint episode, Faith is helped by Barrett when the "anarchy, theft, [and] murder" (80) of city life threaten to overwhelm her. After initially robbing her when she first appears in the city, he reappears approximately midway through the novel when Faith has experienced a spiritual crisis which causes her to exclaim to him: "there isn't any good thing. There never was. It's all an evil lie to keep us happy! There's nothing . . . nothing" (89). Barrett saves her from a crippling nihilism centered in the conviction that "inner and outer worlds were . . . empty" (80) by reinstilling in her a belief in the "good thing" and her ability to pursue it. Outwardly "beaten" (85) and on the verge of death, Barrett becomes for Faith "not so much revolting but revelatory" (85). For it is he who reminds Faith that they are both "questers" (93) driven by a need to always search for the "tenuous belief" that "there had to be a greater good than any many could conceive" (90). He thus converts Faith from a disintegrating drifter into someone who can move with purpose, for it is he who commits her once again to "*the* human adventure, this quest for the Good Thing" (92).

It is Barrett who reinstills her faith in life as a meaningful journey because he convinces her that "The world was allegory . . . it always pointed beyond" (93). And it is he who gives her a powerful emblem of the plasticity and indeterminacy of human experience when he entrusts her with his Doomsday Book, a book with blank pages inviting Faith to create her own self freely by writing the story of her life from scratch. Even though Barrett dies halfway through the novel, he continues to help Faith move meaningfully through life because his "philosopher's spirit" (98) continues to advise her whenever she is threatened with various kinds of traps. As she mechanically makes love to Maxwell in order to squeeze a proposal from him that will enslave them in a loveless marriage, she hears "Barrett's voice just above the wind telling her all this was horribly wrong" (109). At a later point when she fraudulently professes love to Maxwell, she envisions Barrett's face "frowning" (123) in disapproval. Whereas Maxwell is one of the "dead living" (125), Barrett is one of the "living dead" (125), a wise spirit who can caution Faith to resist such bondage. Like Dante's Virgil, he can return from the dead to provide a living voice which helps Faith in her journey away from the various traps which threaten to destroy her. Indeed, he becomes a "wraith" or "conscience that would not let her rest" (96).

Barrett thus enables Faith to journey through Hell to Purgatory and, because of this, her experiences in Chicago do not damn her but purify her. Just as Dante is cleansed by the flames of Purgatory which burn away the material drives which distract him from his spiritual quest, Faith undergoes a purification by fire when she is horribly burned and physically disfigured by fire in Mrs. Beasely's hotel. The fire deprives her of the physical beauty which had earlier made it profitable for her to become a prostitute and had also drawn men like Tippis, Maxwell, and Holmes toward her. Deprived of her outward appearance, "her body seemed already gone, but her mind was clear" (183). And this mental clarity forces her to recognize the importance of burning away what is inessential in her life and committing herself once more to the "necessity" (183) for pursuing truth, the "Good Thing" (183) Ellison's hero can purify himself by burning the contents of his briefcase while underground and thus achieve an existential identity. In the same way, Faith Cross can take "hold of herself" (184) by freeing herself of outward roles and appearances. Like invisible man, she is able to convert an urban hell into a purgatory through her own maturing consciousness.

*   *   *   *   *   *

Put another way, the modern American city contains for both Ellison and Johnson two possibilities. If perceived as a deterministic environment controlled by economic, social, and forces beyond the control of individual people, the city, like the "reconstructed" South, will be an extension of the slave past. But if grasped as a psychological and social frontier, it contains the possibility for dramatic personal growth and social development. In her first weeks in Chicago Faith has a clear sense of how her life pivots on these two possibilities:

Either you were brand new at each instant, innocent, and undetermined and, therefore, free, or you were a bent-back drudge hauling all the world's history on your shoulders across the landscape of your life, limited in all your possibilities, enclosed within the small cage of what had passed before. Each event would weigh you down, alter you, send you through endless changes. You were in bondage. And the other way?—could you be brand new each instant, remade by the power of either your own hand or magical thoughts? (59)

Invisible Man and Faith and the Good Thing certainly do contain many examples of modern urbanites who experience the city as "bondage." Maxwell, for example, in committing himself to a vision of life centering on "money and power" (100) enslaves himself to the same Alger myth which dehumanizes Norton. Tippis's "plastic personality" (83) fails to provide him with a human identity because the many roles he assumes are never generated "from within, only catalyzed from without" (83). Like a host of characters from Invisible Man, including Jack, Wrestrum, Emerson, and Emma, he is enslaved by the flux of urban life because his activities are directed by others who seek to manipulate him.

But the central characters of these two remarkable novels overcome bondage and make themselves free by achieving protean identities arising from the existential consciousness nurtured by urban life. Such consciousness helps them to experience urban reality not as an extension of the slave past but as a new space which empowers them to assimilate their past and then transform it by freely willed actions in the present which create fresh possibilities in the future. In this way, the city provides invisible man with a "new world of possibility (122), in which "you could actually make yourself anew" (377). Likewise, the city inspires in Faith Cross a fresh conception of herself in which she can be "brand new each instant" (59).

NOTES

1. Blanche Gelfant, Women Writing in America (Hanover, N.H.: University Press of New England, 1984), 219.

2. George Rogers Taylor, The Turner Thesis Concerning the Role of the Frontier in American History (Lexington, Mass.: D.C. Heath, 1972), 4.

3. Ralph Ellison, Invisible Man (New York: Random House, 1952), 87. All subsequent references to the text are to this Modern Library edition. Pages numbers appear in brackets after the quotation.

4. Ralph Ellison, Shadow and Act (New York: New American Library), 25–26.

5. Ralph Ellison, Going to the Territory (New York: Random House, 1986), 132, 134, 148, 290.

6. Henry David Thoreau, Walden and On the Duty of Civil Disobedience (New York: Holt, Rinehart, and Winston, 1948), 268.

7. Ellison, Shadow and Act, 174.

8. Most Alger novels espouse a clearly defined formula for success, providing a "paradigm" which books like Washington's Up from Slavery use for serious purposes

but *Invisible Man* inverts for ironic effects. Alger's *Ragged Dick*, for example, centers on the hero's "plan" to achieve "a new life" (New York: Collier Books, 1962: 153) by working hard and then impressing wealthy men who will provide a place for the hero in middle class life. Sponsors such as Mr. Greyson and Mr. Rockwell complete the hero's identity by providing him with a new name (Richard Hunter, Esq.), a steady job, and the prospects of a continued "rise" in American life. Ellison's invisible man earnestly pursues his formula for success for most of the novel but in the end abandons it because he realizes that such "success" will destroy his identity by turning him into a robot. He therefore separates from sponsors such as Norton, Bledsoe, and Jack, simultaneously rejecting the material rewards they have promised him. He also stubbornly refuses the names which others have imposed upon him, preferring to have no name, a symbol of the fluid, indeterminate identity he achieves by existentially descending into the self.

9. Charles Johnson, *Being and Race* (Bloomington and Indianapolis: Indiana University Press, 1990), 15, 17.

10. Charles Johnson, *Middle Passage* (New York: Penguin Books, 1991), 3, 2.

11. Charles Johnson, *Faith and the Good Thing* (New York: Atheneum, 1974), 63–64. All subsequent references to the text are to this edition. Page numbers appear in brackets after the quotation.

12. For an extended discussion of how Ellison describes the city in *Invisible Man* in terms of the hero's descent into hell, see my article "Dante's *Inferno* and Ellison's *Invisible Man*: A Study in Literary Continuity," *College Language Association Journal* 28 (Sept. 1984): 57–76.

9

"But the City Was Real": James Baldwin's Literary Milieu

FRED L. STANDLEY

"UPON entering the last quarter of the twentieth century, man [or woman] seems to be obsessed, in fascination or in horrified contempla-tion, with the theme of the city," declares the opening line of *The City as Catalyst: A Study of Ten Novels* (1979). The author then goes on to suggest that while "an exhaustive study of the city in literature" would require numerous volumes, there would emerge from them "the varied contradicting, mutable, pervasive image, which is the city itself."[1] Indeed, a quick survey of selected excursions into the topic reveals a multiplicity of approaches, analyses, and commentaries about the city. To illustrate that fact, one has only to note, for example: Raymond Williams, *The Country and the City* (1973); Susan Merrill Squire, *Women Writers and the City* (1984); and Lewis Fried, *Makers of the City* (1990).[2] This interest in the city, Squire reminds us, is reflective of an encompassing Western literary tradition in which "po-ets and novelists have written about the city for as long as it echoed their dreams and fears. From the town-country debates in Virgil's *Eclogues* to T. S. Eliot's urban wasteland, the city has provided a moving metaphor for the human condition. And ambivalence has al-ways been a vital part of this literary response."[3] Whether inclined toward negative portrayals of the city, its environs and influence, or toward affirming the human values and virtues inherent to the institutions of the city (and thus, of society), this literary concern, especially within the last three to four decades, attests to the undeni-able fact that contemporary culture is decidedly urban centered.

A compelling rationale for this phenomenon was expressed by Har-vey Cox in *The Secular City: Secularization and Urbanization in Theological Perspective* (1965). Cox cited "the rise of urban civiliza-tion" as one of the hallmarks of our era, "a massive change in the way men live together" which "became possible in its contemporary form only with the scientific and technological advances" which sprang from "the wreckage of religious world views" and made possible the fact that we now "experience the universe as the city of men"; hence, "the world has become his city and his city has reached out to include the world."[4] Cox then points out that this "age of the secular, techno-logical city," just as in all preceding ages, has its own "style—its peculiar way of understanding and expressing itself, its distinctive character, coloring all aspects of its life." Consequently, all political, philosophical, and aesthetic endeavors also are invariably affected:

> Just as the poets and architects, the theologians and lovers of the thir-teenth century all partook of a common cultural substance, so in our time we all share a fund of unspoken perspectives. Just as the straight aisles and evenly clipped hedges of the eighteenth century formal gardens exhibited a style found also in deist theology and neoclassic verse, so our secular urban culture makes itself felt in all our intellectual projects, artistic visions and technical accomplishments.[5]

The literary works of James Baldwin are not unique among African-American authors in the active manifestation of this urban interest, but the fact of this usage has not always been acknowledged or fully appreciated. For example, *The City and Literature: An Introduction* (1983) provides "a historical introduction to the vital and complex relation between literature and the city" and includes a survey of some eighty authors; yet rather curiously no African-American author is even mentioned.[6] Furthermore, a bit earlier David R. Weimer con-ceded in *The City as Metaphor* (1966) that Baldwin evidenced "a familiarity" with the city in his fiction, but also noted that the writer nevertheless failed "to make the urban environment really substan-tial."[7] In contrast to such views, however, a cogent case can be pre-sented for seeing Baldwin not only as a product of the urban environment but also as a writer using the city in numerous literary forms: novels, short stories, dramas, essays, poetry, and interviews. In spite of the fact that he primarily lived abroad for several decades and was often accused of being hopelessly out of touch with American society and culture, he conceived of himself "as a kind of trans-atlantic commuter"[8] who reiterated on numerous occasions that "New York . . . is my big city . . . because I was born there and grew up there"[9] and that Harlem was one of "the only places I'm really at home in the world . . . where people know what I know, and we can talk and laugh, and it would never occur to anybody to say what we all know."[10] Colin MacInnes recognized this focus when he stated to

Baldwin in 1965: "You're a very urban writer."[11] For Baldwin, then—
as for protagonist John Grimes in the first novel Go Tell It on the
Mountain—to a considerable extent, the city's "glories were unimag-
inable—but the city was real."[12] Rather than presenting an exhaustive
survey of Baldwin's use of the city, the function of this essay is to
suggest how the city "has a special significance" for him and how he
has "a unique relationship to the urban environment whether it is
considered as an actual place, or as a symbol of culture, or as the
nexus of concepts and values determining [his] place in history and
society."[13]

Any analysis of the use of the city by Baldwin necessarily requires
the consideration both of literal and figurative imagery with connotations which imply nonliterary assumptions, concepts, and questions.
As Carl Schorske has so carefully noted: "No man thinks of the city
in hermetic isolation. . . . He forms his image of it through a perceptual
screen derived from inherited culture and transformed by personal
experience. Hence the investigation of the intellectual's idea of the
city inevitably carries us outside its own frame into a myriad of concepts and values about the nature of man, society and culture."[14]
Baldwin, thus, rarely uses a literal image of the city without also
expressing a range of associative meanings as in Another Country: "He
was facing Seventh Avenue at Times Square. It was past mid-
night . . . and he had nowhere to go. . . . The avenue was quiet too,
most of its bright lights were out. . . . A sign advertised the chewing
gum which would help one to relax and keep smiling. A hotel's enormous new name challenged the starless sky. The great buildings, unlit,
blunt like the phallus or sharp like the spear, guarded the city that
never slept."[15] Similarly, in Go Tell It on the Mountain the protagonist
walks through the city, but finally with a startling realization:

> He looked straight ahead, down Fifth Avenue, where graceful women
> in coats walked, looking into the windows that held silk dresses, and
> watches, and rings. . . . Niggers did not live on these streets where John
> now walked; it was forbidden. . . . But did he dare to enter this shop out
> of which a woman now casually walked, carrying a great round box? Or
> this apartment before which a white man stood, dressed in a brilliant
> uniform. . . . For him there was the back door, and the back stairs, and the
> kitchen or basement. This world was not for him. If he refused to believe,
> and wanted to break his neck trying, then he could try until the sun
> refused to shine; they would never let him enter.[16]

Underlying this description of the city is a fundamental conception
of a dominant white society whose control of the sources and means
of economic and political power and authority will not permit a mar-

ginalized ethnic group identified by black skin color and presumed as innately inferior to participate on an equitable basis in the search for "life, liberty and the pursuit of happiness." Thus, while New York is Baldwin's city, it is a New York viewed through the lens of Harlem birth, rearing, and residency: "I came from a certain street in Harlem, a certain place and time. And the people I grew up with, my mother and father, my aunts and uncles, all those people in the streets, the people in the church, had a certain life."[17] To be more specific, he would describe and explain the earlier familial experience in this way: "I was born in Harlem, Harlem Hospital, and we grew up—first house was on park Avenue—not the American Park Avenue. . . . We used to play on the roof and in the—I can't call it an alley—but near the river—it was a kind of garbage dump."[18] To give another glimpse of such experience, he said: "I was born in the church, for example, and my father was a very rigid, righteous man. But we grew up in Har-lem—you lived, you know in a terrible house. Downstairs from us there were what my father called 'good-time' people: a prostitute and all of her paramours, all that jazz. I remember I'd met this woman; she was very nice to us; but we were not allowed to go to her house, and if we went there, we were beaten for it."[19] The aura was "that whole order of home-made gin, pigs' feets, chitlin', poverty, and the basement."[20] Still another nonfiction presentation and judgment of this urban environment was the 1948 essay entitled "The Harlem Ghetto" in which is explored white racism, the black press, the black church, and black-Jewish relations; a metaphor expressed in the first paragraph of the physical description of the city hints at a task which he undertakes for himself as writer given the socioeconomic circumstances:

> Harlem, physically at least, has changed very little in my parents' lifetime or in mine. Now as then the buildings are old and in desperate need of repair, the streets are crowded and dirty, there are too many human beings per square block. Rents are 10 to 58 per cent higher than anywhere else in the city; food, expensive everywhere is more expensive here and of an inferior quality; and now that the war is over and money is dwindling, clothes are carefully shopped for and seldom bought. Negroes, traditionally the last to be hired and the first to be fired, are finding jobs harder to get, and while prices are rising implacably, wages are going down. All over Harlem now there is felt the same bitter expectancy with which, in my childhood, we awaited winter: it is coming and it will be hard; there is nothing anyone can do about it.[21]

This ambiance also informed numerous other works, and hence it is not surprising to discover that the treatment of the city delineates explicitly the spheres of separation between blacks and whites through metaphoric allusiveness: "And if you ever did like the city, you don't like it anymore. If I ever get out of this, if we ever get out of this, I swear I will never set foot in downtown New York again. Maybe I used to like it, a long time ago . . . but that was because of our father, not because of the city. It was because we knew our father loved us. Now, I can say, because I certainly know it now, the city didn't. They looked at us as though we were zebras, and you know, some people like zebras and some people don't. But nobody ever asks the zebra. . . . New York must be the ugliest and dirtiest city in the world. It must have the ugliest buildings and the nastiest people. It's got to have the worst cops."[22] Similarly, the first person narrator of the short story, "This Morning, This Evening, So Soon," stands on deck as his ship comes into the New York harbor and reflects on the scene:

There it was, the great unfinished city, with all its towers blazing in the sun. It came toward us slowly and patiently, like some enormous, cunning and murderous beast, ready to devour, impossible to escape. I watched it come closer and I listened to the people around me, to their excitement and their pleasure. There was no doubt that it was real. I watched their shining faces and wondered if I was mad. For a moment I longed, with all my heart, to be able to feel whatever they were feeling, if only to know what such a feeling was like. As the boat moved slowly into the harbor, they were being moved into safety. It was only I who was being floated into danger.[23]

The emotional impact of "the ghetto lines"[24] is hauntingly expressed in the short story "Previous Condition" in which the black protagonist, Peter, is discovered by the white landlady to be living in the room she had rented to his Jewish friend, Jules:

"You can't put me out," I said, "This room was rented in my name."
"You get outta my house!" she screamed. "I got the right to know who's in my house! This is a white neighborhood, I don't rent to colored people. Why don't you go on uptown, like you belong?"[25]

Within Harlem, Baldwin recognized also the differences inherent to the ghetto: "You see, there were two Harlems. There were those who lived in Sugar Hill and there was the Hollow, where we lived. There was a great divide between the black people on the hill and us. I was just a ragged, funky black shoeshine boy and was afraid of the people on the Hill, who, for their part, didn't want to have anything to do with me."[26] Another difference perceived by the author existed among those in Harlem who sought identity, security, and escape within the numerous ecclesiastical organizations:

> It was a storefront church and had stood, for John's lifetime, on the corner of the sinful avenue, facing the hospital to which criminals wounded and dying were carried almost every night. The saints, arriving, had rented the abandoned store and taken out the fixtures; had painted the walls and built a pulpit, moved in a piano and camp chairs, and bought the biggest Bible they could find. They put white curtains in the show window, and painted across this window TEMPLE OF THE FIRE BAPTIZED. Then they were ready to do the Lord's work.[27]

The author's own experiences as an adolescent preacher in just such a Harlem church are refracted not only in that novel but also in *Just Above My Head,* as well as in the widely popular earlier essay *The Fire Next Time*:

> The church was very exciting. It took a long time for me to disengage myself from this excitement, and on the blindest, most visceral level, I never really have, and never will. There is no music like that music, no drama like that drama of the saints rejoicing, the sinners moaning the tambourines racing, and all those voices coming together and crying holy unto the Lord. There is still, for me, no pathos quite like the pathos of those multicolored, worn, somehow triumphant and transfigured faces, speaking from the depths of a visible, tangible, continuing despair of the goodness of the Lord.[28]

This same phenomenon is also exhibited in the opening act of the play *The Amen Corner* in which on a bright Sunday morning, "Before the curtain rises, we hear street sounds, laughter, cursing, snatches of someone's radio; and under everything, the piano, which David is playing in the church" within the tenement. Then, "at rise, there is a kind of subdued roar and humming, out of which is heard the music prologue, 'The Blues Is Man,' which segues into a steady rollicking beat, and we see the congregation singing."[29] Nevertheless, Baldwin was cognizant of the fact that "the post-civil war black church" urban and rural, which had evolved both from expulsions by whites as well as from blacks voluntarily leaving to establish new groups, had become in the time of his childhood and youth "a place of retreat from the dehumanizing forces of white power. It was the one place in which the blacks were 'safe' from the new racist structure that replaced slavery. The black church gradually became an instrument of escape instead of, as formally, an instrument of protest."[30]

Baldwin's experiences with, and awareness of the meaning of the black church is an important contribution to our knowledge of the fact that "by the late nineteenth century . . . the black church in both northern and southern cities had emerged as the most influential institution in the black community, far more independent from white control than the often weak secular institutions of that era."[31] The importance of this literary expression lies in the fact that it serves as a corrective in both urban studies and history to the "tendency to focus on the larger mainstream churches . . . and to avoid the small storefront and Spiritualist churches that were so numerous during the Great Migration era."[32]

The harsh reality of the city also included the historical fact of the black migration from the rural South to the industrialized northern cities in the earlier part of the century. Whether to escape the violence of burnings, beatings, and lynchings; the agricultural depression; or the general discontent over poverty, Jim Crow, and disfranchisement, millions of blacks had fled North and West between the two world wars. As C. Eric Lincoln pointed out in *The Negro Pilgrimage in America*, "the Southern Negro entered the twentieth century looking toward the North as a long-sought promised land."[33] Baldwin was keenly aware of this migration and its impact in his own family background: "My father left the South after a lynch mob wave. My father left the South to save his life. They were hanging niggers from trees in uniforms in 1919 and my father left the South therefore. And came to Chicago where we perish like rats, in New York where you perish like rats."[34] Still, as the narrator of *Go Tell It on the Mountain* explains about Elizabeth: "Her pretext for coming to New York was to take advantage of the greater opportunities the North offered colored people; to study in a Northern school, and to find a better job than any she was likely to be offered in the South. . . . In the winter of 1920, as the year began, Elizabeth found herself in an ugly back room in the home of her aunt's relative."[35] While Houston A. Baker, Jr., recognizes in *Modernism and the Harlem Renaissance* the contributions of Harlem as the "progressive Negro community of the American metropolis" (Alain Locke's phrase) and as "the veritable national seat of Afro-American intellectual and artistic leadership,"[36] a point of which Baldwin was also cognizant, it also is the case that Baldwin emphasized in his works the delimiting factors and features inherent to the circumscribed georgaphical area: "Chicagoans talk about Mississippi as though they had no South Side. White people in New York talk about Alabama as though they had no Harlem."[37]

Still another dimension of the urban environment with its locus in the Harlem ghetto centers upon the degree to which the migrants from the South "still bore the mark of the rural southern world from which they came: a world in which kinship networks, the church and individual white prosecutors represented the sole buffers against the unchecked power of employers and white supremacist organiza-tions. . . . Many Harlemites looked to personal solutions to help them through crises, turning to family members and neighbors to provide them with aid" or they "often turned to religious groups," as David Naison has shown.[38] In this regard it has been fashionable lately in Baldwin studies to analyze his important first novel Go Tell It on the Mountain as primarily a religious novel; indeed it is rich with obvious and frequent scriptural references, allusions, and names and a seeming preoccupation with ecclesiastical and doctrinal matters. However, a more insightful way to view the book is to note its embodiment of a major cultural concept of which religion is merely one segment. A point of entree for interpreting the novel in this manner can be de-duced from a 1970 essay by anthropologist Johnetta Cole entitled "Culture: Negro, Black and Nigger."[39] The essay is an exploratory analysis of "the existence of a black subculture" possessing a unique combination of three components that authenticate its reality and viability in predominantly white America; the three components are (1) those drawn from white America, (2) those shared with all op-pressed people, and (3) those peculiar to blacks.

Within the latter group are elements that help to distinguish the essence of blackness; for example, soul, or style, or a combination. However, the most interesting feature of the essay is the analysis of the four basic life-styles comprising "nigger culture": that is, the street, down-home, militant, and upward bound. "Upward bound" referred to the life-style characterized by the "black bourgeoisie" and centered in better neighborhoods, integrated churches, and clubs, and in short, the black middle class. "Militant" described the political world and life-style of cultural and revolutionary nationalists, especially on col-lege campuses, and in high school black student unions, and their ostensible concern with relief from oppression.[40]

The "Street" life-style—that is, the urban world of American blacks and highly stylized behavior—appears initially to be dominant in Go Tell It on the Mountain. The locale for the novel is the urban North, a setting that the author also refers to as "another country" in a novel of the same name. Within Go Tell It frequent descriptions and depictions of the city are used to express the gutter and the grime, the impersonality and anonymity, the confinement and the isolation of the sprawling and teeming metropolis with its "roar of the damned," a place "where no one cared, where people might live in the same building for years and never speak to one another."[41] While it may be true that "no writer knows the ghetto or its people better than

Baldwin" as Addison Gayle suggests,[42] and that frequent descriptions in Go Tell It reinforce the urban scene as the "gray country of the dead," it is certainly the "down-home" life-style that recurs consistently throughout this first novel, informing and dominating the family experience within the urban setting.

"Down-home" is, according to Cole, "a common expression among black Americans, indicating one's point of origin, down south, or the simple, decent way of life"; as a life-style it is "the traditional way of black folks . . . basically rural and southern" and centering in "the kitchens of black homes, in the church halls for suppers, and in the fraternal orders."[43] Within this broader cultural context, Go Tell It on the Mountain embodies centrally the experiences of the "down-home" life-style. The narrative lines of Gabriel, Florence, and Elizabeth involve flashback reminiscences of their belonging to those traditional generations of the Great Migration when southern blacks left the rural areas of their origin for the northern cities, carrying their cultural heritage (including religion) with them. This "down-home" life-style pervades the novel and possesses inherent ironic implications for interpreting the meaning of the book and of the city; and textual evidence abounds in testimony to this point in the book, as well as in other works such as Another Country, Blues for Mister Charlie, and "Come Out the Wilderness."[44]

Frank asks Florence about a letter she has received: "What's them niggers doing down home? It ain't no bad news, is it?"[45] Florence tells Elizabeth later that "Them niggers down home, they think New York ain't nothing but one long, Sunday drunk," and John teases Elizabeth with his "tell me folks do North they wouldn't think about doing down home."[46]

The interpretive reference point for the novel, then, is a cultural concept rather than a religious concept, though assuredly religion is an aspect of it. Within that context this is not a novel about religion per se; rather, it is a sociopolitical novel which subtly but savagely indicts a white controlled society that has radically delimited the lives and hopes of blacks by the pernicious doctrine and damnable practices of black inferiority that have led to fear, isolation, alienation, hatred, despair, and destruction. The novel is replete with passages of suffused hatred and desired revenge on the white world. After Gabriel learns that a black soldier has been viciously beaten to death by a group of white men, "he dreamed of a white man's forehead against his shoe; again and again, until the head wobbled on the broken neck and his foot encountered nothing but the rushing blood."[47] After her lover, Richard, is jailed for a crime of which he is innocent, Florence "hated it all—the white city, the white world. She could not, that day, think of one decent white person in the whole world."[48] For those whose skin color offers no hope better than "the back door, and the dark stairs, and the kitchen or basement,"[49] the alternatives seem limited to escapism by drugs, drink, and sex, or escape through the church; and both are regarded equally by the author as mere anodynes in the novel. John Grimes must learn the awful realities of the experiences recited in the lives of Florence, Gabriel, and Elizabeth; the options that open to him on the threshing floor in front of the altar are to leave the community of the faithful, and thus court disaster, or to remain among the group and reduce his range of possibilities by embracing a hopeless otherworldliness solely centered in the church and divorced from reality. Thus, the novel indicts not only the white society's racism but also the black society's reliance upon a religious mode of behavior that is irrelevant to the brutalizing and dehumanizing experiences of urban daily living. For Baldwin, refuge in an otherworldly religious orientation rationalized by a conception of God borrowed from the white world and capable only of reinforcing the status quo is an illusion. The larger meaning, then, of *Go Tell It on the Mountain,* resides in the manner by which it is a prefiguration of setting, situations, and motifs that are pursued in other works.

As mentioned earlier, the goal of this essay has been to propose how the city "has a special significance" for Baldwin and to provide examples exemplifying that fact. Additional explanation of the subject is obviously needed in order to complete the portrayal of that interest in and use of the city. Nonetheless, his contribution to the literary treatment parallels the most recent interest in the field of black urban studies in stressing

> the internal values of institutions, and organizations of the black community that have assisted it in surviving long decades of social animosity. . . . In searching for a comprehensive understanding either of a single black community or of the Afro-American urban experience in general, the negative and delimiting effects of white racial attitudes and racial discrimination are too integral to the story to be omitted from the conceptual scheme. . . . Only by a thorough explication of all of the forces at work in the shaping of black urban society at different points in time . . . can we hope to fashion a synthesis that will do justice to both the grandeur and the travail of that history.[50]

NOTES

1. Diana Festa-McCormick, *The City as Catalyst: A Study of Ten Novels* (Cranbury, N.J.: Associated University Presses, 1979), 9, 15.

2. Raymond Williams, *The Country and the City* (New York: Oxford University Press, 1973); Susan Merrill Squire, ed., *Women Writers and the City: Essays in Feminist Literary Criticism* (Knoxville: University of Tennessee Press, 1984); Lewis Fried, *Makers of the City* (Amherst: University of Massachusetts Press, 1990). Squire contains a useful bibliography and notes covering a broad range of matters related to the question of the city and literature.

3. Squire, *Women Writers*, 3.

4. Harvey Cox, *The Secular City: Secularization and Urbanization in Theological Perspective* (New York: Macmillan, 1965), 1.

5. Ibid., 5.

6. Henry Christian, et al. eds., *The City and Literature: An Introduction* (Newark, N.J.: Rutgers University Press, 1983), i–ii, 149–60.

7. David R. Weimer, *The City as Metaphor* (New York: Random House, 1966), 144, 146.

8. Fred L. Standley and Louis H. Pratt, eds., *Conversations with James Baldwin* (Jackson: University Press of Mississippi, 1989), 15.

9. Ibid., 49.

10. Ibid., 107.

11. Ibid., 49. For more on this topic, see James Vopat, "Beyond Sociology? Urban Experience in the Novels of James Baldwin," *Minority Literature and the Urban Experience*, ed. George E. Carter, et al. Selected Proceedings of the 4th Annual Conference for Minority Studies. University of Wisconsin, LaCrosse, 6 (1978): 51–58.

12. James Baldwin, *Go Tell It on the Mountain* (New York: Knopf, 1953), 37.

13. Squire, *Women Writers*, 4.

14. Carl E. Schorske, "The Idea of the City in European Thought: Voltaire to Spengler," *The Historian and the City*, ed. Oscar Handlin and John Burchard (Cambridge, Mass.: MIT Press, 1963), 96; quoted in Squire.

15. James Baldwin, *Another Country* (New York: Dial Press, 1962), 3.

16. Baldwin, *Go Tell It*, 39–40.

17. Standley and Pratt, eds., *Conversations*, 162.

18. Ibid., 32–39.

19. Ibid., 5.

20. Ibid.

21. James Baldwin, "The Harlem Ghetto," *Notes of a Native Son* (New York: Dial Press, 1963), 51. Also see his "A Talk to Harlem Teachers," *Harlem U.S.A.*, ed. John Henrik Clarke (Berlin: Seven Seas Publishers, 1964), 174–83.

22. James Baldwin, *If Beale Street Could Talk* (New York: Dial Press, 1974), 9.

23. James Baldwin, "This Morning, This Evening, So Soon," *Going to Meet the Man* (New York: Dial Press, 1965), 161–62.

24. Baldwin, "Notes of a Native Son," *Notes*, 99.

25. Baldwin, "Previous Condition," *Going to Meet*, 76.

26. Standley and Pratt, eds., *Conversations*, 223.

27. Baldwin, *Go Tell It*, 59.

28. James Baldwin, *The Fire Next Time* (New York: Dial Press, 1963), 47. Other similar uses are found in the novel *Just Above My Head* (New York: Dial Press, 1978).

29. James Baldwin, *The Amen Corner* (New York: Dial Press, 1968), 5–6.

30. James H. Cone, *Black Theology and Black Power* (New York: Seabury Press, 1969), 104.

31. Kenneth L. Kusmer, "The Black Urban Experience in American History," *The*

State of Afro-American History, ed. Darlene Clark Hine (Baton Rouge: Louisiana State University Press, 1986), 120.

32. Ibid.

33. C. Eric Lincoln, *The Negro Pilgrimage in America* (New York: Bantam Books, 1967), 84.

34. Standley and Pratt, eds., *Conversations,* 123.

35. Baldwin, *Go Tell It,* 218.

36. Houston A. Baker, Jr., *Modernism and the Harlem Renaissance* (Chicago: University of Chicago Press, 1987), 74–75, 83–84.

37. Standley and Pratt, eds., *Conversations,* 12.

38. Mark Naison, *Communists in Harlem During the Depression* (Urbana: University of Illinois Press, 1983), 32.

39. Johnetta B. Cole, "Culture: Negro, Black and Nigger," *New Black Voices,* ed. Abraham Chapman (New York: New American Library, 1972), 491–98. Also Fred L. Standley, "*Go Tell It on the Mountain:* Religion as the Indirect Method of Indictment," *Critical Essays on James Baldwin,* eds. Fred L. Standley and Nancy Burt (Boston: G. K. Hall, 1988), 188–94.

40. Standley, "*Go Tell It on the Mountain.*"

41. Baldwin, *Go Tell It,* 219.

42. Addison Gayle, Jr., "Cultural Nationalism: The Black Novelist in America," *Black Books Bulletin* 1(1971): 7.

43. Cole, "Culture," 497–98.

44. Baldwin, *Another Country,* 20; *Blues,* 42; "Come Out the Wilderness," *Going to Meet,* 192.

45. Baldwin, *Go Tell It,* 77.

46. Ibid., 186.

47. Ibid., 123.

48. Ibid., 150.

49. Ibid., 33.

50. Kusmer, "Black Urban Experience," 121–22.

10

If the Street Could Talk: James Baldwin's Search for Love and Understanding

YOSHINOBU HAKUTANI

$\mathcal{N}$o $\mathcal{N}$ame in the Street, a book of essays Baldwin wrote immediately before If Beale Street Could Talk, is about the life of black people in the city just as the story of Beale Street takes place in the city. While $\mathcal{N}$o $\mathcal{N}$ame in the Street is a departure from Baldwin's earlier book of essays in expressing his theory of love, If Beale Street Could Talk goes a step further in showing how black people can deliver that love. In $\mathcal{N}$o $\mathcal{N}$ame in the Street, Baldwin does not talk like an integrationist; he sounds as if he is advocating the ideas of a militant separatist who has no qualm about killing a white enemy. Although the book turns out to be a far more sustained examination of the falsehood to which Americans try to cling than his previous works, it still falls short of a vision in which love can be seized and recreated as it is in If Beale Street Could Talk.

Whenever Baldwin wrote about American society, he became the center of controversy, for his career coincided with one of the most turbulent eras in American history, marked by the civil rights movement at home and the Vietnam War abroad. A realist as he was, he was forced to take a stance in dealing with the current issues of society and of race in particular. He has been both extolled and denounced for his unique vision of racial harmony in America. Praising him for his ideas is not difficult to understand, because he is not only an eloquent writer but an acute historian. Modern American society is predominantly urban; black and white people live and work together in the city. Those who look forward to the future embraced him as a prophet; those who want to place politics over history and impose the past on the future dismissed him as a dreamer.

Some black readers also disparaged Baldwin's work. "The black writer," Joyce Carol Oates observed in her review of If Beale Street

Could Talk, "if he is not being patronized simply for being black, is in danger of being attacked for not being black enough. Or he is forced to represent a mass of people, his unique vision assumed to be symbolic of a collective vision."[1] A black writer like Richard Wright is seldom assailed because he not only asserts being black but openly shows his anger as a black man. To Baldwin, Wright's portrayal of the life of black people seems to be directed toward the fictional but realistic presentation of a black man's anger. Although sympathetic to this rage, Baldwin sees a basic flaw in Wright's technique, contending that the artist must analyze raw emotion and transform it into an identifiable form and experience.[2] Baldwin cannot approve of Wright's use of violence, which he regards as "gratuitous and compulsive because the root of the violence is never examined. The root is rage."[3]

This basic difference in vision and technique between Wright and Baldwin has a corollary in the difference between the two types of novels exemplified by *Native Son* and *If Beale Street Could Talk*. Both stories take place in the city, Chicago of the thirties in Wright's novel and New York of the sixties in Baldwin's. Bigger Thomas is accused of murder in the first degree for the accidental death of a white girl, and Fonny Hunts is imprisoned for the rape of a Puerto Rican woman, which he did not commit. Behind similar scenes of racial prejudice, lie fundamentally different ideas about the existence of black people in American society. During his act of liberation, Bigger becomes aware of his own undoing and creation, but he achieves his manhood through murdering his girl friend. Fonny, an artist and an intellectual, consciously aware of the primacy of love, is able to revive that relationship and achieve his deliverance. Wright's novel, whether it is *Native Son* or *The Outsider*, ends tragically with the death of its hero, and neither of the victims can lead others to the discovery of love. Fonny's search for love and liberation, on the other hand, is accomplished through his sense of love, which others can emulate and acquire. Not only does he survive his ordeal, but his child is to be born.

Baldwin's technique of elucidating this idea of love and deliverance differs with that of a protest novel. *Native Son* was intended to awaken the conscience of white society, and Wright's strategy was necessarily belligerent. To survive in his existence, Bigger is forced to rebel, unlike Fonny who defends himself in the interior of his heart. Bigger learns how to escape the confines of his environment and gain an identity. Even before he acts, he knows exactly how Mary, and Bessie later, have forced him into a vulnerable position. No wonder he convinces himself not only that he has killed to protect himself but also that he has attacked the entire civilization. In contrast to *If Beale Street Could Talk*, *Native Son* departs from the principles of love and sympathy which people, black or white, have for their fellow human beings. In "How 'Bigger' Was Born," Wright admits that his earlier *Uncle Tom's Children* was "a book which even bankers' daughters could read and weep over and feel good about."[4] In *Native Son,* however, Wright could not allow for such complacency. He warns that the book "would be so hard and deep that they would have to face it without the consolation of tears" (xxvii).

The salient device in *If Beale Street Could Talk* is the narrative voice of a nineteen-year-old black girl named Tish. She is Fonny's fiancée and is pregnant with his child. Not only is she a compassionate and lovable woman, but the reality of her pregnancy inspires others to generate love and hope. Baldwin's concept of love and liberation is conveyed realistically by many of those involved in the story, her husband-to-be, their relatives, the lawyer, the landlord, the restaurant owner, and others regardless of their race. But what makes Baldwin's concept vibrant is Tish's voice through which it grows enriched and spiritualized. Her manner of speech is warm but calm and completely natural. Only through her vision can the reader learn to know the meaning of love and humanity.

By contrast, Wright's authorial voice, as Baldwin noted, succeeds in recording black anger as no black writer before him has ever done, but it also is the overwhelming limitation of *Native Son.* For Baldwin, what is sacrificed is a necessary dimension to the novel: "the relationship that Negroes bear to one another, that depth of involvement and unspoken recognition of shared experience which creates a way of life . . . it is this climate, common to most Negro protest novels, which has led us all to believe that in Negro life there exists no tradition, no field of manners, no possibility of ritual or intercourse, such as may, for example, sustain the Jew even after he has left his father's house."[5]

What Baldwin calls "ritual or intercourse" in black life is precisely the catalyst for the attainment of love and deliverance in *If Beale Street Could Talk.* To see the relationship of Tish and Fonny as spiritual rather than sexual, genuine rather than materialistic, is commonplace, but to make it thrive on the strength of the communal bond in black life is Baldwin's achievement. Baldwin seizes upon this kinship in family members, relatives, friends, and associates. Tommy in Saul Bellow's *Seize the Day,* like Fonny, falls a victim of circumstance, and changes his family name to Wilhelm but retains his Jewish heritage in his battle of life. "In middle age," Bellow writes about Tommy, "you no longer thought such thoughts about free choice. Then it came over you that from one grandfather you had inherited such and such a head of hair . . . from another, broad thick shoulders; an oddity of speech from one uncle, and small teeth from another, and the gray eyes . . . a wide-lipped mouth like a statue from Peru. . . . From his mother he had gotten sensitive feelings, a soft heart, a brooding nature."[6]

The antithesis to Baldwin's idea of bondage is the focus of an existentialist novel of Richard Wright's. Cross Damon in *The Outsider*, rejecting his heritage, wishes to be renamed. His mother, the product of the traditional Christianity in the South that taught black children subservient ethics, tries to mold her son's character accordingly. He thus rebels against his mother, who moans, "To think I named you Cross after the Cross of Jesus."[7] As he rejects his mother because she reminds him of southern black piety and racial and sexual repression, he, in so doing, discards genuine motherly love altogether. He resembles Meursault in Albert Camus's *The Stranger*, who stands his trial for the murder of an Arab.[8] Meursault is not only accused of murder, but condemned as immoral because he did not weep at his mother's funeral. Damon's action, like Meursault's, derives from his nihilistic belief that "man is nothing in particular" (135). At the end of the story, however, Wright expresses a sense of irony about Damon's character. Tasting his agonizing defeat and dying, Damon utters:

> "I wish I had some way to give the meaning of my life to others. . . . To make a bridge from man to man . . . Starting from scratch every time is . . . no good. Tell them not to come down this road. . . . Men hate themselves and it makes them hate others. . . . Man is all we've got. . . . I wish I could ask men to meet themselves. . . . We're different from what we seem. . . . Maybe worse, maybe better. . . . But certainly different. . . We're strangers to ourselves." (439)

As if to heed Damon's message, Baldwin challenged the climate of alienation and estrangement that pervaded black life. Not only did he inspire black people to attain their true identity, but, with the tenacity and patience seldom seen among radical writers, he sought to build bridges between black and white people. In contrast to African-American writers like Richard Wright and John A. Williams, who fled the deep South to seek freedom and independence in the northern cities, Baldwin always felt that he was a step ahead in his career. "I am a city boy," he declared. "My life began in the Big City, and had to be slugged out, toe to toe, on the city pavements."[9] For him the city was a place where meaningful human relationships could evolve through battle and dialogue. As in any confrontation of minds, there would be casualties but eventually a resolution and a harmony would emerge. In *Another Country*, a novel of black life in the city, Rufus Scott, once a black drummer in a jazz band but now lonely and desperate, meets with a poor white girl from Georgia. They are initially attracted to each other, but eventually she becomes insane and he commits suicide. Even though hate overrules love in their relationship, it is the traditional southern culture in which she was ingrained rather than the estranged environment of New York City that ruins their relationship.

Because *Another Country* is not a polemical tract but a powerful novel, as Granville Hicks recognized,[10] it seems to express a subtle but authentic dilemma a black man faces in America. The novel suggests not only that the South is not a place where black people can have their peace of mind and happiness, but also that the city in the North is not a place where they can achieve their identity and freedom. And yet the novel is endowed with an ambivalent notion that America is their destined home. It is well known that Baldwin loved to live in another country. Paris was his favorite city, where he felt one was treated without reference to the color of skin. "This means," he wrote, "that one must accept one's nakedness. And nakedness has no color" (*No Name* 23). But Baldwin returned home, as did American expatriates in the twenties, and trusted his fortune in America.[11] In "Many Thousands Gone," he stated, "We cannot escape our origins, however hard we try, those origins which contain the key—could we but find it—to all that we later become" (*Notes* 20).

In search of home, black writers quite naturally turn to the city in the North, where black and white citizens live side by side and talk to one another. In *No Name in the Street*, Baldwin intimated his sentiments: "Whoever is part of whatever civilization helplessly loves some aspects of it, and some of the people in it. A person does not lightly elect to oppose his society. One would much rather be at home among one's compatriots than be mocked and detested by them" (194–95). The black citizen would be drawn to city living only because the interracial relationship in a melting pot could thrive on mutual respect and understanding, the lack of which has historically caused black people's exodus from the South. Such a relationship, as Baldwin quickly warns, is possible only if white people are capable of being fair and having goodwill and if black people themselves are able to achieve their true identity.

The burden that falls upon the shoulders of both white and black citizens is poignantly expressed with a pair of episodes in *No Name in the Street*. For the white people's responsibility, Baldwin recounts a white juror's attitude toward the American system of justice. The juror spoke in court:

"As I said before, that I feel, and it is my opinion that racism, bigotry, and segregation is something that we have to wipe out of our hearts and minds, and not on the street. I have had an opinion that—and been taught never to resist a police officer, that we have courts of law in which to settle . . . that I could get justice in the courts"—And, in response to Garry's [the defense attorney's] question, "Assuming the police officer pulled a gun and shot you, what would you do about it?" the prospective juror, at length, replied, "Let me say this. I do not believe a police officer will do that." (159–60)

The juror's reply not only provides a "vivid and accurate example of the American piety at work," as Baldwin observes, but also demon-strates the very honesty in Baldwin that makes his feeling credible to the reader.[12]

Baldwin calls for responsibility on the part of black people as well. In the middle of the chapter "Take Me to the Water," he now plunges himself into the dreary waters of urban society. This part of the narra-tive, in contrast to the personal and family episodes preceding it, abounds with experiences that suggest impersonality and superficiality in human relationships. After a long sojourn in France, Baldwin saw his school chum, now a U.S. post office worker, whom he had not seen since graduation. At once Baldwin felt a sense of alienation that separated the one who was tormented by America's involvement in Vietnam and the one who blindly supported it. Baldwin felt no con-ceivable kinship to his once friend, for "that shy, pop-eyed thirteen year old my friend's mother had scolded and loved was no more." His friend's impression of the famous writer, described in Baldwin's own words, is equally poignant: "I was a stranger now . . . and what in the world was I by now but an aging, lonely, sexually dubious, politically outrageous, unspeakably erratic freak?" What impressed Baldwin the most about this encounter was the fact that despite the changes that had occurred in both men, nothing had touched this black man. To Baldwin, his old friend was an emblem of the "white-washed" black who "had been trapped, preserved, in that moment of time" (No Name 15–18).

No Name in the Street is an eloquent discourse intended for all Americans to attain their identity and understanding. It takes its title from the speech by Bildad and Shuhite in the Book of Job that de-nounces the wicked of his generation:

> Yea, the light of the wicked shall be put out,
> And the spark of his fire shall not shine.
> His remembrance shall perish from the earth,

And he shall have no name in the street.
He shall be driven from light into darkness,
And chased out of the world.[13]

Baldwin sees in Bildad's curse a warning for Americans: without a
name worthy of its constitution, America will perish as a nation. "A
civilized country," he ironically observes, "is, by definition, a country
dominated by whites, in which the blacks clearly know their place"
(177). He warns that American people must remake their country
into what the Declaration of Independence says they wanted it to be.
America without equality and freedom will not survive; a country
without a morality is not a viable civilization and hence it is doomed.
Unless such a warning is heeded now, he foresees that a future generation of mankind, "running through the catacombs: and digging the
grave . . . of the mighty Roman empire" (178) will also discover the
ruins of American cities.

The responsibility for American people to rebuild their nation,
Baldwin hastens to point out, falls upon black people as heavily as
upon white people. This point echoes what he has said before, but it
is stated here with a more somber and deliberate tone. It sounds
comfortable to hear Baldwin speak in *Notes of a Native Son* that
"blackness and whiteness did not matter" (95). He thought then that
only through love and understanding could white and black people
transcend the differences in color to achieve their identity as human
beings and as a nation. In *No Name in the Street,* such euphoria has
largely dissipated; the book instead alludes to the reality that black
Americans are descendants of white Americans. "The blacks," Baldwin stresses, "are the despised and slaughtered children of the great
Western house—*nameless* and *unnameable* bastards" (185, my italics).
A black man in this country has no true name. Calling himself a black
and a citizen of the United States is merely giving himself a label
unworthy of his history and existence. To Baldwin, the race problem
is not a race problem as such; it is fundamentally a problem of how
black Americans perceive their own identity.[14]

No Name in the Street also addresses their cultural heritage. Baldwin admonishes the reader that the term *Afro-American* does not
simply mean the liberation of black people in this country. The word,
as it says, means the heritage of Africa and America. Black Americans,
he argues, should be proud of this heritage. He demands they discard
at once the misguided notion that they are descendants of slaves
brought from Africa, the inferiority complex deeply rooted in the
American psyche. An Afro-American, in Baldwin's metaphysics, is
defined as a descendant of the two civilizations, Africa and America,

both of which were "discovered" not by Americans but by European settlers.

Baldwin's prophecy, moreover, is rendered in epic proportion. "On both continents," Baldwin says, "the white and the dark gods met in combat, and it is on the outcome of this combat that the future of both continents depends" (194). The true identity of an Afro-American, the very term that he finds the most elusive of all names, is thus given a historical light. To be granted this name, as he stresses, "is to be in the situation, intolerably exaggerated, of all those who have ever found themselves part of a civilization which they could in no wise honorably defend—which they were compelled, indeed, endlessly to attack and condemn—and who yet spoke out the most passionate love, hoping to make the kingdom new, to make it honorable and worthy of life" (194). Historically, then, Baldwin bears out his old contention that both black and white citizens on this continent are destined to live together on the same street and determine their own future.

No Name in the Street, however, ends on a dark note, as some critics have suggested,[15] precisely because Baldwin had not yet discovered the true name for American people. The most painful episode in the book that influences his outlook on the racial question is his journey into the deep South. There he discovered not only a sense of alienation between black and white people, who had lived together over the generations, but an alienation within the white man himself. While a Southerner was conceived in Baldwin's mind as a man of honor and human feeling like a northern liberal, he struck Baldwin as a man necessarily wanting in "any viable, organic connection between his public stance and his private life" (53–54). Baldwin was in fact conscious that white people in the South always loved their black friends, but they never admitted it. This is why Baldwin characterizes the South as "a riddle which could be read only in the light, or the darkness, of the unbelievable disasters which had overtaken the private life" (55).

But Baldwin's search for a national identity in the name of brotherhood and love does not end in the South. Baldwin returns to the streets of the North. In the eyes of a middle-aged black writer, the potential for a truly American identity and understanding emerges in the city of the North through the black and white coalition with the radical students, and even in the black and white confrontation in the labor unions. Moving to Chicago in the thirties, Wright witnessed a coalition that existed between black men and white underground politicians, but this interracial cooperation, as he realized, did not arise out of the brotherhood on the part of the white men but out of their political and economic motives.[16] Such a white and black relationship as Baldwin envisioned in the sixties was a rallying cry for the black people who have seized the opportunity to make the once pejorative term *black* into what he calls "a badge of honor" (189). Although this encounter may entail hostile and dangerous reactions, it is, he asserts, a necessary crucible for black people to endure in achieving their identity. In the context of the late sixties, this is what he meant by the experience which a person, black or white, must face and acquire so that the person might attain identity. Baldwin hoped that the estrangement he witnessed in the South would not repeat itself in the North.

His most romantic quest in *No Name in the Street* involves the "flower children" he saw walking up and down the Haight-Ashbury section of San Francisco in the late sixties. Observing the young black men putting their trust not in flowers but in guns, he believed that the scene brought their true identity to the threshold of its maturity. The flower children, in his view, repudiated their fathers for failing to realize that black Americans were the descendants of white fathers; they treated the black children as their denied brothers as if in defiance of their elders. "They were in the streets," he says in allusion to the title of this work, "in the hope of becoming whole" (187). For Baldwin, the flower children were relying upon black people so that they could rid themselves of the myth of white supremacy. But he was undeniably a realist. He had no confidence in the black men who were putting their trust in guns, nor did he trust the flower children. In this episode he is quick to warn black listeners: "this troubled white person might suddenly decide not to be in trouble and go home—and when he went home, he would be the enemy" (188). In Baldwin's judgment, the flower children of the city in America became neither true rebels nor true lovers, either of whom would be worthy of their name in their quest for a national identity. In either case, he says to chide himself, "to mistake a fever for a passion can destroy one's life" (189).

The spectacle of the flower children thus figures as one of the saddest motifs in *No Name in the Street*. Although the vision of the young Baldwin was centered in love and brotherhood, the sensibility of the older Baldwin here smacks of shrewdness and prudence. Idealism is replaced by pragmatism, and honesty and sincerity clearly mark the essential attitude he takes to the problem of identity in America. His skeptical admiration for the flower children casts a sad note, for the encounter symbolizes the closest point to which black and white Americans had ever come in their search for love and understanding.

But at heart Baldwin was scarcely a pessimist. These pages, filled with love and tenderness, vividly express his feeling that, through these children, black Americans have learned the truth about themselves. And this conviction, however ephemeral it may have been, contributes to his wishfulness and optimism of the seventies. He has come to know the truth, stated before,[17] that black Americans can free themselves as they learn more about white Americans and that "the truth which frees black people will also free white people" (129). Baldwin's quest continues in *If Beale Street Could Talk*, for the novel is the catalyst for disseminating the truth. Even though Baldwin stresses the human bondage that exists within the black community, he also recognizes, in his imagination at least, the deep, universal bonds of emotion that tie the hearts of people regardless of their color of skin.

For Baldwin, the bondage that exists on Beale Street is hardly visible from outside. City life, as depicted by American realists from Stephen Crane and Theodore Dreiser down to James T. Farrell and Richard Wright, often brings out isolation and loneliness to the residents. The city is a noisy, crowded place, yet people scarcely talk to one another. New York City, Baldwin's home town, also struck Baldwin as emblematic of the impersonality and indifference that plagued city life in America. On his way to the South on a writing assignment, he stopped by the city to rest and to readjust his life, spent on foreign soil for nearly a decade. But all he heard was "beneath the nearly invincible and despairing noise, the sound of many tongues, all struggling for dominance" (*No Name* 51). The scene is reminiscent of what Crane, in the guise of a tramp, faces at the end of "An Experiment in Misery": "The roar of the city in his ear was to him the confusion of strange tongues, babbling heedlessly; it was the clink of coin, the voice of the city's hopes, which were to him no hopes."[18]

Unlike an existentialist in search of individual autonomy in the face of the void, chaotic, and meaningless universe, Baldwin seeks order, meaning, and dream in one's relation to others. A critic has dismissed *If Beale Street Could Talk* as "pretentious and cloying with goodwill and loving kindness and humble fortitude and generalized honorableness."[19] But because Baldwin is a confirmed romantic, his concept of love and honor is expressed with a sense of idealism. Neither the turbulence that embroils the urban ghetto nor the indifference that sweeps over it can disperse his dream.

It is ironic that the impersonality and estrangement which permeate Beale Street compel its residents to seek a stronger and more meaningful relationship with others. Tish, separated from her fiancé in jail, reflects on her happy childhood days, "when Daddy used to bring me and Sis here and we'd watch the people and the buildings and Daddy would point out different sights to us and we might stop in Battery Park and have ice cream and hot dogs."[20] Later in the story, Baldwin portrays the crowded subway, an epitome of city life, and suggests the notion that city inhabitants are forced to protect themselves. When a crowded train arrives at the platform, Tish notices her father instinctively puts his arm around her as if to shield her from danger. Tish recalls:

> I suddenly looked up into his face. No one can describe this, I really shouldn't try. His face was bigger than the world, his eyes deeper than the sun, more vast than the desert, all that had ever happened since time began was in his face. He smiled: a little smile. I saw his teeth: I saw exactly where the missing tooth had been, that day he spat in my mouth. The train rocked, he held me closer, and a kind of sigh I'd never heard before stifled itself in him. (52)

This motif of human bondage also appears as a faint noise coming from Tish and Fonny's unborn child. Tish hears it in the loud bar where she and her sister Ernestine talk about their strategy to get Fonny out of jail:

> Then, we are silent. . . . And I look around me. It's actually a terrible place and I realize that the people here can only suppose that Ernestine and I are tired whores, or a Lesbian couple, or both. Well. We are certainly in it now, and it might get worse. I will, certainly—and now something almost as hard to catch as a whisper in a crowded place, as light and as definite as a spider's web, strikes below my ribs, stunning and astonishing my heart—get worse. But that light tap, that kick, that signal, announces to me that what can get worse can get better. (122)

The bondage of black and white people in *If Beale Street Could Talk* could also be solidified, as could the black kinship, if the relationship were based upon a mutual understanding of others as individual human beings rather than as blacks who have typically been victimized by white society, or as whites who have habitually oppressed blacks under the banner of racial supremacy. No sooner does one treat another human being for an economic or political purpose than such a relationship ceases to exist. To show the possibility of a prosperous relationship between black and white people in the city, Baldwin has created many sympathetic portraits of white people. The Jewish lawyer the black families hire to defend Fonny is initially an ambitious man bent on advancing his career but later becomes an altruistic individual. The Italian woman who owns a vegetable stand informs the police of a racial harassment committed by a white hoodlum, thereby helping Fonny to be exonerated of his action to protect Tish, a victim of the white man's insult. The owner of a Spanish restaurant willingly allows Tish and Fonny to have dinner on credit out of his compassion for their unjust plight.

For Baldwin, black people in the North, in contrast to those in the South, can move freely and talk frequently with fellow residents. His white characters, unlike those in Wright's fiction, are seldom stereotyped. Whether they are prejudiced or fair-minded, materialistic or humanistic, they are always individuals capable of making their own judgments. It seems as though the spirit of individualism in which they have grown up becomes, in turn, contagious among the black people. In *No Name in the Street,* Baldwin shows why black men living in Paris were treated as individuals as Algerians were not. "Four hundred years in the West," he argues, "had certainly turned me into a Westerner—there was no way around that. But four hundred years in the West had also failed to bleach me—there was no way around *that,* either" (42).

The westernization of black people in America, as Baldwin would have agreed with Wright, has taken place by far at a swifter pace in the North than in the South. Southern life for black people, as vividly portrayed in *No Name in the Street,* was not only stagnant and dark, but it created terror. Baldwin traveled down the Southland at the time of the racial turmoil in Little Rock, Arkansas, in the late fifties, when black children attempted to go to school in front of a hostile army and citizenry to face the white past, let alone the white present. During his stay he encountered one of the most powerful politicians in the South, who made himself "sweating drunk" to humiliate another human being. Baldwin distinctly recalls the abjectness of this incident: "With his wet eyes staring up at my face, and his wet hand groping for my cock, we were both, abruptly, in history's ass-pocket." To Baldwin, those who had power in the South still lived with the mentality of slave owners. The experience convinced him that a black man's identity in the South was defined by the power to which such white men tried to cling, and that a black man's humanity was placed at the service of their fantasies. "If the lives of those children," he reflects, "were in those wet, despairing hands, if their future was to be read in those wet, blind eyes, there was reason to tremble" (61–62). It is characteristic of his narrative that the height of terror, as just described, is set against the height of love the child Baldwin felt when his life was saved by his stepbrother. His narrative thus moves back and forth with greater intensity between the author's feelings of abjectness and exaltation, of isolation and affinity.

Baldwin's style becomes even more effective as his tendency toward rhetorical fastenings and outbursts is replaced by brief, tense images that indicate a control of the narrative voice. For instance, one summer night in Birmingham, Baldwin met in a motel room one Rev. Shuttlesworth, as marked a man as Martin Luther King, Jr. Gravely concerned with Shuttlesworth's safety for fear that his car might be bombed, Baldwin wanted to bring it to his attention as Shuttlesworth was about to leave the room. But the minister would not let him. At first, there was only a smile on Shuttlesworth's face; upon a closer observation, he detected that "a shade of sorrow crossed his face, deep, impatient, dark; then it was gone. It was the most impersonal anguish I had ever seen on a man's face." Only later did he come to realize that the minister was then "wrestling with the mighty fact that the danger in which he stood was as nothing compared to the spiritual horror which drove those who were trying to destroy him" (*No Name* 67). A few pages later, this shade of dark and sorrow is compensated for by that of light and joy. Baldwin now reminisces about his Paris days—how little he had missed ice cream, hot dogs, Coney Island, the Statue of Liberty, the Empire State Building, but how much he had missed his brothers, sisters, and mother: "I missed the way the dark face closes, the way dark eyes watch, and the way, when a dark face opens, a light seems to go on everywhere." (71).

Unlike W. E. B. Du Bois and Jean Toomer, who viewed the South with deep nostalgia, Baldwin, like Richard Wright and John A. Williams, was repulsed by it, Even though at times he felt an affinity with the black people in the South and found his home there, he also found, as does Richard Henry in *Blues for Mister Charlie,* that once he had lived in the North he could not go home again. Baldwin's quest for humanity in *If Beale Street Could Talk* is not merely to seek out affinity with black people; it is to search the interior of city life. He is in search of a human bond in the hearts and souls of people. It stresses the conventional and yet universal bondage innate in man, a human affinity that can grow between man and woman, members of a family, relatives, friends—any group of individuals united in the name of love and understanding.

Fundamental to Baldwin's concept of human bondage is the relationship of love between a man and a woman that yields posterity. What saves Fonny and Tish from loneliness and despair is their expecting the child in her womb. Every time she visits him in jail, they focus their talk on the unborn baby. Whenever he sees her face during the visit, he knows not only does she love him, but "that others love him, too. . . . He is not alone; we are not alone." When she looks ashamed of her ever expanding waistline, he is elated, saying, "Here she come! Big as *two* houses! You sure it ain't twins? or triplets? Shit, we *might* make history" (162). While at home, she is comforted by Ray Charles's voice and piano, the sounds and smells of the kitchen, the sounds and "blurred human voices rising from the street." Only then does she realize that "out of this rage and a steady, somehow triumphant sorrow, my baby was slowly being formed" (41).

However crowded, noisy, and chaotic Baldwin's city may be, one can always discover order, meaning, and hope in one's life. The street talks as though conflict and estrangement among the residents compel them to seek their ties with smaller human units. Not only does the birth of a child, the impending birth of Tish and Fonny's baby, constitute the familial bond, but it also signals the birth of new America. Baldwin has earlier conceived this idea in *No Name in the Street*, in which the first half of the book, "Take Me to the Water," depicts the turmoil of American society in the sixties and the second, "To Be Baptized," prophesies the rebirth of a nation. In the epilogue he writes: "An old world is dying, and a new one, kicking in the belly of its mother, time, announces that it is ready to be born." Alluding to the heavy burden falling upon American people, he remarks with a bit of humor: "This birth will not be easy, and many of us are doomed to discover that we are exceedingly clumsy midwives. No matter, so long as we accept that our responsibility is to the new born: the acceptance of responsibility contains the key to the necessarily evolving skill" (196).

Baldwin's extolment of the relationship between Tish and Fonny also suggests that the interracial relationships of love and sex as seen in *Another Country* are often destroyed by the forces of society beyond their control. In such a relationship, genuine love often falls a victim of society, a larger human unit. Baldwin's love story in *If Beale Street Could Talk* also suggests that a homosexual relationship is an antithesis to the idea of rebirth. Levy, Fonny's landlord, is a personable, happily married young man. Being Jewish, he values the closeness in family life and the offspring marriage can produce. He willingly rents his loft to Fonny, who needs the space to work on his sculptures, because he is aware of his own happiness in raising children and wants his tenants to share the same joy. "Hell," Levy tells Fonny, "drag out the blankets and sleep on it. . . . Make babies on it. That's how *I* got here. . . . You two should have some beautiful babies . . . and, take it from me, kids, the world damn sure needs them." Out of sympathy for Fonny's situation, he even forgoes payment of the rent while Fonny is in jail, saying, "I want you kids to have your babies. I'm funny that way" (133–34).

As urban society disintegrates because of its indifference and impersonality, the love and understanding that can unite smaller communities, couples, families, relatives, and friends become essential to the pursuit of happiness. Those who are deprived of such relationships cannot survive. Daniel Carty, Fonny's childhood friend, who is also arrested by the D.A.'s office, is a loner. Without ties to his family and relatives, he is doomed.

Tony Maynard, Baldwin's former bodyguard, who appears in *No Name in the Street,* is reminiscent of Daniel Carty. Tony is imprisoned on a murder charge arising from a mistaken identity.[21] Since the title "To Be Baptized" in *No Name in the Street* suggests the idea of rebirth, Baldwin's motif of alienation, which Tony's episode illustrates in the latter portion of the book, seems incongruous. In any event, Tony is treated as a victim of the indifference and hatred that exists in society; like Daniel, he is without the protection of his family and relatives. Ironically, he is a professional bodyguard for a man but no one else can guard him.

While Baldwin often evokes the idea of rebirth in *No Name in the Street* by biblical references, he has a penchant to assail, in *If Beale Street Could Talk,* those who find their haven in the church. To him, a long history of the Christian church has partly resulted in the enslavement of black people in this country, and the black people "who were given the church and nothing else"[22] have learned to be obedient to the law of God and the land but failed to be independent thinkers.[23] Mrs. Hunt, Fonny's mother, like Cross Damon's mother in *The Outsider,* has a blind trust in Christ. She even believes that Fonny's imprisonment is "the Lord's way of making my boy think on his sins and surrender his soul to Jesus" (64). Her doctor convinces Mrs. Hunt, who has a heart problem, that her health is more important than her son's freedom. By contrast, Fonny's father Frank is a defiant disbeliever. "I don't know," Frank tells his wife, "how God expects a man to act when his son is in trouble. *Your* God crucified *His* son and was probably glad to get rid of him, but I ain't like that. I ain't hardly going out in the street and kiss the first white cop I see" (65). Although it is tragic that Frank commits suicide when he is caught stealing money to raise funds to defend his son, Frank's action suggests the genuine feeling of love and tenderness a father can have for his son.

Baldwin ends *If Beale Street Could Talk* on a triumphant note. Fonny is out of jail, however temporary it may be, because of the efforts by those who are genuinely concerned about his welfare. Not only has he been able to endure his ordeal, but his experience in jail has renewed his human spirit. The last time Tish visits him in jail, he tells her: "Listen, I'll soon be out. I'm coming home because I'm glad I came, can you dig that?" (193). The final scene once again echoes the voice that conveys Baldwin's idea of love and rebirth.

Fonny is now a sculptor at work in his studio: "Fonny is working on the wood, on the stone, whistling, smiling. And, from far away, but coming near, the baby cries and cries and cries and cries and cries and cries and cries and cries, cries like it means to wake the dead" (197).

Baldwin completed this scene of freedom and rebirth on Columbus Day, 12 October, as indicated at the end of the book. The reference to Columbus Day may easily remind one of Pudd'nhead Wilson's calendar note for that day in the conclusion of Mark Twain's classic novel of racial prejudice: "October 12, *the Discovery. It was wonderful to find America, but it would have been more wonderful to miss it.*"[24] While Twain's intention in the book is a satire on American society and on slavery in particular, Baldwin's in *If Beale Street Could Talk* is to discover a new America. When Baldwin declares in the epilogue for *No Name in the Street* that "the Western party is over, and the white man's sun has set. Period" (197), one can be puzzled. The question remains whether or not Baldwin had come away from the turbulent sixties as a disillusioned American. Throughout *No Name in the Street* he has fluctuated between his feelings of love and hatred as his episodes betray. From the perspective of his hatred and resignation, the book clearly bodes ill; from the perspective of his love and understanding, though avowedly less frequent, it nevertheless suggests its author remains hopeful. But in *If Beale Street Could Talk* Baldwin's ambivalence has largely disappeared, and the book tells that the sun will also rise in America, this time for black citizens as well as for white citizens.

NOTES

1. Joyce Carol Oates, "A Quite Moving and Very Traditional Celebration of Love," *New York Times Book Review,* 26 May 1974, 1–2.

2. I agree with Kichung Kim, who advances the theory that the difference between Wright and Baldwin arises from the two different concepts of man. Kim argues that the weakness Baldwin sees in Wright and other protest writers "is not so much that they had failed to give a faithful account of the actual conditions of man but rather that they had failed to be steadfast in their devotion . . . to what man might and ought to be. Such a man . . . will not only survive oppression but will be strengthened by it." See Kim, "Wright, the Protest Novel, and Baldwin's Faith," *CLA Journal* 17 (March 1974): 387–96.

3. James Baldwin, "Alas, Poor Richard," *Nobody Knows My Name* (New York: Dial, 1961), 151.

4. Richard Wright, "How 'Bigger' Was Born," *Native Son* (New York: Harper, 1966), xxvii.

5. James Baldwin, *Notes of a Native Son* (New York: Bantam Books, 1968), 27–28.

6. See Saul Bellow, *Seize the Day* (New York: Viking, 1956), 25. Tish in *If Beale*

Street Could Talk often wonders if their baby would inherit Fonny's narrow, slanted, "Chinese" eyes.

7. Richard Wright, *The Outsider* (New York: Harper, 1953), 23.

8. Albert Camus, *The Stranger,* trans. Stuart Gilbert (New York: Vintage Books, 1942).

9. James Baldwin, *No Name in the Street* (New York: Dell, 1972), 59.

10. See Granville Hicks, "Outcasts in a Caldron of Hate," *Saturday Review* 45 (1962): 21.

11. Saunders Redding observed that Wright, who paid homage to Africa, failed to find home there. See Redding, "Reflections on Richard Wright: A Symposium on an Exiled Native Son," *Anger and Beyond: The Negro Writer in the United States,* ed. Herbert Hill (New York: Harper, 1966), 204. Like Wright, John A. Williams, who hailed from Mississippi, has said, "I have been to Africa and know that it is not my home. America is." See Williams, *This Is My Country Too* (New York: New American Library, 1956), 169.

12. To reveal this kind of malady in society as Baldwin attempts to do in *No Name in the Street* requires an aritist's skills. The juror's response is reminiscent of Aunt Sally's to Huck Finn, who reports that a steamboat has just blown up a cylinder-head down the river:

> "Good gracious! Anybody hurt?"
> "No'm. Killed a nigger."
> "Well, it's lucky; because sometimes people do get hurt."

See Mark Twain, *Adventures of Huckleberry Finn,* ed. Henry Nash Smith (Boston: Houghton, 1958), 185. What Twain and Baldwin share is the genuine feeling an intense individualist possesses; both writers feel their own great powers and yet recognize the hopelessness of trying to change the world overnight.

13. *Prose and Poetry from the Old Testament,* ed. James F. Fullington (New York: Appleton, 1950), 77.

14. In a later volume of essays, Baldwin makes a similar assertion about black Americans' somber realization of themselves: "This is why blacks can be heard to say, *I ain't got to be nothing but stay black, and die!*: which is, after all, a far more affirmative apprehension than *I'm free, white and twenty-one.*" See *The Devil Finds Work* (New York: Dial, 1976), 115.

15. See, for example, Benjamin DeMott, "James Baldwin on the Sixties: Acts and Revelations," in *James Baldwin: A Collection of Critical Essays,* ed. Keneth Kinnamon (Englewood Cliffs, N.J.: Prentice-Hall, 1974), 158.

16. See Richard Wright, *12 Million Black Voices* (New York: Viking, 1941), 121–22.

17. In 1961 Baldwin wrote in his essay "In Search of a Majority:" "Whether I like it or not, or whether you like it or not, we are bound together. We are part of each other. What is happening to every Negro in the country at any time is also happening to you. There is no way around this. I am suggesting that these walls— these artificial walls—which have been up so long to protect us from something we fear, must come down" (*Nobody Knows My Name:* 136–37). In 1962 he wrote in "My Dungeon Shook": "Well, the black man has functioned in the white man's world as a fixed star, as an immovable pillar: and as he moves out of his place, heaven and earth are shaken to their foundations. . . . But these men are your brothers—your lost, younger brothers. And if the word *integration* means anything, this is what it means: that we, with love, shall force our brothers to see themselves as they are, to

cease fleeing from reality and begin to change it." See *The Fire Next Time* (New York: Dial, 1963), 23–24.

18. See *Great Short Works of Stephen Crane* (New York: Harper, 1968), 258.

19. John Aldridge, "The Fire Next Time?" *Saturday Review*, 15 June 1974: 24–25.

20. James Baldwin, *If Beale Street Could Talk* (New York: Dial, 1974), 9.

21. I agree with Benjamin DeMott, who regards Tony Maynard as an undeveloped character despite much space given for that purpose, but the weakness of Baldwin's characterization results from his use of a sterile man in the context of creation and rebirth (DeMott, "James Baldwin on the Sixties," 158).

22. See Baldwin's interview by Kalamu ya Salaam, "James Baldwin: Looking towards the Eighties," *Critical Essays on James Baldwin*, ed. Fred L. Standley and Nancy V. Burt (Boston: Hall, 1988), 40.

23. Sandra A. O'Neile observes in her essay, "Fathers, Gods, and Religion: Perceptions of Christianity and Ethnic Faith in James Baldwin," that "more than the heritage of any other Black American writer, Baldwin's works illustrate the schizophrenia of the Black American experience with Christianity." Black people, she argues, needed a distinction "between Christianity as they knew it to be and Christianity as it was practiced in the white world." See *Critical Essays on James Baldwin*, 125–43.

24. Mark Twain, *Pudd'nhead Wilson* and *Those Extraordinary Twins*, ed. Sidney E. Berger (New York: Norton, 1980), 113.

11

Metonymy and Synecdoche: The Rhetoric of the City in Toni Morrison's *Jazz*

JOCELYN CHADWICK-JOSHUA

"I want . . . well, I didn't always . . . now I want. I want some fat in this life."

(*Jazz* 1)

SINCE the eighteenth century, the city and the African American have had a unique relationship, particularly with the northern city. In a type of rhetorical paradox the city offered the free person of color the access to freedom while simultaneously constraining the depth and degree of that freedom. In some ways, one might view this rela- tionship as a love-hate relationship destined for disillusionment and desertion. But as we trace the path of the African American during the nineteenth and twentieth centuries, while disillusionment and desertion have occurred, the opposite has happened as well. Southern African Americans, so long denied voice, thought, emotion, and just simple presence, viewed the city as the path, the venue, the metonymi- cal and synecdochal representation and promise of a better way of life, a vehicle by which they could gain the parity and freedom denied. Critics and sociologists agree that two primary reasons for the allure of the city during the early twentieth century were the increasing Jim Crowism and over segregation and violence in the rural South as well as the economic shift from agriculture to industry.[1]

While writers have depicted various perspectives of the city and its influence on the African American, American women writers of color such as Ida Barnett Wells, Frances Ellen Watkins Harper, Alice Walker, Zora Neale Hurston, Gloria Naylor, and Ntozake Shange, have rendered the city in womanist[2] terms. It is from this rhetorical frame that this paper will explore Toni Morrison's rendering of Harlem—*the city*—in *Jazz*. Using what psychologist Carol Gilligan and rhetor Karlyn Kohrs Campbell refer to as speaking in a different voice, a voice that relies on symbolic reversal and woman-centered use of metonymy and synecdochy, Toni Morrison uses the city to reflect the empowerment of those voices, voices that at once see themselves free and constrained.[3]

Kenneth Burke in *A Grammar of Motives* identifies metonymy and synecdoche as not only tropes for figurative use but also as tropes for "the discovery and description of 'the truth'."[4] Burke delineates among what he calls the "four master tropes." Of the four, this study is concerned with metonymy and synecdoche. Metonymy, according to Burke, has a "basic 'strategy'" that conveys

> some incorporeal or intangible state in terms of the corporeal or tangible. . . . 'Metonymy' is a device of 'poetic realism'—but its partner, 'reduction,' is a device of 'scientific realism.' Here 'poetry' and 'behaviorism' meet. . . . [The poet] knows that 'shame,' for instance, is not merely a 'state,' but a movement of the eye, a color of the cheek, a certain quality of voice and set of muscles. . . .[5]

Burke distinguishes metonymy from synecdoche by deducing that because metonymy reduces, then "reduction is a *representation*."[6] He says that "[a]s a mental state is the 'representation' of certain material conditions, so we could—reversing the process—say that the material conditions are 'representative' of the mental state."[7] Merging this definition with Campbell's definition of symbolic reversal used in womanist rhetoric reveals how Morrison accomplishes character development and revelation, particularly among the novel's primary women, using her *characterization* of the city as a synecdochal and metonymical conduit.[8] The material nature of the city represented through the eyes and ears and brains of these women who symbolically reverse the city's material conditions allows Morrison to establish her theme of endurance and survival.

Specifically, Morrison's rhetorical use of metonymy and synecdoche, then, renders the city in this novel as nurturer and agitator as well as *birth-mother* of *Jazz*'s characters—Joe Trace, Violet Trace, Alice Manfred, and Felice. The city and its frenetic motion also reflect the innermost desires, frustrations, and fears of these characters. *Jazz*'s unseen but participatory and vocal narrator reveals this multifaceted trait of the city early in the novel after providing a microcosmic summary of the tragic love triangle involving Joe, Violet, and Dorcas:

> A city like this one makes me dream tall and feel in on things. Hep. . . .
> When I look over strips of green grass lining the river, at church steeples

and into cream-and-copper halls of apartment buildings, I'm strong. Alone, yes, but top-notch and indestructible—like the City in 1926 when all the wars are over and there will never be another one.[9]

Like the tall buildings and the church steeples and the fertile, green grass juxtaposed with anticipated isolation synecdochally described by the narrator, Morrison's city empowers *because* of the paradox it compels each character to acknowledge and experience.

Violet's telling Alice that she wants "some fat in this life" (110) echoes the sentiment of all migrating people of color threaded throughout the novel. It is the same fat to which the narrator alludes at the beginning, a surplus of opportunity and freedom and voice that the city paradoxically offers and denies. Joe and Violet synecdochally represent what African Americans hoped to achieve in the city— economic independence, but

> job discrimination, which ironically was practiced in the heart of the black ghetto, exacerbated these employment problems. During the 1920's the vast majority of Harlem's retail establishments would only lure blacks for menial jobs such as porter, maid, or elevator operator. As a result of this . . . most of Harlem's residents lived . . . on the verge of poverty. . . .[10]

This paradox Joe and Violet reflect in Joe's descriptions between what he has heard about the prospects of the city and what he and Violet actually accomplish:

> He loved the woods. Loved them. [But] Joe knew people living in the City and some who'd been there and come home with tales to make Baltimore weep. . . . (106)

Joe has heard that "whitepeople literally [throw] money at you—just for being *neighborly*: opening a taxi door, picking up a package" (106, emphasis mine). Ironically the *neighborly* tasks Joe lists are synecdochal components of the menial jobs the city offers to people of color. Despite this reality, however, Joe makes the best of the menial jobs in the city, then procures a "little sideline selling Cleopatra products in the neighborhood" and says that opportunity in the city allows Violet to cut out day work and just do hair so that, after awhile, they are economically able to move from Tenderloin to 140th and Little Africa to Lenox Avenue and larger living quarters (127–28).

The city metonymically rendered as *the Promise Land* thematically permeates the novel. This promised land is what migrating African Americans like Joe and Violet Trace see and hear. By the time Joe and Violet arrive in the city, 1906, almost 90,000 had migrated from

the South, most seeking economic and social opportunity and independence.[11] As much as Joe and Violet—along with thousands like
them—loved the land and relished the idea that once the fourteenth
and fifteenth amendments became law they could themselves own and
control their destinies, the harsh reality was that life in the South
was more uncertain, uncontrolled and frenzied.

Morrison depicts this chaotic state of affairs with Rose Dear, Violet's mother when her land is parcelled off piece by piece. This pathetic
scene with white movers tilting Rose Dear out of her last chair as she
sits at an invisible repossessed table, sipping imaginary boiled coffee
from a cherished china teacup—that also becomes imaginary—with
her little finger extended synecdochally represents the dream deferred
for many southern African Americans, a dream metonymically depicted in the cup that falls from Rose Dear's hands, ". . . unbroken
. . . and lying a bit beyond her hand. Just out of reach" (98). The
"teacup" scene that the city offers is a promise that is at once tangible
and yet "just out of reach." But the risk that people like Joe and Violet
take is well worth it. Joe and Violet earned their wages in the fields
picking cotton—"ten cents a day for the women and a case quarter
for the men" (103). Violet's grandmother, True Belle, earned hers as
a domestic—"with twenty-two years of the wages Miss Vera initiated
as soon as the War was over (but held in trust lest her servant get
ideas), True Belle . . . got the money—ten eagle dollars" (142). Those
wages, as Wintz stresses, "were paltry when juxtaposed to those in
the City. Women domestics . . . who received $2.50 per week in the
South, could earn $2.10 to $2.50 per day in the North, while their
husbands could increase their earnings from $1.10 per day to $3.75
per day by taking a job in a northern factory."[12]

Such apparent economic improvement lured more and more African
Americans to the city and some did, like Joe and Violet, experience
modest success. From the moment they arrived, the city would begin
its metonymical message of freedom, independence, and voice, making
moot whatever risks they might experience to the personal and moral
codes they observed in the rural woods of the South. Morrison ex-
pertly conveys this sense of city-inspired euphoria by combining a
series of descriptive synecdochies:

> However they came, when or why, the minute the leather of their soles
> hit the pavement—there was no turning around. Even if the room they
> rented was smaller than a heifer's stall and darker than a morning privy,
> they stayed. . . . Part of why they loved it was the spectre they left behind.
> . . . The minute they arrive . . . and glimpse the wide streets and wasteful
> lamps lighting them, they know they are born for it. There, in a city,

they are not so much new as themselves: *their stronger, riskier selves.* (33, emphasis mine)

It is not just their soles and imaginations that hit the pavement of the city and fall in love but their very souls, for as the narrator states, the city *makes* them love it with such intensity and single-mindedness that they have a tendency to lose focus of what real love, love among and between people, is without the city as frame.[13]

What Morrison depicts over and over through this series of metonymies and synecdochies is the city's paradoxical promise—a promise that is at once positive and negative, and therefore, metamorphic, to all newcomers as well as veterans of the city. This bifurcated persona of the city extends its persuasive promise to include a variety of social motifs: economic and social advancement as well as adolescent initiation. The most profound metamorphosis and promise experienced by people of color in the city occurs, however, within the love relationship between men and women: husband and wife, girlfriend and boyfriend, Sweetbacks and "high-heeled shoes with graceful straps across the arch" (55). All encounters, of course, are subject to the city's inevitable paradox that lies beneath each *promise* of success or failure.

Just as the city offers paradoxical economic advancement, it also presents itself as social facilitator, and it is the social frame that Morrison renders in some detail before exploring the romantic one. In many ways, one can conclude that the city's social frame is not simply tangential but precursory to comprehending more personal relationships. Cynthia Hamilton states that "[w]hen ordinary working people reach out to reappropriate from their oppressions the whole of everyday life, societal transformation may occur."[14] Such transformation takes place in *Jazz* among Joe, Violet, Alice, and Felice, each transformation forced to happen because the city itself engineers it. No character better relates how the city functions as social facilitator and subsequently transformer than Alice Manfred. Although Alice Manfred makes a point of distinction between where she lives, Clifton Place, and the heart of Harlem, Lenox Avenue and surrounding area, the city yet proved to be for her a social facilitator. Harlem itself developed into a "cultural center and a Mecca for its aspiring young"[15] and its fledgling middle class, a fact that Alice and her Civic Daughters' luncheon meeting demonstrates. It is the same city which Alice so fears and of which she disapproves that allows her to gather socially with her group to plan a Thanksgiving fundraiser for the National Negro Business League (69). It is the same city that allows the narrator to foreshadow Alice's social affiliations and overall social perspective when in her synecdochal, encyclopedic list of the city's positive *and* negative traits she includes "... and every club, organization, group, order, union, society, brotherhood, sisterhood, or association imaginable" (10).

Clearly, the city offers positive opportunities for social advance-ment, advancement both direct and indirect. Through a series of syn-ecdochies woven throughout the novel, Morrison allows the narrator and Alice to inform the audience that the city allows for colored clerks at the A&P, Negro surgeons at Harlem Hospital, "colored nurses" at Bellevue, master seamstresses—like Alice, and independent, licensed *as well as* unlicensed beauticians—like Violet. Such renderings, from one perspective, metonymically reduce the city to the role of positive social facilitator, thus engendering self-reliance and race pride.

But while this role is not only accurate but indeed one to be desired, true to the symbolic reversal Morrison uses, it is the city's contradic-tions *within* this facilitating context that reveals the deep-structured and complex nature and personality of the city with its effect on its citizens of color. Yes, the Negro surgeon operates at Harlem hospital, but he is operating on his people coming into the emergency room who have injured one another, according to the narrator, in a violent crime. Yes, the A&P has a colored clerk, but only one. The "first class of colored nurses" at Bellevue metonymically represent social progress, but in the midst of their undeniable accomplishment and dedication, they are "declared unseemly for the official Bellevue nurse's cap" be-cause of their hair (8–9). And the opportunity for a better life and social opportunity for the average blue-collar worker appears within reach, but the city frames these accomplishments as well against a backdrop of what Alice Manfred describes as the city being a place

> ... where whitemen leaned out of motor cars with folded dollar bills ... where salesmen touched her and only her as though she was a part of the goods they had condescended to sell her ... where she, a woman of fifty had no surname. Where women who spoke English said, Don't sit there, honey, you never know what they have. (54)

With each cause for concern and qualified accomplishment, pride is an indispensable requirement, for the theme of endurance and sur-vival emerge.

Through Alice Morrison amplifies her paradoxical vision of the city and its role as social facilitator when she extends the symbolic reversal to include that part of the city which microcosmically *should* provide a safe haven but, paradoxically, does and does not. This part of the city Alice describes synecdochally through clothes rather than through consumer goods as she did earlier. "High-heeled shoes with graceful straps," "vampy hats . . . with saucy brims," "makeup of any kind," and "coats clung low in the back and not buttoned but clutched, like a bathrobe or a towel around the body" (55) contribute to the dual, paradoxical image of the city as social facilitator.

By relying on stylistically juxtaposing the positive with the negative aspects of the city as a social facilitator for its people of color, or antanagoge, Morrison empowers the reader to *see and feel* the paradox that the characters themselves see and hear, particularly the women. It is Morrison's unrelenting repetitious style of synecdochal listing and then framing those lists within metonymy that reveals what she is representing as well as what she hopes the reader will perceive.[16] The confusion, frustration, and utter contradiction with the city as social facilitator and as omnipresent power and inspiration come to the reader as experienced by Alice and later Violet and Felice. And each, by the novel's conclusion, surmises that all of the emotions experienced and shared between them—Alice, Felice, and especially Violet, *the City's contradiction*—have been worth the frustration and confusion (222–25).

Perhaps more than any other character in *Jazz*, Violet, in her para-doxical relationships with Joe, Alice, and Felice, reflects the positive and negative paradox of the city. Violet's schizophrenia displays one of the most provocative metonymies of how the city licenses both, Violet and "*that* Violet"—the Violent—to live and flourish, for a time, in the same body, the same flesh (90–97). The city allows *that* Violet to transcend traditional social boundaries normally observed by Violet so that she can violate—*kill*—the corpse of Joe Trace's lover in her casket. The city also allows the boys who subdue her to violate "the teachings they had followed all their lives about the respect due their elders" (91), again rendering metonymically and synecdochally Morrison's city of paradox.

As we see with Violet's character, only through privileging oneself to feel and experience the diversity and paradox of sights, sounds, and emotions emitted by the city can one find one's real, inner self. Echo-ing Virginia Woolf, Violet realizes *only* after having experienced the city that she must *kill the angel in the house*,[17] or in this case *that* Violet, the violent one (208–9) if she is ever to regain not just her *old* self but, more importantly, her *reborn* self, the woman-self that her "mother didn't stay around long enough to see. . . . The one she would have liked and the one [Violet] used to like before . . ." (208).

For Violet to articulate this action to Felice, she has had to experi-ence and survive all that the city has had to "dish out," even when she herself did not fully comprehend what she was doing or what was being done to her. The city with its seductive call, for example, to impressionable young girls like Alice's niece Dorcas sets the frame for Alice and Violet to meet and ironically *share* an experience. Because the city sings music that Alice calls "dirty, get-on-down music" (58), music that transforms the city into the *Beast* that desires its own filth, that wants its own self raped, that wants to be its own slaughtered children (78), Alice unsuccessfully attempts to navigate her niece away from people represented by Violet and Joe Trace, the synecdo- chal representations of "[the] embarrassing kind" (79). More specifi- cally, to Alice, Joe and Violet become a metonymy for impending danger and their actions synecdochal proof:

> The husband shot; the wife stabbed. Nothing her niece did or tried could equal the violence done to her. And where there was violence wasn't there also vice? Gambling. Cursing. A terrible and nasty closeness. Red dresses. Yellow shoes. And, of course, race music to urge them on. (79)

Each sight, sound, experience is strengthened and subsidized by the city.

Again, true to the paradox and symbolic reversal demonstrated within the novel, Alice and Violet find themselves paradoxically drawn together. As women, they can, by using their own voices, find the solace necessary to make sense out of what on the surface appears to have been a senseless act of violence—"love" gone wrong. By using their voices to construct questions heretofore unasked, Alice and Vio- let see into each other's pain —not just Joe's shooting Alice's niece or Violet's attempted violation of the niece's corpse—but into Alice's stunted, puritanical childhood and Violet's traumatic one. As a result of the sharing, Violet acknowledges her *other* self and reintroduces *that* Violet into herself. Alice begins to understand her own psycho- logical aberrations with sex and her own sexuality. In Morrison's own words regarding African-American women, Alice and Violet begin to see and understand their own paradoxical natures.[18] Without the city's framing and engineering circumstance and event, however, nei- ther woman would ever have identified or confronted her own self so earnestly and completely. Given the city's pervasive and permeating persona, they actually have no choice in the matter, a sentiment that the narrator foreshadows early on in the novel:

> Do what you please in the City, it is there to back and frame you no matter what you do. And what goes on on its blocks and lots and side streets is anything the strong can think of and the weak will admire. All you have to do is heed the design—the way it's laid out for you, consider- ate, mindful of where you want to go and what you might need tomor- row. (9)[19]

Whereas Alice's sharing with Violet empowers her to continue her identification and acknowledgement of her sources of her emotional and psychological pain on her own, it takes Alice to see and hear and experience the second young girl "with an Okeh record under her arm and carrying some stewmeat wrapped in butcher paper . . . with four marcelled waves on each side of her head" (6) to complete her identification and acknowledgement.[20] When Felice seeks out Joe and Violet, initially to locate her opal ring that she loaned to Dorcas, she establishes a relationship with Joe and Violet—much to the surprise of them all. In her three visits to the Trace home, Felice—whose name means happy, according to Joe (212)—engages Violet in conversations that cause Violet to articulate how she understands herself in relation to the city: its impact on her home, Rome in Vesper County, and her relationship with her husband Joe and the dead girl, Dorcas. The most important truth to emerge from this sharing is Violet's finding her own voice, her real self.

It is the narrator who most ably clarifies the effect the paradox of the city has on its inhabitants, an effect that is itself paradoxical. Foreshadowing another tragic triangle framed and inspired by the city (6), the narrator "predicts" that just like the Violet-Joe-Dorcas triangle that ended in murder and attempted (re)murder, love requited, unrequited and stunted, the Violet-Joe-Felice triangle will suffer the same fate. With the last, and most significant symbolic reversal in the novel, the "doomed three"not only do not become a triangle but each finds a part of him and herself that had at one time been lost—Joe, a sense of his mother and their spiritual bond; Violet, the woman she has wanted to be; and Felice, a sense of self and voice, an enhanced awareness that will never allow her to be anyone's ". . . alibi or hammer or toy" (222).

Only the city with its metonymies and synecdochies combining to create its paradoxical persona interacting with its inhabitants could produce such character transformations. Only the city, Harlem, with its ability to mean different things to different people at the same time, a city that was simultaneously the aspiration and desperation of its citizens could contain such people and make such cultural meaning. Wintz supports this depiction of Harlem during the twenties:

> Harlem reflected the confusing and contradictory position of blacks in the early twentieth century. It was a symbol of the black migrant who left the South and went north with dreams of freedom and opportunity. It also symbolized the shattered pieces of those dreams which lay half-buried beneath the filth and garbage of the city slum.[21]

It is Morrison's rhetorical cataloguing of this rhythm of paradox primarily experienced *through the women* that the reader begins to comprehend what the narrator refers to as the irresistible "clicking" pulse of the city. With *Jazz*, then, Morrison renders the city's "primal scenes"[22] which provide in this work metonymic vignettes that reflect the paradox of the lives of its inhabitants. And by the novel's conclusion, the characters and the city's synecdochal rhythm merge into one. The narrator states:

> I wonder, do they know they are the sound of snapping fingers under sycamores lining the streets? . . . Even when they are not there, when whole city blocks downtown and acres of lawned neighborhoods in Sag Harbor cannot see them, the clicking is there. (226)

And so Morrison's depiction of the city in this most unusual novel deliberately does not provide a neatly-wrapped, contained, and linear world view. Rather, this world, synecdochally represented by the city, the world of the migrating southern African American, teems with contradiction and danger and loving and history as well as herstory. It is also a world that Langston Hughes aptly described, forshadowing Morrison's own compelling depiction:

> Harlem, like a Picasso painting in his Cubistic period. Harlem—Southern Harlem—the Carolinas, Georgia, Florida—looking for the Promised Land —dressed in rhythmic words, painted in bright pictures, dancing to jazz—and ending up in the subway at morning rush time—*headed downtown*. . . . Melting pot Harlem—Harlem of honey and chocolate and caramel and rum and vinegar and lemon and lime and gall. Dusky dream Harlem rumbling into a nightmare tunnel. . . .[23]

Amid the unrelenting paradox, these characters endure, survive, and emerge the better for having experienced the city.

NOTES

1. Cary D. Wintz, *Black Culture and the Harlem Renaissance*, 6. See also Wintz, 8–9; *Encyclopedia of Black Americans; Nathan Irvin Huggins, Harlem Renaissance*, 57–58; James Weldon Johnson, "Harlem: The Cultural Capital of the World"; Molefi Asante and Mark Mattson, *Historical and Cultural Atlas of African Americans*, 159–61; W.E.B. Du Bois, "The Migration of the Negroes," 185–90.

2. According to the *Amazons: A Feminist Dictionary Bluestockings and Crones*, womanist includes the commitment "to survival and wholeness for the entire people, male *and* female. Not a separatist, except periodically, for health."

3. Carol Gilligan, *In a Different Voice*, 173. Gilligan asserts that women make meaning not only phallologocentrical but woman-centered as well. This *different voice* is one that reveals her "ethic of care, the tie between relationship and responsibility,

and the origins of aggression in the failure of connection." Karlyn Kohrs Campbell, "The Rhetoric of Women's Liberation: An Oxymoron" (390; 392–94). Campbell further elucidates on the *different*, rhetorical way women construct meaning by saying that this kind of liberating rhetoric "attacks the entire psychosocial reality, the most fundamental values, of the cultural context in which it occurs. She goes on to state that this kind of rhetoric of "intense moral conflict . . . highlights . . . 'consciousness raising' . . . [that encourages each person] to express her personal feelings and experiences . . . to create awareness (through shared experiences)." Morrison weaves such a relationship between Violet Trace and Alice Manfred and Violet and Felice. As each relationship evolves, the audience experiences along with each woman the intensity of conflict, the emotion of aggression with love lost, and, more importantly, a woman who becomes aware of herself, her city, its power, and her place in it.

4. Kenneth Burke, *A Grammar of Motives* (Berkeley: University of California Press, 1945), 503.

5. Ibid., 506–7.

6. Ibid., 506.

7. Ibid., 507.

8. Campbell, 397–98. "Symbolic reversals transform devil terms society has applied to women into god terms and always exploit the power and fear lurking in these terms as potential sources of strength. . . . Quite evidently, they are attempts at the radical affirmation of new identities for women." Morrison allows Alice, Violet, and Felice to reverse the impact of the city at will, thereby creating the rhetorical paradox and subsequent dialectic necessary for each woman to experience her own development. Each woman also symbolically reverses such concepts and ideas as friendship, love, sexuality, and independence.

9. *Jazz*, 7. Further references to this novel will be cited by page number(s) internally.

10. Wintz, 24; 26. According to Wintz, of the more than 224,000 African Americans living in New York by 1930 only 258 African-American owned businesses existed. Employers other than those cited earlier such as Metropolitan Life Insurance Company while it insured over 100,000 people of color, it employed none. And those white-owned businesses that did employ African Americans did so at the menial level as heretofore cited. Utility companies hired 1%, and vocational schools refused to train African Americans for jobs traditionally held by whites. Langston Hughes also relates his surprise at this revelation. See Hughes' essay "My Early Days in Harlem," 59.

11. Wintz, 13. See also *Jazz*, 33.

12. Wintz, 15–16. See also Gilbert Osofsky, "Harlem: The Making of a Ghetto," 7–19; Kenneth B. Clarke, "HARYOU-ACT in Harlem—The Dream that Went Astray," 80–85; Paula Giddings, *When and Where I Enter: The Impact of Black Women on Race and Sex in America*, 141–48; Walter F. White, "'Work or Flight' in the South," 237–41.

13. See *Jazz*, 33–34. The narrator asserts that those in the city essentially *unlearn* how they loved before their migration, and assume a new approach to loving, one dictated by the city itself. One's ability to love another, according to the narrator, is based on "the way a person is in the City."

14. Hamilton, 147.

15. Wintz, 20; 27; and Giddings, 187–215; Langston Hughes, Milton Meltzer, and Eric Lincoln ed. *A Pictorial History of Black Americans*, 272.

16. Morrison herself states that she never actually says what a character looks like or how a state of mind should be interpreted. Rather, she asserts that in order to

assure a participatory audience, she allows the character to be a "simile" or a metaphor or a painting. See *Black Women Writers at Work,* ed. Claudia Tate, 127.

17. Woolf, *A Room of One's Own.*

18. In the Tate interview Morrison states that African-American women *are* paradoxes in that they can without conflict acknowledge and combine "the nest and adventure." "They are both safe harbor and ship; they are both inn and trail. We, black women, do both" (122).

19. This sentiment is repeated in throughout the novel (33; 117–18; 120). What is interesting here, too, is Morrison's feminization of the city. While at times its voice is neuter or masculine, it also possesses a womanist voice that is itself a womanist voice of paradox—a voice that entices and seduces to one's regret yet a voice that nurtures and omnisciently *knows* what an individual will need and sets about appropriate preparations.

20. While this girl is introduced synecdochally very early in the novel, Morrison elects to allow the city to reveal her piece-meal—a slowly-evolving synecdoche. Interestingly, the girl is referred to by name as friend and companion to Alice's niece, Dorcas, even on the night Joe shoots Dorcas. But the real connection and the substantive characterization of Felice, or the girl with the Okeh record, evidences itself only the final third of the novel (197ff).

21. Wintz, 29. See also a compelling personal narrative written by George S. Schuyler, journalist, essayist, and novelist during the twenties who after having moved slowly to the Right, wrote "From Job to Job: A Personal Narrative," chronicling the adversities many African Americans encountered on the job search.

22. Rushdy, "'Rememory': Primal Scenes and Constructions in Toni Morrison's Novels," 303. Rushdy asserts that Morrison's use of a traditionally Freudian primal-scene "is . . . an opportunity and affective agency for self-discovery through memory and through what Morrison felicitously calls 'rememory'" (303). The city as Morrison uses it in *Jazz* functions as unavoidable catalyst that at once seduces and compels its citizens to engage in the process of *rememoring* the conscious and sub-conscious layers of their lives and experiences. This process of rememory, according to Rushdy, empowers outside of the actual experience to "enter the sphere of the action" (303).

23. Hughes, 60.

WORKS CITED

Amazons: A Feminist Dictionary Bluestockings and Crones.

Asante, Molefi, and Mark T. Mattson. *Historical and Cultural Atlas of African Americans.* New York: Macmillan, 1992.

Burke, Kenneth. *A Grammar of Motives.* Berkeley: University of California Press, 1962.

Campbell, Karlyn Kohrs. "The Rhetoric of Women's Liberation: An Oxymoron." In *Methods of Rhetorical Criticism: A Twentieth-Century Perspective,* 3rd ed., edited by Bernard L. Brock, Robert L. Scot, and James W. Cheseboro, 388–402. Detroit: Wayne State University Press, 1989.

Clarke, Kenneth. "HARYOU-ACT in Harlem—The Dream that Went Astray." In *Harlem USA,* edited by John Henrik Clarke, 80–85. New York: Collier, 1964.

Du Bois, W.E.B. "The Migration of the Negroes." *The Crisis* 15 (June 1917): 63–66. Rpt. in vol. 3 of *A Documentary History of the Negro People in the United States,* 6 vols., edited by Herbert Aptheker, 185–90. 1951; New York: Citadel, 1990.

Giddings, Paula. *When and Where I Enter: The Impact of Black Women on Race and Sex in America.* New York: Bantam, 1988.

Gilligan, Carol. *In A Different Voice: Psychological Theory and Women's Development.* Cambridge: Harvard University Press, 1982.

Hamilton, Cynthia. "Work and Culture: The Evolution of Consciousness in Urban Industrial Society in the Fiction of William Attaway and Peter Abrahams." *Black American Literature Forum* 21, 1–2 (1987): 147–63.

Huggins, Nathan Irvin. *Harlem Renaissance.* New York: Oxford, 1971.

Hughes, Langston. "My Early Days in Harlem." In *Harlem USA*, edited by John Henrik Clarke, 57–61. New York: Collier, 1964.

Hughes, Langston, Milton Meltzer, and Eric Lincoln, eds. *A Pictorial History of Black Americans.* 1956. New York: Crown, 1983.

Johnson, James Weldon. "Harlem: The Cultural Capital of the World." In *The New Negro: Voices of the Harlem Renaissance,* edited by Alain Locke. 1925. New York: Atheneum, 1992.

Low, W. Augustus, and Virgil A. Clift, eds. *Encyclopedia of Black America.* New York: Da Capo, 1981.

Morrison, Toni. *Jazz.* New York: Plume, 1993.

———. "Toni Morrison." In *Black Women Writers at Work,* edited by Claudia Tate, 117–31. New York: Continuum, 1988.

Osofsky, Gilbert. "Harlem: The Making of a Ghetto." In *Harlem USA*, edited by John Henrik Clarke, 7–19. New York: Collier, 1964.

Rushdy, Ashraf H.A. "'Rememory': Primal Scenes and Constructions in Toni Morrison's Novels." *Contemporary Literature* 21 (1990): 300–323.

Schuyler, George S. "From Job to Job: A Personal Narrative." *The World Tomorrow* 6 (May 1923): 147–48. Rpt. in vol. 3 of *A Documentary History of the Negro People in the United States,* 6 vols., edited by Herbert Aptheker, 427–30. 1951; New York: Citadel, 1990.

White, Walter F. "'Work or Fight' in the South." *New Republic* 18 (March, 1919): 144–46. Rpt. in vol. 3 of *A Documentary History of the Negro People in the United States,* 6 vols., edited by Herbert Aptheker, 237–41. 1951; New York: Citadel, 1990.

Wintz, Cary D. *Black Culture and the Harlem Renaissance.* Houston: Rice University Press, 1988.

Woolf, Virginia. *A Room of One's Own.* New York: Harcourt, 1929.

12

The Wall and the Mirror in the Promised Land: The City in the Novels of Gloria Naylor

MICHAEL F. LYNCH

1

THE vision of America as the modern Eden, an ideal or virtually perfectible land, has roots deep in the national history and psyche. William Carlos Williams points out in In the American Grain, however, that the Puritans strangely had no wonder for the New World and that their primary urge was to impose a European sense of order by dominating and controlling the environment. As part of this project of mastery, the destruction of the Indian was sanctioned by his failure to be what he was not—a European. As a result of these inherited attitudes of hypocrisy and hostility, Williams sees America today as "the most lawless country in the civilized world, a panorama of murders, perversions, a terrific ungoverned strength, excusable only because of the horrid beauty of its machines" (68). Many American writers have maintained a qualified vision or myth of Eden, locating it paradoxically far from our prided technological centers of control, the cities. Writers such as Cooper, Thoreau, Melville, Whitman, and Twain idealized the non-urban settings of the West, the woods, the sea, the open road, and the river, suggesting the need for escape from the man-made city in order to develop oneself and to realize freedom. This essentially romantic quest, which offers a return to "nature" as the answer to disillusionment with society, often assumes the fundamental innocence of the individual when uncorrupted by society. However, this attempt to reassert or recapture innocence tends to deny the responsibility of individuals either for creating the "corrupt" city or for working toward its regeneration. The Edenic quest for an idealized non-urban setting in American literature, in spite of its emphasis on freedom, ironically shares some of the deterministic implications of naturalism insofar as it portrays the individual as the product of environment.

The black experience in America has not encompassed the luxury of belief in an earthly, American Eden. The conditions of slavery encouraged blacks to look not backwards, to the garden before the fall (slavery itself being the most horrible evidence of that fall), but forward to heaven's promise of relief and the end of all suffering. The rural southern environment continued to be oppressive and dangerous after the ending of slavery, discouraging the idealization of the rural life. Dreams of the northern city as a promised land faded with the massive migration after World War I and the realities of tenement housing, unemployment, and increasingly overt racism. Many black writers have focused on the inequities and evils found in the city, yet they have not been able or willing to envision an ideal pastoral alternative. This refusal to seek an elusive, and perhaps illusory innocence (in a setting which might perfect the individual) somewhere out in nature, stands as one of the prime contributions of black writers to American literature. For this refusal calls us back from the romanticized, at times narcissistic quest, to make a more sober analysis of actual values and realities in contradiction of our highest ideals.

Black American authors generally have been neither "pro-urban" nor "anti-urban," have neither simply celebrated nor damned the city. Instead, they have attempted to depict the city and its effects on blacks as realistically as possible, recognizing it as the environment in which most black Americans find themselves. Individuals' need for escape from this environment usually takes the form either of temporary, self-destructive measures such as drugs and violence, or of upward mobility to a more refined urban or suburban area. Black writers influenced by naturalism emphasize the power of environment to the point of personifying its crushing effect on the individual. Some of these writers (e.g., Wright, Ellison) rejected naturalism for its bleakness and its minimizing of individual responsibility and freedom, both on the part of those who perpetuate unjust social conditions and those who struggle against them. But throughout the varied characterizations of the city one usually finds both a concentrated willingness to describe and confront a frequently hostile environment, as well as a reluctance to offer an idealized escape. Baldwin sees the racial problem as a result of the typical failure of Americans to know themselves and to face reality. Speaking of the white world beyond Harlem he says,

I didn't meet anyone in that world who didn't suffer from the very same affliction that all the people I had fled from suffered from and that was that they didn't know who they were. . . . This failure to look reality in the face diminishes a nation as it diminishes a person, and it can only be described as unmanly. (122, 125)

While blacks share in these problems of seeking identity and facing reality, black writers often insist on the disturbing but salutary self-examination of the individual and of society. Before proceeding to a discussion of the novels of Gloria Naylor, we will briefly consider a few key works in order to set Naylor's in a more specific context.

2

Ann Petry's *The Street* presents one of the bleakest images of the city in black American fiction. Working the naturalistic vein in a manner similar to the early Richard Wright, Petry depicts the city as a "jungle" (8) whose wind does "everything it could to discourage the people walking along the street" (2), and whose images of enclosure and entrapment deny human dignity. In spite of Lutie Johnson's responsibility, courage, and tenacity in fighting the degradation of her environment, the hostility of the street drives her to self-destructive violence as an expression of her anger and her humanity. Petry shows grimly how even the best individuals are destroyed: "Streets like the one she lived on were no accident. They were the North's lynch mobs" (307). The endless cycle of human destruction claims the young while their parents expend their energies providing for them and attempting to escape. Petry's city virtually guarantees the defeat of a person in the deforming environment.

In "The Ethics of Living Jim Crow," Richard Wright relates his experiences in southern cities of being insulted and assaulted while observing ritual denial of other blacks' dignity. Much of his subsequent work shows how the northern city tantalizes blacks and cruelly frustrates their visions of possibility. He observes in "How 'Bigger' Was Born" that blacks react more violently in the northern city than in the South because the former seems to offer so much more but actually denies blacks' hope for a better life, causing disillusionment and bitterness:

It was not that Chicago segregated Negroes more than the South, but that Chicago had more to offer, that Chicago's physical aspect—noisy, crowded, filled with the sense of power and fulfillment—did so much more to dazzle the mind with a taunting sense of possible achievement that the segregation it did impose brought forth from Bigger a reaction more obstreperous than in the South. (xv)

The city in *Native Son* is a deadly environment where violence becomes practically the only response available in a climate dominated by deprivation and fear. Bigger's naturalistic city cramps his growth and threatens his identity and manhood, and he responds violently in order to assert his self-worth. In condemning Bigger to death, society denies its responsibility for creating the environment which virtually forces such self-destructive acts and for condemning blacks to separate but quite unequal opportunities.

In "The Man Who Lived Underground" and *American Hunger,* Wright develops the underground as a symbol of black's relegation to sub-human status in the American city. Fred Daniels's psychic journey underground awakens him to personal and universal responsibility for all suffering, and he chooses to share his insight with the dangerous city above. But society rejects his knowledge and ignores his newly established innocence as he is brutally murdered. In *The Outsider* the sense of the city as an oppressive environment dissipates as Wright stresses existential themes. Cross Damon has much more education and greater opportunities than Bigger. He asserts his absolute freedom to recreate himself and to live beyond good and evil, in revolt not against society or injustice but against the "emptiness" of existence.

Against the backdrop of the Harlem Renaissance, which celebrated at least part of one city as an arena of exuberance and possibility, Jean Toomer in *Cane* draws a stark contrast between the rural South as a flawed but mysterious, nurturing setting and the northern city as an alien, corrupting world. Toomer uses Washington, D.C., to represent the corrosive effect of the city on blacks:

A crude-boned, soft-skinned wedge of nigger life breathing its loafer air, jazz songs and love, thrusting unconscious rhythms, black reddish blood into the white and whitewashed wood of Washington. Stale soggy wood of Washington. Wedges rust in soggy wood. (39)

In the second section of *Cane,* set in Washington, blacks striving for middle-class achievement experience diminished vitality as well as confusion over identity. Materialism and the wish for status engender a split in the individual between body and mind, desire and will, so that he chooses against that which he really wants. While Toomer offers the "swan-song" (Turner, xxii) of an era in the South with passion and wonder, he does not idealize the South, showing plainly its violence and racial hatred. Yet he reveals southern blacks as whole individuals, unlike northern ones who suffer from the debilitating effects of institutionalized education and religion. Ralph Kabnis, one such northern black, has been rendered disillusioned and impotent by his education; but because of his southern experiences there are signs of hope for his translation into the semi-mystical leader-savior figure for which all of *Cane* prepares. Although Toomer does not share Claude McKay's acrimony for "the harsh, the ugly city" (60) which arouses McKay's "life-long hate" (61), he does regard the city as foreign, unnatural soil for the displaced seeds of the rural South.

One finds further treatment of the city as harsh soil for the southern emigrants in Toni Morrison's *The Bluest Eye* and Claude Brown's *Manchild in the Promised Land*. Neither book has the naturalistic grimness of *Native Son* or *The Street*, but both emphasize the destructive power of an environment where black Americans' lives are discounted. Throughout *The Bluest Eye* Morrison reflects on the soil as a metaphor for the city and for American society:

> I even think that the land of the entire country was hostile to marigolds that year. This soil is bad for certain kinds of flowers. Certain seeds it will not nurture, certain fruits it will not bear, and when the land kills of its own volition, we acquiesce and say the victim had no right to live. (160)

An extremely competitive and racist society demands scapegoats and people to despise because they differ from an artificial standard of beauty. Pecola Breedlove and her family symbolize the psychic violence done when blacks accept white standards of appearance and internalize white people's hatred as self-hate. Southern women such as Pauline Breedlove, transplanted to towns like Lorain, Ohio, find no family or community support, because many northern blacks enforce white standards of beauty and exercise their need for someone to look down upon. Morrison juxtaposes the progression of the seasons with the unnatural self-loathing of the Breedloves and its consequences, Cholly's rape of his daughter and Pecola's escape into madness. There is hope in narrator Claudia's sensitivity and concern for Pecola and in her belief in the efficacy of action for others. But for Morrison the smaller urban landscape rigidly conveys society's rejection of black people's identity and beauty, and it disguises their effacement as self-destruction.

In *Manchild in the Promised Land*, the city disillusions its black pilgrims of the forties and traps many of them in a cycle of violence, drugs, and death. The southern pioneers have become "a misplaced generation," "a misplaced people" (vii) who consciously had sought the promised land on their journey to the city, only to find "too many people full of hate and bitterness crowded into a dirty, stinky, uncared-for closet-size section of a great city" (viii). Brown succinctly states both the despair and the resolution of many black Americans for whom the city is lacking in opportunity and humanity but who simply have nowhere to go: "Where does one run when he's already in the promised land?" (viii) He details the plague of heroin which ravaged Harlem in the fifties, killing or enslaving most of his generation. Yet the darkness of his account is leavened by his own good fortune in escaping Harlem and pursuing work and education in the outside world. As signs of hope he relates his feeling of freedom and a new spirit of compassion and strength in the Harlem community which helped to battle the reign of drugs. Brown's return to Harlem shows his desire to contribute to a stronger community and his faith that the city can become good soil.

3

The novels of Gloria Naylor, which take place long after the initial stages of black people's disillusionment with the city, do not evoke the idea of the promised land. Naylor continues in the tradition of much black fiction, rejecting the innocence of society and the individual and exploring the failure of the Edenic quest, whether within the city or in a non-urban place, while affirming values of self-knowledge and community as means of survival and of helping others. *The Women of Brewster Place* presents the ghetto section of the city as a wall which restricts people's lives without destroying entirely their freedom. In a far less pessimistic manner than Petry or Wright, Naylor offers realistic evidence of the city's harshness, yet she avoids hope-lessness in the depiction of women whose bonds with each other inspire them to challenge their environment. The people in *Linden Hills* have the illusion of an Eden in that they think they have "made it" by advancing to the most prestigious black neighborhood in the country and by acquiring the material advantages of the American dream. Yet their man-made paradise is really a hell of self-destruction caused by betraying the "internal mirror" of self. *Mama Day* contrasts New York City to the island of Willow Springs, which in many ways seems to be an idealized world set apart from civilization's greed and violence. But here also Naylor shows the limitations of escape from the city, as well as the potential for evil anywhere.

The wall that makes Brewster Place a dead end functions as the novel's central symbol of containment and frustrated possibility. The black residents have clung to the street with a desperate acceptance that whatever was here was better than the starving southern climates they had fled from. Brewster Place knew that unlike its other children, the few who would leave forever were to be the exception rather than the rule, since they came because they had no choice and would remain for the same reason. (4)

Naylor observes this "desperate acceptance" as a realistic response, parallel to Brown's question of where one can run in the promised land. Yet over the course of the novel the residents' heightened consciousness of and anger about the wall contribute to their gradually increasing belief in the efficacy of their united action. The wall proclaims that their lives and possibilities must end here; it is partly responsible for stunted personal growth, disappointed dreams, rape, death, and madness. But it also becomes a scene of mourning, expiation, and unity, and it inspires the symbolic regeneration of the community. Mattie Michaels's dream of the destruction of the wall prophesies the residents' temporary victory over the environment, with the "death" of Brewster Place. They move on to new, though mostly not better streets; but the women especially, like the "ebony phoenix" (5), have grown and risen to some new life.

The very existence, not to mention the perpetuation of streets such as Brewster, testifies to the responsibility of white society. Naylor's analysis, however, goes deeper than mere sociology or accusations of blame, focusing on the individuals in this community and their responsibility to face themselves in order to gain more control over their difficult circumstances, or at least over their responses to those circumstances. Ben, Etta Mae, and Mattie left the South largely because of their inability to face a personal failure. Ben seeks solace in alcohol for the memory of his prostituted daughter, Etta for her vanished youth in frequent shifts of scene, and Mattie for her mistakes bringing up Basil in her concern for her sisters in the neighborhood. Mattie was forced to leave the confines of her moralistic rural upbringing because her judgmental father could not forgive her human error of pregnancy out of wedlock; luckily, she happened upon the motherly Eva Turner before she was almost driven from Asheville by similar attitudes. As Basil grew up, she denied that his irresponsibility was founded on her wanting a dependent child. Even when he skipped town on her bail, Mattie deluded herself that he would return. Her new life in the northern city, and that of the residents of Brewster generally, is symbolized by her plants, brought up from the South and fighting "for life on a crowded windowsill" (7). Correcting her approach with Basil, Mattie offers her sisters and daughters her generous compassion and support, but lets them be responsible for their decisions.

The other women in the novel also illustrate the idea that an individual's self-knowledge and self-acceptance can modify even such a degrading environment, that cumulatively a community of such individuals evolving in this manner can hope for and create a better life. Etta Mae Johnson's rebellious nature broke free of her rural southern origins and found northern cities better able to accommodate her independence. But her life of constant mobility has reinforced her flight from serious self-examination and her illusion that a man would settle down with an indolent and too-easy woman. Staring at the wall on the night she starts to realize her folly, Etta is saved from despair by Mattie's loving support. Once Etta accepts her situation and stops seeing freedom in mobility, she emerges as a contented, active member of the community who helps to minimize judgmental attitudes.

Brewster Place does not trap Kiswana Browne, who can see over the wall from her apartment and into Linden Hills, where her parents beckon her to give up her plan of living with poor folk in order to make positive changes. Kiswana has an oversimplified understanding of these people and a somewhat condescending attitude about their struggles. Yet because of her mother's visit she recognizes that blacks who are proud and committed to improving conditions need not be dramatic in their efforts nor necessarily poor. Kiswana's deepened knowledge and acceptance of her mother and of her own need for education make her much more effective over the rest of the novel. She is able to inspire Cora Lee to take an interest in her children, and she organizes the tenants' organization for some concrete changes. Cora Lee denies she is an uncaring, negligent mother interested only in escapist television and the comfortable dependence of her latest baby. She emerges from her reverie after Kiswana reminds her that babies become people and challenges her to take pride in all her children. As Cora begins to adjust her identity to that of a more concerned mother, she immediately begins to improve Brewster Place. Lorraine's failure to accept her lesbianism has made her weak and unhappy, and she has fled shame and embarrassment until she, too, faces the wall. Ben's fatherly support helps Lorraine to accept herself in spite of many people's rejection and her own partner's wish to maintain her weakness. Ben and Lorraine become victims of the ugliest impulses on this street, but his death and her madness are sacrificial because they hold up a mirror to the community and force a general, tacit admission of complicity in their fates.

The block party of Mattie's dream, threatened by the apocalyptic week of rain after Lorraine's rape and Ben's death and by the widespread guilt surfacing in various women's dreams, is a sign of the "phoenix" of this neighborhood rising from destruction and achieving solidarity in realistic hope for a better place to live. Naylor under' stands that the punks who rape Lorraine are themselves victims of a rigidly confining environment, "a world that was only six feet wide" (170), but she insists on individuals' power and responsibility to op' pose their own degradation. Naylor does not shrink from depicting frightening acts which might induce despair about black people's ex' perience in the city. But the whole novel prepares for a feeling of confidence with the positive, gradual changes in the responses of these women to themselves and to their world. Each grows stronger through the acceptance of her own limitations and mistakes and consequently each woman has more to offer others. If the wall becomes a kind of mirror in which they look in order to survive, their destruction of the wall is a symbolic eradication of their old, lesser selves. As they spontaneously remove the horrid structure brick by brick, they defy and transcend the severe limitations the city imposes on them. Their victory is qualified, for although they survive the destruction of the wall and the condemnation of Brewster Place, they go on, "some to the arms of a world that they would have to pry open to take them, most to inherit another aging street and the privilege of clinging to its decay" (191). But they take with them their inner strength, their confidence, and their dreams, which "ebb and flow, ebb and flow, but never disappear" (192)

In *Linden Hills* Naylor develops the idea of the person's need for self-knowledge and fidelity to self, showing how the lack of these can lead to ruin even if one has a very high level of personal comfort and material security. Linden Hills is still in the city, physically not far from ghetto areas such as Brewster Place and Putney Wayne, but quite removed from poverty, violence, and fear. Those who live in Linden Hills, as well as many who aspire to do so, conceive of it as an Eden, a jewel of black pride and also the surest symbol of one's success. Yet whereas the women on Brewster Place begin to forge a better community through individual strength, the people in Linden Hills fail to develop a strong sense of self because, acceding to the demands of materialist American culture, they dismiss knowledge of self in the interest of acquisition and advancement. They have achieved their tenuous success, in fact, largely through buying into the American fever for competition to the point of ignoring others and denigrating the very idea of community. Consequently, there liter' ally is no community for them to turn to which might help them to better understand themselves. The only physical walls here serve to keep the lowly out, yet metaphorical walls of isolation and despair entrap these people at least as much as Brewster's edifice contains its residents. As Willie Mason and Lester Tilson make their journey into the appalling vacuum of Linden Hills, they reflect on "that silver mirror propped up in your soul" (epigraph) as the individual's guide to identity and sanity. They come to confront themselves in a deeper sense as they witness the waste of potential among some very gifted people.

With the upper-class, Linden Hills Naylor portrays the antithesis of the stereotypical black city neighborhood. Yet she suggests that the absence of struggle for physical survival paradoxically fosters a Darwinian ruthlessness and betrayal of blacks in other areas of the city. With few exceptions such as the Reverend Hollis, who enter-tains poor children at Christmas, most of Linden Hills does not want to know that Putney Wayne or Brewster Place exist. The people of Linden Hills virulently oppose the city's proposed low-income housing project on the edge of Putney Wayne. They claim that renovations on the extremely dilapidated housing would be adequate, blaming poor blacks for their own health problems and complaining of the welfare drain. Their excuses for their position, echoing those of racist whites, include fears of crime and lowered standards in schools. These well-off blacks form a diabolical alliance with a white racist organiza-tion in order to block the housing, revealing the depths of their moral degradation. Defending their action with the ironic and hypocritical phrase "we're part of a whole city" (135), they choose to deny their kinship and responsibility to their immediate neighbors, who are also black. Willie sees the cannibalistic nature of this behavior: "These days of disinheritance, we feast on human heads. . . . The plates never seemed empty of the brown and bloody meat" (133). Luther Nedeed, himself part witness and part architect of the general decay in Linden Hills, pierces the self-deception and identifies its destructive power: "Never lie to yourself because that's the quickest road to destruction. . . . The Alliance is free to engage in myths about inferior schools and deteriorating neighborhoods while all they're really fearing is the word *nigger*" (137). Although Willie senses Nedeed's evil, he applauds his honesty here. He notes that the residents of Linden Hills can be more vicious and cruel than the worst in Putney Wayne; but, with the exception of Luther, they lack the honesty "to pick up a knife and really cut a man's throat" (193).

Luther Nedeed's original concept of Linden Hills as a symbol of black pride and power to oppose "the white god" (11) has degenerated into a corrupting materialism with the result that "Linden Hills wasn't black; it was successful" (17). Accepting what Baldwin refers to as the typical American substitution of status for identity (111), the residents take pride in their self-created Eden; although they go to church they believe that they save themselves. Mrs.Tilson, Les's mother, on the lowest rung of the ladder of status within the develop-ment, feels sharply her social inferiority. According to Les, she drove her ill husband to a fatal heart attack with her insistence on his working two jobs so they could have the expected comforts. Winston Alcott betrays his gay lover and himself with his socially prudent marriage, which guarantees him a prestigious Tupelo Drive mortgage but which also threatens him with decay from within. The pressures of being a black executive or "Super Nigger" (99) in a major corpora-tion are illustrated in Xavier Donnell and Maxwell Smyth, who de-form their personalities with their required denials of their blackness and personal desires. The moral decline of Reverend Hollis intensified with his arrival years ago in Linden Hills, where he has exploited the community's selfishness for his own gain by offering them comfortable assurances of their righteousness instead of reminders of their mortal-ity and their need for spiritual values.

The case of Laurel Dumont epitomizes the self-destruction caused by the estrangement from self so prevalent in this exclusive part of the city. Like many people here, she has been a victim of uninterrupted success, never having experienced a failure which might have forced her to look within and realize an identity: "She might have had time to think about who she was and what she really wanted, but it never happened. And when she finally took a good look around, she found herself imprisoned within a chain of photographs and a life that had no point" (228). On Tupelo Drive, perceived by many as the social summit but physically and morally the lowest point in Linden Hills, it seems virtually impossible for Laurel or anyone to find or create a true home with sustaining values. Thus, after ten years at this address, Laurel finds nothing but a void inside herself, and she commits suicide out of her despair, the destruction of her face underscoring her tragic lack of identity. Dr. Braithwaite, who plays the role of the objective academic in his studies of the area, merely watches as many of these people destroy themselves, and he feels neither responsibility nor any ability to stop them. Luther not only watches but as holder of mort-gages actually incites individuals' movement down toward his mortu-ary at the bottom of the hill. Although disillusioned by the failure of Linden Hills to become "a beautiful, black wad of spit right in the white eye of America" (9), he holds on to his power over so many lives and cruelly allows people such as Laurel to die as he looks on.

The central characters Willa Nedeed, Les, and Willie undergo par-allel symbolic journeys at the same time they discover the emptiness at the heart of this community. While Willa is locked in the basement of her home she suffers the death of her child, but through "meetings" with her predecessors in the Nedeed family she comes to understand and accept the roles she has chosen for herself. The loneliness, pain, and emotional sterility that Willa finds in the writings and photos of the other Mrs. Nedeeds force her to admit these realities in her own life, but also to see that the fault lies not with herself but with her brutally insensitive husband. She rises above the insanity and self-destruction of these women with her determination to live. Set against the novel's motif of facelessness, she recognizes her face in the water and finds "a healing calm" (268) as she moves toward the world above.

Willie and Les, although from the vastly different areas of Putney Wayne and Linden Hills, attended the same schools and have rejected education as society's instrument of conformity and mediocrity. The city has disillusioned them but also inspired them with the possibility of becoming poets with a sense of fidelity to disadvantaged blacks. They see Linden Hills not as an Eden but as a fallen place whose inhabitants have sold the mirror in the soul and lost themselves. But over the course of their journey both young men come to view these people primarily not as betrayers of their people but as victims of self-betrayal, objects not for judgment but compassion. Their deepening sense of the priority of self-knowledge as seen in others' lives leads them to examine their own need for change. Les's guilt over his relatively easy life in Linden Hills manifests itself in his condemnation of his neighbors as selfish, empty people. But he grows to recognize his indolence and need for greater challenges as he witnesses others' decline. Willie also looks into the "mirror" of self, deepening his considerable compassion for blacks in this alien neighborhood and acquiring a more social ethos by deciding to write down his poetry and make his contribution to the larger community. His strong intuitive bond with the captive Willa, whom he has never met and whose name he does not even know, symbolizes his increasing psychic connection with and responsibility to black people.

With *Mama Day* Naylor shifts her focus for the most part from the city to a non-urban setting that would seem an ideal escape from the dangers and corruption of the urban experience. She explores certain Edenic aspects of the island of Willow Springs, including the inhabitants' safety and ability to survive without much struggle, their sense of community, their closeness to nature and fidelity to tradition, and their stubborn wish to remain untainted by the degrading influences of civilization. Yet the novel suggests the limitations of this escape from urban reality, showing this environment's natural dangers and its own share of universal human evil. The counterpoint between the island and the city results ironically in a softening of the city's image and a qualified defense of its viability.

The older people of Willow Springs exhibit little of the potentially ruinous striving for physical and social mobility common on Brewster Place and in Linden Hills. They protect their cynicism about "any-thing coming from beyond the bridge" (7), and they usually regard with disdain those young folk who choose to live there, like Reema's boy, who has had all of his good sense "educated" out of him. Proud of their independence of the mainland and of their sense of community, they wisely refuse to sell any part of their shoreline to greedy devel-opers. A mythical, otherworldly sense of place pervades Willow Springs, which is neither part of South Carolina nor of Georgia. The people here prefer to maintain a wooden bridge in spite of its vulnera-bility to destruction in storms, to underscore their tenuous tie to the outer world. Mama Day watches the "Phil Donahue Show" and observes with wonder the variety of moral corruption in the cities up North.Those residents of the island who work beyond the bridge, however, are touched by that corruption, becoming more selfish and more materialistic and diminishing the spirit of community. The image of Willow Springs as a possible paradise dissipates with evidence of human evil and its awful consequences. Ruby's irrational anger against Cocoa and her attempt to kill her disturb the relative moral equanim-ity of this environment. Cocoa's near death and the sacrificial death of George, together with the terrible destructive force of the hurricane, darken the pastoral scene and discourage any romanticizing of this non-urban setting.

Cocoa carried her neighbors' anti-city feelings North to New York, where for seven years she has found it a center of feverish, often pointless activity and impersonality, and also a place where "racism moved underground like most of the people did" (18). She especially objects to the lack of decent men available in the city. Cocoa fears the multiplicity and variety of people in New York, and she has limited her exposure to the city, confining herself to "the ghettos for our permanent tourists" (65). George, on the other hand, grew up in one of the city's homes for orphans, which provided a cold but decent environment and a spur to an active, productive life. He enjoys the neighborhoods and ethnic communities that make up New York, and he recognizes that Cocoa needs to see the true city and to stop repress-ing her natural country ways. Under the influence of his openness and friendship, she admits "how small and cramped my life had been" (98) and begins to appreciate the city's beauty. Although he's a city boy, George shows an unusual appreciation for the delights of Willow Springs, referring to the town as a "paradise" and "another world"

(175). After his death, Cocoa understandably finds the city unattrac-
tive and leaves it, but she does settle in Atlanta, a compromise between the northern city and the southern retreat which indicates her
openness to the possibilities of the urban environment. Mama Day
knows of the vice and danger of New York, but on her visit after
George's death she reciprocates his affection for Willow Springs as
she finds the city "full of right nice folks" (305).

The main characters of *Mama Day* become involved in each other's
lives and influence each other's views on the city and the country
out of their need for a deeper connection with themselves and their
pasts. George helps Cocoa to resolve her conflict of antagonism toward
the city she lives in, and Mama Day increases Cocoa's respect for her
background by using mysterious powers to counter Ruby's actions
and save Cocoa's life. George is drawn to the Days' "paradise" because
of his lack of family history and his desire to be a part of a family
with a long line of strong individuals. Mama Day welcomes George,
the representative of the city, as the key in her search for the name
and identity of her great-grandmother Sapphira Wade and for an understanding of her own power as the offspring of the seventh son of
a seventh son. Through George's acceptance of Mama Day's seemingly
insane instructions to save Cocoa's life, he offers up his own. He also
allows Mama Day to make a psychic connection with Sapphira and
to understand that Candle Walk night commemorates "a light that
burned in a man's heart" (308) as well as the beauty of a woman who
was never really a slave.

4

Naylor's work reflects the reluctance in African-American literature to join in the romantic quest for an Eden which is so common
in American literature. In one sense her novels rival the grimness of
naturalism in their depictions of degrading conditions and human evil,
yet in another sense they offer much hope for the individual and the
community with their emphasis on self-knowledge and interdependence. The wall of Brewster Place must not be accepted but confronted and dismantled and the mirror of self faced, for there is no
escape from the city to an ideal environment that will perfect man or
offer complete happiness. To Brown's question of where one can run
to in the promised land, Naylor demonstrates that a fallen or false
Eden such as Linden Hills or Willow Springs is not the answer.

Baldwin suggests that many white Americans live with an assump-
tion of their innocence, an illusion many blacks cannot afford:

The things that most white people imagine that they can salvage from the storm of life is really, in sum, their innocence. . . . I am afraid that most of the white people I have ever known impressed me as being in the grip of a weird nostalgia, dreaming of a vanished state of security and order, against which dream, unfailingly and unconsciously, they tested and very often lost their lives. (172)

Naylor rejects any Eden based on dangerous assumptions of innocence, and she asserts the individual's power and responsibility to look within and thereby to transform the world without.

WORKS CITED

Baldwin, James. *Nobody Knows My Name*. New York: Dell, 1961.

Brown, Claude. *Manchild in the Promised Land*. New York: New American Library, 1965.

McKay, Claude. "The Tired Worker," "The White City." In *The Black Poets*, edited by Dudley Randall, 60, 61. New York: Bantam, 1971.

Morrison, Toni. *The Bluest Eye*. New York: Washington Square Press, 1970.

Naylor, Gloria. *Linden Hills*. New York: Penguin, 1985.

———. *Mama Day*. New York: Vintage Books, 1988.

———. *The Women of Brewster Place*. New York: Penguin, 1982.

Petry, Ann. *The Street*. Boston: Beacon Press, 1946.

Toomer, Jean. *Cane*. New York: Liveright, 1923.

Turner, Darwin T. Introduction to *Cane*, by Jean Toomer. New York: Liveright, 1923.

Williams, William Carlos. *In the American Grain*. New York: New Directions, 1956.

Wright, Richard. "How 'Bigger' Was Born." In *Native Son*, vii–xxxiv. New York: Harper & Row, 1940.

13

The Sensory Assault of the City in Ann Petry's *The Street*

LARRY R. ANDREWS

ANN Petry's first novel, *The Street* (1946), reflects black disillusion-ment with the northern city after the 1920s. Lutie Johnson, its pro-tagonist, sees her street, and by extension the city, as her monstrous antagonist. Like Petry's novella "In Darkness and Confusion" (1947), the work is set in Harlem, here largely on 116th Street. Her third novel, *The Narrows* (1953), with its appropriately claustrophobic ti-tle, is also set in a ghetto, but in a New England town. *The Street* has remained one of the most vivid and compelling evocations of city life in African-American literature, and it anticipates the superb urban landscapes of Paule Marshall and Gloria Naylor.

As a novel of the city, *The Street* touches on all of the major themes in modern urban literature. In a few passages, Petry suggests that the city can be aglow with life and that it can offer occasional experiences of community:

> The glow from the sunset was making the street radiant. The street is nice in this light, she [Lutie] thought. It was swarming with children who were playing ball and darting back and forth across the sidewalk in complicated games of tag. (64)

But the picture is largely negative. Barbara Christian speaks of the work's "relentless presentation of the dreary despair of the inner cit-ies" (*Black Feminist Criticism* 11). Overcrowding deprives the inhabit-ants of needed personal space—on the subway, in the street, in the apartment houses, "so that the black folks were crammed on top of each other—jammed and packed and forced into the smallest possible space until they were completely cut off from light and air" (206). The dominant images of the novel are claustral and suffocating—walls, cages, cellars, even other people's stares. Alienation and isola-

196

tion are a corollary of this spatial deprivation. Self-interest in the name of survival squeezes out compassion, and Lutie, on her own, working and raising a small boy, has no one to turn to whom she can trust. The street dehumanizes its inhabitants, destroying their spirit, as in the case of the aimlessly staring man in the hospital (201–2) or the resigned young girls. An endless cycle of poverty is especially destructive. "The most memorable quality of *The Street*," as Theodore Gross notes, "is its direct, unsentimental, ruthless, bitter description of poverty: the black characters are caught in a suffering that fills them with meanness and hatred, that diminishes their humanity" (45). Prostitution, crime, and sudden death complete this typically modern picture of the artificial urban environment bereft of nature's softer influences. In her growing awareness near the end, Lutie sums it up with understatement: "Perhaps living in a city the size of New York wasn't good for people. . . . Certainly it wasn't a good place for children" (Petry 396).

Many commentators on the novel have assigned this portrayal of the city to the naturalism of the Richard Wright "school." Petry herself laid the groundwork for this emphasis in an interview with James Ivy in *The Crisis* in February 1946:

> "In *The Street* my aim is to show how simply and easily the environment can change the course of a person's life. . . .
>
> "I try to show why the Negro has a high crime rate, a high death rate, and little or no chance of keeping his family unit intact in large northern cities." (49)

Class oppression is part of this picture, as the vastly unequal distribution of wealth creates extremes of rich and poor neighborhoods, the latter effectively trapping the inhabitants for life. Vernon Lattin and Marjorie Pryse have shown how the novel ironically explodes the American economic dream of the founding fathers. Robert Bone classifies the work as an "environmentalist" novel of the Wright school in its treatment of slum neighborhoods (157). Noel Schraufnagel says that it "indicates how a ghetto shapes the lives of its inhabitants into a rigid framework of poverty and hopelessness. . . . The environment is the controlling factor of the novel" (40–42). Addison Gayle especially emphasizes the forces of the environment: "Miss Petry is more interested in the effects of the environment upon her characters than she is in the characters themselves. The characters are products of the street; their lives are dominated by forces beyond their control" (192). More recently Barbara Christian has concurred that "Petry's major concern in the novel was most emphatically the hostile environment of Harlem and its effects on the people who must endure it" (*Black Women Novelists* 63). Bernard Bell calls the work "a conventional novel of economic determinism in which the environment is the dominant force against which the characters must struggle to survive" (107). Arthur Davis, on the other hand, denies the total domination of the environment (193–94). Lattin also has urged that the novel "cannot be discussed merely in environmentalist terms" (69), and he stresses Lutie's revolt and discovery. Mary Helen Washington agrees that the novel is naturalistic but complains that it tends to marginalize women and thus ignore "many of the deeply felt realities of women's lives" (298), whereas Gloria Wade-Gayles argues that the work treats gender issues as part of its naturalism (152). But again in her excellent recent essay Pryse points out positive alternatives to the supposedly determined choices Lutie makes, alternatives suggested by her grandmother's values, the conjuring tradition of Prophet David, and the successful revolt of her foil Min.

Beyond this larger naturalist tradition that portrays the city in general as a hostile environment impossible to overcome, critics have amply demonstrated that racism is the determining factor more than the city per se. The system of socioeconomic oppression that the white power structure has created is responsible for the heightened suffering of the Harlem ghetto. Lutie comes to realize that "streets like the one she lived on were no accident. They were the North's lynch mobs, she thought bitterly; the method the big cities used to keep Negroes in their place" (323). The lesson of her experience is that white people have caged blacks in the ghetto, tossed them their refuse, and systematically destroyed the black family: "Streets like 116th Street or being colored, or a combination of both with all it implied, had turned Pop into a sly old man who drank too much; had killed Mom off when she was in her prime" (56). White people refuse to hire black men and overwork black women, leaving the street to educate the children. White butchers, lawyers, detectives, landlords, bar owners, schoolteachers, and affluent women with hostile stares are merely the front for white capitalists like the Chandlers who live at a distance and pull the strings: "It wasn't just this city. It was any city where they set up a line and say black folks stay on this side and white folks on this side. . . . It all added up to the same thing, she decided—white people. She hated them. She would always hate them" (206). As Gross points out, Petry "does not permit the reader to forget that the white world has drawn the limitations and consequently caused the bitter despair of black people" (44). And Christian finds that "Petry clearly indicts the white society for the failure of many black marriages and implies that it consciously is seeking the fragmentation of the black family" (*Black Women Novelists* 66).

In addition to racism, sexism is a dominant force against which Lutie Johnson must struggle, for all of the white characters and many of the black characters, including Mrs. Hedges, see her primarily as a sexual object. Wade-Gayles and Beatrice Royster have been instrumental in analyzing the impact of sexual oppression on Lutie and other black women portrayed in the novel. Wade-Gayles finds that male critics who draw parallels between Lutie and Wright's Bigger Thomas "ignore the added burdens that being a woman places on her" (149). She says that Petry "reaches into the souls of black women for their peculiar agony. *The Street* is an explosion of sounds of racial and sexual agony" (154). Royster says that all of the violence of the street "grows out of, or is precipitated by, sexual encounters between men and women" (qtd. Petry 154).

Thus the interpretation of the role of the city in the novel has been well developed in terms of naturalism, class oppression, racism, and sexism. The ideology of this protest novel is manifest in the text itself, which contains thematic generalizations and numerous symbolic and metaphorical references to the street that represent this whole array of forces. But the work is far more than a *roman à thèse* of the Wright school. It strikes the reader above all as an act of imagination and literary art. What I would like to focus on in this respect is the powerful physical way in which the city assaults the characters' senses through concrete detail. Some critics have noted this aspect of style in passing. Lattin gives some examples of the images of traps, cages, and walls (70), and Gross notes Petry's compelling portrayal of details of setting (42). Christian stresses her "voluminous use of external detail" in contrast to Wright's approach in *Native Son,* but focuses on the "tone of the commonplace" in these details (64).

What strikes me, however, is the extraordinary, nightmarish character of most of the sensory detail. Characters in the novel typically feel pressed upon or actually invaded physically, often to the point where their perceptions are distorted and they feel terror or hysteria. In this often surreal vision of the modern city the novel is thus akin not only to the naturalism of Zola, Crane, Dreiser, and Wright but also to the urban evocations of Poe and Dickens, and to the great modern portrayals of the city—St. Petersburg of Gogol, Dostoevsky, and Bely, the Paris of Baudelaire and Rilke's *Die Aufzeichnungen des Malte Laurids Brigge,* the Berlin of Döblin's *Berlin Alexanderplatz,* the Prague of Kafka's *Der Prozess,* and the Harlem of Ellison's *Invisible Man.* In these works, as in *The Street,* the psychological stress the characters undergo as a result of urban socioeconomic structures combines with the sensory assault of the urban physical environment to produce a dislocation rendered in an intense and nightmarish style.

In *The Street* this sensory assault occurs on several levels. To a small extent it is a general urban condition that creates crowded subways and streets and bombardments of noise and smells that affect more or less all inhabitants, black and white people alike. But clearly the city can be benign to the white and well off. The sensory assault is heightened, then, for inhabitants of the black ghetto, where poverty and racism are suffocating and "people were packed together like sardines in a can" (206). Yet even here people can occasionally expand compared to their sense of encroachment and violation in the downtown white world. Lutie reflects that

> once they are freed from the contempt in the eyes of the downtown world, they instantly become individuals. Up here they are no longer creatures labeled simply 'colored' and therefore all alike. She noticed that once the crowd walked the length of the platform and started up the stairs toward the street it expanded in size. The same people who had made themselves small on the train, even on the platform, suddenly grew so large they could hardly get up the stairs to the street together. She . . . stood watching them as they scattered in all directions, laughing and talking to each other. (57–58)

In most physical ways Harlem is claustrophobic and evokes a protective, survivalist response, or it is openly violent and breeds violence within characters. Most central to the novel, however, is the sensory assault related to sexual exploitation. As an attractive black woman on her own, Lutie is subjected to the lustful looks of white men, the hostile stares of white women, the sexual propositions of Junto and Mrs. Hedges, and the attempted rapes by Boots and the Super Jones. What is particularly effective stylistically is Petry's use of all the other detailed assaults of the setting on Lutie's senses as an indirect way of expanding and intensifying this vulnerability of black women. The walls that press in on her and the silence that threatens to get inside her constitute a kind of rape against which she must constantly protect herself. Such details, often repeated, thus express Lutie's gender situation as distinct from, though related to, her racial and urban situation.

Stylistically the city is palpable in a negative way to every character through powerfully described detail touching every sense, including the sense of movement and perception of space. Characters experience even inert objects as threatening and other people as invasive. Even natural elements such as the wind are often perverted by the city so that they participate in its punishing effects. Characters under stress from other causes are especially susceptible, and if they have lively imaginations and intuitive powers, their sense perceptions may become distorted and exaggerated to the point of disorientation. To some extent the ability of characters like Lutie to experience heightened sensation is a result of instincts that can be a powerful source of protection. Her grandmother had tried to tell her that evil was palpable: "'Some folks so full of it you can feel it comin' at you—oozin' right out of their skins'" (20). What counts is what other resources one has with which to act on these perceptions—folk wisdom, flight, conjuring, communal support. Tragically, Lutie relies instead on rationalism, individualism, and the American myth of success until at the end violence explodes from her uncontrollably. Thus the sensitivity to the city's sensory bombardment is not in itself a weakness but may be a strength if it is supported by other qualities. The numbing of Harlem's inhabitants ("sleepwalkers") into insensibility is a death-in-life, a fate worse than the fears with which Lutie has to live.

The physical assault on Lutie is established vividly in Petry's brilliant opening chapter, when she first arrives on the street and takes an apartment. The initial description of the wind on the street is filled with vigorous verbs:

> It rattled the tops of garbage cans, sucked window shades out through the top of opened windows and set them flapping back against the windows; and it drove most of the people off the street . . . except for a few hurried pedestrians who bent double in an effort to offer the least possible exposed surface to its violent assault. (1)

The refuse the wind picks up from the street becomes a "barrage" that "swirled into the faces of the people" (2). The natural element is corrupted by the wind-tunnel effect of the narrow street and the dirt mingled with the wind as it hits the pedestrians:

> It found all the dirt and dust and grime on the sidewalk and lifted it up so that the dirt got into their noses, making it difficult to breathe; the dust got into their eyes and blinded them; and the grit stung their skins. It wrapped newspaper around their feet entangling them until the people cursed deep in their throats, stamped their feet, kicked at the paper. . . . And then the wind grabbed their hats, pried their scarves from around their necks, stuck its fingers inside their coat collars, blew their coats away from their bodies.
> The wind lifted Lutie Johnson's hair away from the back of her neck so that she felt suddenly naked and bald, for her hair had been resting softly and warmly against her skin. She shivered as the cold fingers of the wind touched the back of her neck, explored the sides of her head. It even

blew her eyelashes away from her eyes so that her eyeballs were bathed in a rush of coldness and she had to blink in order to read the words on the sign swaying back and forth over her head.

Each time she thought she had the sign in focus, the wind pushed it away from her so that she wasn't certain whether it said three rooms or two rooms. (2)

This small opening passage encompasses the invasive, multisensory assault of the city, the sexual overtones of Lutie's vulnerability ("naked," "fingers . . . explored"), and the clouding of perception. Minutes later the angry wind again blows dust, ashes, and paper into her face, eyes, nose, and ears (4).

Lutie's first encounter with Mrs. Hedges as she enters the apartment building begins a series of "staring" assaults on Lutie by people who represent the hostile influences of the city:

> It wasn't that the woman had been sitting there all along staring at her, reading her thoughts, pushing her way into her very mind, for that was merely annoying. . . . It was the woman's eyes. They were as still and as malignant as the eyes of a snake . . . flat eyes that stared at her—wandering over her body, inspecting and appraising her from head to foot. (5–6)

Minutes later she encounters the Super Jones' lustful stare: "after his first quick furtive glance, his eyes had filled with a hunger so urgent that she was instantly afraid of him" (10). As she mounts the stairs ahead of him she feels that "he was staring at her back, her legs, her thighs. She could feel his eyes traveling over her—estimating her, summing her up, wondering about her" (13). Back downstairs, she feels him "eating her up with his eyes" (25). Later on she refers to the "moist" looks of white men and the hostile stares of white women. The entrepreneur Junto, her ultimate nemesis, watches her, studies her in the mirror of the bar (146–49), and Boots Smith, with his hard, expressionless, predatory eyes, watches her react to his job offer (150–52). In all of these cases her personal space is invaded physically and she is the object of sexual appraisal.

When Lutie first sees her house's interior, she is disturbed by its claustrophobic atmosphere. The dim light in the entrance hall deceives her into thinking she sees a piano there. The hall is narrow, the stairs steep and dark, and the upstairs halls very narrow and smelly. As she ascends to the fifth floor the temperature gets colder and colder, and she imagines that it must get hotter and hotter in summer until "your breath would be cut off completely" (12). When she reaches the fourth floor, "instead of her reaching out for the walls, the walls were reaching out for her—bending and swaying toward her in an effort

to envelop her" (12). The rooms in her apartment are small and dark
and face the back—a rubbishy backyard and a blind air shaft. Petry
carefully describes the size and feeling of each nook of the apartment,
and later repeats the same claustral adjectives whenever she refers to
Lutie's apartment. In recognizing her limited choice in apartments,
Lutie creates a metaphor from the corridors: "You've got a choice a
yard wide and ten miles long" (19).

All of her perceptions of the physical setting are colored by the
threat of Super Jones, who shows her the apartment. Her sense of
this threat begins when she rings his doorbell. Petry gives astonishing
emphasis to the assaultive force of the doorbell and Jones' dog:

> It made a shrill sound that echoed and re-echoed inside the apartment and
> came back out into the hall. Immediately a dog started a furious barking
> that came closer and closer as he ran toward the door of the apartment.
> Then the weight of his body landed against the door and she drew back
> as he threw himself against the door. Again and again until the door began
> to shiver from the impact of his weight. There was the horrid sound of
> his nose snuffing up air, trying to get her scent. And then his weight
> hurled against the door again. She retreated toward the street door. (8–9)

It continues with the "hot fetid air" and hissing steam that come at
her out of his rooms. She feels stalked by Jones up the dark stairs,
with his physical presence behind and beneath her.

In the apartment, with his flashlight pointed down, he becomes "a
figure of never-ending tallness. And his silent waiting and his appearance of incredible height appalled her . . . he looked as though his
head must end somewhere in the ceiling. He simply went up and
up into darkness" (14–15). The repetition emphasized Lutie's sensory
disorientation. At this moment she feels Jones' monstrous desire: "the
hot, choking awfulness of his desire for her pinioned her there so that
she couldn't move. It was an aching yearning that filled the apartment,
pushed against the walls, plucked at her arms" (15). She thinks that
he reaches out for her but is uncertain in the dimness. When she hears
the choking sound of his repressed desire she imagines his turning out
the light and attacking her in the dark. She senses the force of his will
against her: "When he finally started down the hall, it seemed to her
that he had stood there beside her for days, weeks, months, willing
her to go down the stairs first" (18). And even though she gets him
to go first on the descent, he still controls the pace. His effect on her
is completed by the denizens of his apartment—Min, whom she mistakes for furniture in a Kafkaesque touch, the cowed dog, and the
canary—all "huddled" and "shrinking."

What does Lutie offer in resistance to this initial onslaught? She tries humor, imagining the landlord renting out cots in the entrance hall and thinking that the bathroom wasn't big enough for Methu-selah's beard and that the only source of fresh air was the toilet vent pipe. She also tries rational common sense, reassuring herself that she is imagining things and that there is no cause for fear. She offers "determination," a fighter's will to overcome adversity. She also recalls her grandmother's storytelling wisdom and hums her grandmother's song about "no restin' place" (17). She falls back on a naive faith in urban order:

> If he [Jones] tries to include making love to the female tenants, why this is New York City in the year 1944, and as yet there's no grass growing in the streets and the police force still functions. Certainly you can holler loud enough so that if the gentleman has some kind of dark designs on you and tries to carry them out, a cop will eventually rescue you. That's that. (19)

Yet she is compelled to accept in herself "the instinctive, immediate fear she had felt when she first saw the Super" (20). She throws a final menacing look at him

> just in case some dark left-over instinct warned me of what was on your mind—just in case it made me know you were snuffing on my trail, slather-ing, slobbering after me like some dark hound of hell seeking me out, tonguing along in back of me. (25)

Although she can click her heels and click her purse shut with an air of angry determination, her defiant departure is undercut by the dog's yelps, Mrs. Hedges' flat stare, and the biting wind.

In the course of the novel Lutie's senses continue to be assailed by the apartment house and street. It is impossible to walk around in her rooms without bumping into something. As she washes dishes with the radio on, a "stillness that crept through all the rooms" becomes so palpable that "she found she kept looking over her shoulder, half-expecting to find someone had stolen up in back of her *under cover of the quiet*" (78, my emphasis). The halls are dank with the smell of urine, and every time she enters the apartment "the walls seemed to come in toward her, to push against her" (79). These two images of silence and of the pushing walls are constantly reiterated as Lutie struggles harder and harder to get out of the street. In chapter 6 she sees Junto's bar as an escape from small dark rooms and the silence, and like the other patrons, she responds to "the sound of laughter, the hum of talk, the sight of people and brilliant lights, the sparkle of the big mirror, the rhythmic music from the juke-box" (145). But the big mirror behind the bar distorts everything in the bar. Underneath the illusory "gaiety and charm" reflected there is the reality of Junto (also magnified by the mirror), whose "squat figure managed to dominate the whole room" (146). The mirror lies to her when she feels "free here where there was so much space," where the mirror "pushed the walls back and back into space" (146). For this is the beginning of her ultimate entrapment by Junto, who first sees and desires her here. Her disoriented perceptions seem benign but are just as dangerous as her earlier fearful ones. When she returns home after the ride with Boots, she is depressed again by the "silence and the dimly lit hallway and the smell of stale air. . . . It was like a dead weight landing on her chest" (186).

In chapter 8 Lutie has a remarkable nightmare of pursuit. When she finds out that Super Jones has been in her apartment she feels invaded and remembers the first day there. She now connects Jones with a life of "basements and cellars" and sees him as an embodiment of the street that threatens to destroy her. In her terrifying nightmare she sees him whining and crawling down the street after her with a building chained to his shoulders. Although she feels sympathy for him as an emasculated black man also imprisoned by the street, she must protect herself from his assault; he has merged with his dog and become the slavering hell-hound from chapter 1:

> She reaches out her hand toward the padlock and the long white fangs closed on her hand. Her hand and part of her arm were swallowed up inside his wolfish mouth. She watched in horror as more and more of her arm disappeared until there was only the shoulder left and then his jaws closed and she felt the sharp teeth sink in and in through her shoulder. The arm was gone and blood poured out. (192–93)

Along with this image of Jones in the dream, the goadings of Mrs. Hedges and the transformation of the street's inhabitants into rats with houses chained to their backs bring to a climax Lutie's response to the city's assault. She awakens to a new "dread" of her room. "In the darkness it seemed to close in on her until it became the sum total of all the things she was afraid of and she drew back nearer the wall because the room grew smaller and the pieces of furniture larger until she felt as though she were suffocating" (194). It is then that she remembers the shoes of the murdered man in the street, the stabbed girl's "gaudy mask" of a face, and the psychopath's stare in the hospital. She vows to fight against becoming inured to the violence of the city and to escape the street with the added money from her hoped-for singing job.

For two days her new dream blinds her to the wind and the dim hallway (230), but this respite is short-lived. When Jones attempts to rape her, she is jolted back to reality and beyond it into surreality. Under the horror "not to be borne" of Jones's contorted face and sweating body and the stench of the dog on her back,

> She screamed until she could hear her own voice insanely shrieking up the stairs, pausing on the landings, turning the corners, going down the halls, gaining in volume as it started again to climb the stairs. And then her screams rushed back down the stair well until the whole building echoed and re-echoed with the frantic, desperate sound. (236)

Saving her, Mrs. Hedges appears balloon-like to Lutie's disordered perception, with her white nightgown against her intensely black and scarred skin, so that she looked like "a creature that had strayed from some other planet" (237). Henceforth Lutie will continually picture the trap of the street as Jones's "pulling her down, down into the cellar."

After her disillusionment with the no-pay singing job, which has been a ploy of Junto's to make her his mistress, she again succumbs to the assault of her building—its pushing walls, its noises of flights that prevent privacy, its stairs "like a high, ever-ascending mountain" (313). On her visit to the Crosse School for Singers, the repulsive appearance of Mr. Crosse that assails her senses—his fat body, his soggy, shredded cigar, his rank smell, the skin of his hand "the color of the underside of a fish—a grayish white" (321)—is but the extended expression of yet one more attempt to exploit her sexually. In her righteous rage (throwing the inkwell at him) she finds herself increasingly violent and savage in her "cage," like the zoo tigers she remembers in vivid detail.

When Lutie discovers that Bub has been caught and detained by the police for the postal theft for which Jones has framed him, she begins to realize how the system has worked to destroy black families, a white system embodied in the "crisp, crackling white paper" of the court notice. Her sobs pervade the house and are echoed by the inhabitants' own pain, as if these cries are already within them (390). Without Bub in the apartment "the furniture had diminished in size, shrinking against the wall" (401), and the living room becomes "a vast expanse of space—unknown and therefore dangerous" (405). Under this new stress Lutie's perceptions are increasingly distorted.

In the last part of the novel (the last day) leading to Lutie's killing of Boots, the most vivid sensor stimulus is, remarkably, *silence*. Lutie's earlier sense of an invasive silence now becomes overwhelming as she desperately attempts to get money from Boots to keep Bub out of reform school. She is first "assailed by the stillness" at the Children's Shelter emanating from the "shrinking, huddled" women there (408–9). She begins "to believe the silence and the troubled waiting that permeated the room had a smell—a distinct odor that filled her nose until it was difficult for her to breathe" (409–10). The silence then successively drives her out of the apartment, where her throat is "constricting"; the movie house, where it "crouched along the aisles, dragged itself across the rows of empty seats . . . coming at her . . . coming nearer and nearer"; and the beauty shop, where it "crouched down in the next booth" and might leave with her and "somehow seep into the apartment before she got there, so that when she opened the door it would be there. Formless. Shapeless. Waiting. Waiting" (412–13). She begins to realize that she is "smelling out evil as Granny said." Finally, back in her apartment and again "assailed by the deep, uncanny silence that filled it," she is able to give the disembodied silence she could only "sense" before a clear shape in a terrifying but enlightening hallucination:

> It was Junto. Gray hair, gray skin, short body, thick shoulders. He was sitting on the studio couch. . . .
> If she wasn't careful she would scream. She would start screaming and never be able to stop, because there wasn't anyone there. Yet she could see him and when she didn't see him she could feel his presence (418)

She hopes soon to "be free of this mounting, steadily increasing anger and this hysterical fear that made her see things that didn't exist" (419). But when she arrives at Boots's, hallucination becomes real as the squat white Junto sitting on the couch whom she sees literally as "a piece of that dirty street itself" (422). At the moment she strikes Boots with the candlestick, motivated by a desire to kill Junto, her sense perception is seriously disoriented. She no longer "sees" Boots but instead sees the street and the small rooms, stairs, and halls. Ironically, the silence she would have destroyed, the evil represented by Junto, remains—it makes her feel as if she is "wading through water, wading waist-deep toward the couch, and the water swallowed up all sound. It tugged against her, tried to pull her back" (432). It nearly prevents her from getting to the door:

> The four corners of the room were alive with silence—deepening pools of an ominous silence. She kept turning her head in an effort to see all of the room at once; kept fighting against a desire to scream. Hysteria mounted in her because she began to believe that at any moment the figure on the

sofa might disappear into one of these pools of silence and then emerge
from almost any part of the room, to bar her exit. (433)

When all of the sensory assaults on her being coalesce into a clear
white male enemy, Lutie finds that in succumbing to uncontrollable
violence and striking out against him and his environment she has
succumbed to the very mechanisms of control of that environment.
She feels that she can only abandon her child and flee to yet another
big city—Chicago—that could "swallow her up" (434).

Although Lutie is the central character who registers the sensory
bombardment of the city, most of the other characters also react
strongly to the physical environment and experience some of the same
nightmarish disorientation. Super Jones has come to be defined and
deformed by loneliness and lust. Mrs. Hedges labels him "cellar
crazy"—a creature of cellars and basements (and ships' holds), as if
the physical environment of his work has made him an imbalanced
lecher seeking to express emasculated power through possession of
women. On his first visit to Bub, the duress of his desire causes him
to overreact to the sensory stimulation of Lutie's lipstick, the smell of
her talcum, and the clothes in her wardrobe that "bent toward him
as he looked inside" (108). When Min conjures him with a cross, he
becomes so obsessed with its shape that he sees it everywhere. After
she has left him he is uncertain whether her making the sign of the
cross was real or hallucinatory. His misperception of Lutie's facial
expression incites him to rape: "She seemed to fill the whole hall with
light. There was a faint smile playing around her mouth and he
thought she was smiling at the sight of him and bending and swaying
toward him" (234). He is extremely vulnerable to Mrs. Hedges' invasive gaze not just because she mocks him and prevents his enjoying
the street scene but because he thinks she can read his thoughts, can
get inside him. The claustral ghetto environment has made Jones both
victim and predator. His psychic imbalance makes him susceptible to
heightened and distorted sense perceptions which in turn make him
vulnerable to sexual desire, fear, and his own violence.

Bub's fear of being alone in the apartment at night may seem to be
a normal child's anxiety, but it too is linked to the city's menace and
it reinforces the reactions of other characters. His sensory orientation
is dislocated: "The furniture changed in the dark—each piece assumed
a strange and menacing shape that transformed the whole room" (211–
12). He, too, feels invaded: "The floor would creak and the wind
would rattle the windows like something outside trying to get in at
him" (212). The corners are "wiped out in the dark," the chair becomes a "bulge of darkness," as though "quick, darting hands had

substituted something else" (213). Sounds are magnified—heavy foot-steps, a violent fight next door, the woman's sobbing so that "the room quivered with it until he seemed almost to *see the sound running through the dark*" (218, my emphasis). He was "lost in a strange place filled with terrifying things" (218).

Min, the Super's drudge, had retreated from the kind of lively engagement of the senses Lutie experiences, but as she begins to reas-sert control over her life by getting help from the Prophet David and later by deciding to leave Jones and the street, her responses are reawakened. From her point of view Jones's gloomy, silent anger "filled the small rooms until they were like the inside of an oven—a small completely enclosed space where no light ever penetrated" (352). At the same time her bed without Jones increases in size night after night until it seems to "stretch vast and empty around all sides of her." She has won protection from Jones, but now she no longer wants to stay:

> Having room to breathe in meant much more. Lately she couldn't get any air here. . . . It was because of the evilness in Jones. She could feel the weight of it like some monstrous growth crowding against her. He had made the whole apartment grow smaller and darker; living room, bedroom, kitchen—all of them shrinking, their walls tightening about her. (362)

Jones himself has become a monster in her distorted perception: "Every sound he made was magnified. His muttering to himself was like thunder, and his restless walking up and down, up and down, in the living room seemed to go on inside her in a regular rhythm that set her eyes to blinking so that she couldn't stop them" (363). She knows that she will die if she stays. With a final look at the street she thinks, "It wasn't somehow a very good place to live, for the women had too much trouble, almost as though the street itself bred the trouble" (355).

To a lesser extent other characters also suffer distortion of percep-tion from the assault of the city. Mrs. Hedges' vision has been partly defined and distorted by being trapped in a burning house, stuck in a basement window, and being terribly burned. Her pain over her loss of any attractiveness centers on her burned-off hair, and her obsession with other women's hair occurs eight times in the space of four pages. She is capable of a kind of nurturing, as Pryse points out (124), but primarily she uses people's suffering and serves Junto's ends with schemes derived "from looking at the street all day" (251).

Boots's perceptions have been molded by the sounds of the bells and the racist commands of passengers on the Pullman cars where he formerly worked, and by the "curtains blowing in the breeze" in his apartment that have imprinted his girl's affair with a white lover on his brain.

Even Miss Rinner, Bub's neurotic white teacher, suffers from heightened and distorted sense perceptions. Educated in racist stereotypes by a segregated society, she is suffocated by the odors of the school, of the black children, and of "Harlem itself—bold, strong, lusty, frightening" (328). When she opens her classroom door on Monday morning "the smell had gained in strength as though it were a living thing that had spawned over the week-end and in reproducing itself had now grown so powerful it could be seen as well as smelt" (328). She is hysterically afraid of the black people she passes on the street "as though she had run a gantlet" (331). As a result of her obsessively exaggerated perceptions, she retreats from teaching the children anything and contributes to the oppression of the system.

The city, then, and particularly the ghetto streets and buildings, can create a disoriented perception that combines disastrously with the psychic imbalance created by other more abstract forms of oppression through class, race, and gender. Is the country any better? Lutie learns about "Country Living" from Chandlers' sleek magazines and their life in Lyme, Connecticut. Despite her memories of the wide, beautiful main street with its overarching elms, she senses the injustice it implies for her and the hollowness of its beauty, given the disintegration of the Chandler family. Her life on the Chandlers' country estate is largely spent indoors, where she is subjected to guests' stereotyping her as a black wench. Later, on the drive with Boots, she finds that the hills along the Hudson River outside the city close in on her too much. Although two or three references point to the desirability of sun, sky, space, and farm work, the novel contains no clear opposition between city and country, as does, for example, Gloria Naylor's *Mama Day*.

And after all, the general descriptions of the street are not exclusively negative. Yet, in the sleet the "blobs of light" from windows make "no impression on the ever-lengthening shadows" (414), the buildings "loom darkly" against the distant sky, and the snow gets dirty quickly. But Lutie delights in the rope-jumping girls, Jones enjoys the activity on the street and yearns to join the circles of joking men, and the snow can momentarily transform the street, "gently obscuring the grime and the garbage and the ugliness" (436). Implied in the novel, however faintly, is the hope that one's senses may also be receptive to beauty, that one may gather resources to accept realistically, as well as resist, the menacing and the ugly, and that human community may transcend the inhuman environment.

WORKS CITED

Bell, Bernard W. "Ann Petry's Demythologizing of American Culture and Afro-American Character." In *Conjuring: Black Women, Fiction, and Literary Tradition,* edited by Marjorie Pryse and Hortense J. Spillers, 105–15. Bloomington: Indiana University Press, 1985.

Bone, Robert A. *The Negro Novel in America.* New Haven: Yale University Press, 1958.

Christian, Barbara. *Black Feminist Criticism: Perspectives on Black Women Writers.* New York: Pergamon Press, 1985.

————. *Black Women Novelists: The Development of a Tradition, 1892–1976.* Westport, Conn.: Greenwood Press, 1980.

Davis, Arthur P. *From the Dark Tower: Afro-American Writers 1900 to 1960.* Washington, D.C.: Howard University Press, 1974.

Gayle, Addison. *The Way of the New World: The Black Novel in America.* Garden City, N.Y.: Doubleday, 1973.

Gross, Theodore. "Ann Petry: The Novelist as Social Critic." In *Black Fiction: New Studies in the Afro-American Novel since 1945,* edited by A. Robert Lee, 41–53. New York: Barnes & Noble, 1980.

Ivy, James. "Ann Petry Talks about Her First Novel." *The Crisis* 53 (February 1946): 48–49.

Lattin, Vernon. "Ann Petry and the American Dream." *Black American Literature Forum* 12 (Summer 1978): 69–72.

Petry, Ann. *The Street.* Boston: Beacon Press, 1985.

Pryse, Marjorie. "'Pattern against the Sky': Deism and Motherhood in Ann Petry's *The Street.*" In *Conjuring: Black Women, Fiction, and Literary Tradition,* edited by Marjorie Pryse and Hortense J. Spillers, 116–31. Bloomington: Indiana University Press, 1985.

Schraufnagel, Noel. *From Apology to Protest: The Black American Novel.* Deland: Everett Edwards, 1973.

Wade-Gayles, Gloria. *No Crystal Stair: Visions of Race and Sex in Black Women's Fiction.* New York: Pilgrim Press, 1984.

Washington, Mary Helen. "'Infidelity Becomes Her': The Ambivalent Woman in the Fiction of Ann Petry and Dorothy West." In *Invented Lives: Narratives of Black Women 1860–1960,* edited by Mary Helen Washington, 297–306. New York: Doubleday, 1987.

14

John A. Williams: The Black American Narrative and the City

PRISCILLA R. RAMSEY

DESPITE their own rural origins, John A. Winthrop and the Puritans who made the Atlantic crossing in 1630 brought with them an essentially urban notion of what America would become, envisioning it as "a city on a hill." This conception of an urbanized America did not become a historical reality until late in the nineteenth century; however, the Puritans' own Protestant work ethic, combined with their own industriousness and religious outlook, produced a series of villages and towns loosely connected by large tracts of agrarian lands. Later in the nineteenth century these villages and towns would evolve into cities of various sizes in the form that we know them as cities today. In any event, this urban conceptualization was the original intent of those founding fathers who first came to the new world (Marx 165).

Simultaneously, as early as 1619 and unrelated either culturally or philosophically to the Puritans' Anglo-Saxon tradition came the introduction of chattel slavery into the American colonies of the South. While these two cultural groups bore no relation to each other, slavery's economic bondage to the Europeans forced an unholy alliance between the two groups. Cotton and tobacco would be kings. Cheap labor had to be imported from Africa to sustain European capitalistic hegemony. Considering the dictated purposes for their introduction to the New World, Africans initially met the New World experiences for the most part as a rural rather than as an urban group.

Slavery ended, Reconstruction failed, and the great migratory shift of black people from the rural South to the urban North began. This shift, lasting from the late 1890s through the 1920s, owed its causes to reasons which are by now familiar: racial violence, boll weevil destruction to cotton crops, and farm technology which replaced black farm workers' jobs.

But not all black people moved to the North. Although the population was statistically altered, there were people who heeded both Booker T. Washington's warning to remain southward and Paul Lawrence Dunbar's Rake's Progress reworking of black urban experience in *The Sport of the Gods*. Quite literally, Dunbar's message was a cautionary tale to would-be migrants that the city held terrible traps for those who had known only the southern rural environment. As Gilbert Osofsky points out in *Harlem: The Making of a Ghetto*, migrants were usually younger than the age of forty because those older than forty were willing to expose themselves to the hazards of southern life. Additionally, those more willing to go to the North could further see black urban experience reflected in Alain Locke's *The New Negro*, W. E. B. Du Bois's *The Philadelphia Negro*, and Urban League founder Charles Johnson's periodical, *Opportunity*. All of this writing contributed to a new reality for these black Americans: an urban reality. Clearly, by the beginning of the Harlem Renaissance after World War I, Dunbar's version of black experience in the city was losing its effect. People were coming to the North primarily for economic reasons and for other more frivolous reasons as well: among them, curiosity about the city after attending summer school in the North, and the attraction to a perceived glamour of city life after reading exaggerated letters sent back South by relatives.

In all, given this kind of black experience, how does a modern writer like John A. Williams shape a symbolic reconstruction of an urban reality in all its economic, political, and psychological dimensions? The organizing principles readily adaptable to Williams's reading of black experience are indeed economic, political, and psychological because these figure more prominently as the fundamental categories which lie at the sources of conflict in the selected novels by Williams.

Night Song (1961) discloses our notions of social or racial homogeneity in the urban setting by creating a human milieu which undermines any kind of usual conceptions about these issues. Urban America is characterized by its fragmented, isolated human beings and its alienation from earlier communal nineteenth-century institutions such as church, school, and civil organizations. It becomes both backdrop and investigating prism through which Williams looks at a series of social configurations representing a psychological quagmire—a fluid idea and variegated collection of alienated human beings.

The urban setting becomes coldly indifferent and so William's characters must create a human community supportive enough to help them survive the predatory assaults of the setting. This urban tableau does not project a metropolis of glamour or excitement; instead, New York as described in *Night Song* functions at best as coolly detached and at worst as cruelly rapacious. *Night Song* embodies a New York underworld, one filled with human parasites who regularly attach their personal mediocrity to the world of black musicians in order to provide themselves an identity. Black parasites, usually jazz musicians, also exploit this world.

To create a human community, Williams shapes a revolutionary vision, one that undermines our concepts of class and our stereotypes of interracial alliances. Conservative critics considered the novel too anti-establishment for its time. In 1962 the American Academy of Arts and Letters Prix de Rome Award rescinded its award ostensibly because of the novel's subject matter: drug addiction, alcoholism, and interracial affairs.[1]

First, Keel Robinson, one of the three shifting narrators in the novel, is a "drop out" from a divinity school and an establishment career in the ministry. Keel is committed to caring for others, a humanitarian philosophy derived both from his middle-class family background and his divinity school training. His commitment is not without cost to himself. Keel suffers from a racially grounded rage which has rendered him sexually impotent. He comes to terms with his anger at white society and gradually gains insight about his situation and that of others around him in his urbanized setting.

Second, however, he must resolve his guilt and rage, which stem from his interracial relationship with his lover, Della. These emotions underscore his misperception of her as a symbol of white society. She wrongly becomes symbol and embodiment of bourgeois hegemony, and even of white oppression. He cannot successfully integrate his love for her with this kind of underlying unconscious perception of her.

The reality is quite the opposite, for Della is to herself anything but a white middle-class symbol. If she is classifiable at all, she is an Afrophile, a woman who relishes her contact with the black jazz underworld in Greenwich Village. More importantly, she represents the standard fare one finds in a multi-ethnic urban setting. Her cultural and psychological portraits are filled with the hip and coolly detached—an idiom of the black jazz underworld. In fact, from the standpoint of her years of exposure and length of her relationship with Keel which has created this exposure, she is far more deeply involved with the black world than is the other central white character, Hillary.

Hillary, another person who remains close to Sadak's, the coffee house which Della and Keel run, comes to the Village out of despair, suffering a self-punishing guilt over being the driver in his wife's fatal car accident. He has reached the twin nadirs of his life: alcoholism and dereliction. Formerly Hillary was a professor of English. It is significant that Williams assigns Hillary this particular profession because we assume here a certain sensitivity, a certain intelligence and insight indicative of those who work in universities in quest of truth. In Hillary's case, his quest toward truth has brought him to the truth of himself: a devastating clarity about the fact that he cannot rise above the circumstances in which he finds himself, the belief that he does not deserve to live. Thus he follows a path of self-destruction, whether we see him foolishly attempting to seduce Della behind Keel's back or drinking heavily. In either case, he is playing out a slow and painful ballet locked in his death wish.

Hillary's downward progression is no worse than that of Richie Stokes, who is equally devastated by life. Richie is a black jazz saxophonist who will eventually die of a drug overdose and simple disillusionment but will overcome his destruction with the help of a black man, Keel Robinson. Elaborating from this situation, Williams again illustrates the possibilities of existence while underscoring the impossibility of the journey for black men who make mistakes. Richie Stokes, a portrait based on saxophonist Charlie Parker, cannot have another chance because he is a black man. The world is not forgiving of black illusions.

All of these people, to one degree or another, represent the human condition in an urban setting. All suffer varying degrees of alienation and fragmentation. Williams resolves their predicaments with differing kinds of controls: Della and Keel find each other again physically and emotionally while Hillary returns to college teaching, much wiser about the depths of human caring. Eagle, like the self-destructive yet cynically perceptive character Williams creates, dies of a drug overdose. This is indeed Williams's most pessimistic commentary on city life. The jazz underworld is essentially heartless and so is the city which surrounds the only protective setting possible: Sadak's. Little hope lies in this world other than that of the protected coffee house— a bitter commentary on city life.

In *The Man Who Cried I Am* (1967), Williams places into the narrative both social and political ideologies which allow him to voice the contradictions between the black individual's situation and the historical forces defining the black American experience. Max Reddick, Williams's protagonist, is dying of rectal cancer, but that cancer in the individual situation is merely a symbol for the racist cancer eating at the broader social and economic realities of black American society. Despite the fact that Williams creates a sophisticated Max Reddick who travels throughout American, Africa, and Europe, his perceptions are never far removed from the terrifying incidents of history which mark and shape the black American consciousness in the contemporary world.

The Black Power Movement, a response in the 1960s to what black people called an oppressive political situation in America, becomes one of the book's major issues. Historical forces conspire to destroy even this kind of political affirmation on the part of black people. Max Reddick and his writer friend, Harry Ames (an approximation of Richard Wright), discover the King Alfred Plan and the Alliance Blanc. This organization has an agenda to incarcerate more than 22,000 black people should their political strivings constitute what the government considers a "national emergency." Black Power is ostensibly not to be more than rhetorically effective in America because both the CIA and the Federal government will be certain to terminate its slightest assertions. In fact, Ames first, then Reddick will be killed for even "knowing."

Moreover, Williams works across a large and complicated tableau in this novel, handling the professional rise and political fall of his protagonist, Max Reddick, as Williams examines what being a black writer actually means in both a bourgeois America and in Europe. Williams points to the tenuous grasp of this particular bourgeois class context against the devouring competitive publishing market. He works out the unconscious conflicts that mark interracial romantic alliances, exposing the Southern Civil Rights Movement. Finally, he develops object lessons in human ambiguity, greed, competition, and personal corruption as these organically develop across the cities of the United States, Africa, and Europe.

These issues structure and constitute this complex novel which places its central figure, Max Reddick, primarily into urban settings. Indeed, Reddick projects a consciousness living at the margins of two cultures at once. Reddick carries within him the historical lessons gained in America which have built his racial sensitivities. His capacity to blend into other environs while sustaining his own black identity causes his narrative to reflect recurringly his heightened awareness to relevant distinctions between the habits of living in different cultural settings.

Much of what Max registers about these cities reflects a sense of his own psychological freedom in Europe, specifically in Amsterdam. Williams initiates Max's story in Amsterdam via a retrospective on the last twenty-four hours of Max's life. Thinking that he will soon be dead of rectal cancer, he attempts to form some understanding with his estranged wife, Magrit, about the termination of their marriage.

Instead, he will actually be killed by CIA agents who discovered his knowledge of the King Alfred Plan. Ironically, after three hundred pages of reminiscences, memories, and flashbacks over the years of Max's life, Magrit will wait, instead, for him, this time in a European restaurant. Unfortunately, she is not aware that she is already a widow.

What is significant about many of his glosses on cities like Paris and Amsterdam is that Max genuinely registers a sense of racial freedom in these cities. New York provides, perhaps, one of the few places left for him to live comfortably in America, although New York is not without its racial faults. In Europe Max would feel a relief from the historical legacy of slavery. This feeling about Europe, however, does not excuse the fact that he has not yet fully forgiven its colonialist history. Finally, what is most ironic about Max and his perceptions of European cities is that he will die in one, not because European authorities kill him but because it is the very historical legacy of slavery and its aftermath which destroy him. Specifically, he will be shot by CIA agents who come to kill him for knowing too much about the King Alfred Plan, a plan designed to quell American urban unrest, that is, Black Power movements should they escalate beyond mere rhetoric. Black Power movements emerged, in essence, as a response to the very unequal and enraging conditions embodied in American racism. Despite this sense of freedom in Europe, despite the generosity of being away from the balls and chains of Black American history, Max will be killed by its very agent in this very freest of all cities.

Using New York as his locus, Williams's *Sons of Darkness, Sons of Light: A Novel of Some Probability* (1969) creates a dialectic in which political power relationships clash against each other. These relationships destroy each other while paradoxically they also reconstruct each other. Each power group's relationship to the other one dictated by the proximity of urbanization makes this discord possible. The plot of the novel which centers around the cataclysmic results of a Black Power vendetta against a white policeman who kills a young black man, affirms this reality. New York City erupts in rage and murder. The subtitle of the novel, "A Novel of Some Probability," echoes the prophetic nature of Williams's intentions in this highly physical and violent novel, which reflects the height of the Black Power Move- ment's most active decade in the sixties. In fact, the physicality and violence portrayed in the novel have caused critics and Jerry Bryant, in particular, to complain. In contrast to the novel of violence, Bryant outlines the superior direction Williams's books have taken as novels of thought:

The avenue in which he [Williams] is most comfortable is the world of the black intellectual. His prototypical character is the man of thought whose creativity is sapped by racism. The strength of the character and his interests for the reader live in the power of self analysis and understanding. (82)

Although Bryant's words might themselves also be prophetic and in this case critically prophetic, this book did not receive extraordinarily high praise from academic critics nor from Williams himself. Williams admits writing the book quickly but its appropriateness to the political climate of the time brought high popular acclaim and high sales. According to Gilbert A. Muller, the popular audiences supported the novel (86).

Although Black Power movements seem to be the subject of the novel, racial matters are never the primary goal of Williams's thought, despite the political climate of the country and despite his growing pessimism and lack of faith in a racially equalitarian America by the time he wrote this novel. The problem of race becomes the way in which he explores the massive complexities of a much broader human condition translating across race and gender. In this particular case, he examines the intricate social forces coming into conflict with established authority.

Adding to this reality is the fact that his tone projects a cynicism toward the political corruption lying beyond the illusion of power in this large city, New York. The legal system compromises its alleged standards, allowing evil to go unpunished among its ranks. For example, Captain Corrigan, a white policeman, kills a young black man without legal penalty. Hence, Black Power groups conspire as vigilantes to bring the law to order.

The characters, for the most part, participate in this series of disjunctures as they move about this nightmare world of New York. Certainly the book underscores the potential naivete built into any belief in a black political American dream of peace and harmony between the races. The book examines the collapse of this notion from both ends of the class and color spectrum: Eugene Browning, a central figure and ex-college professor, essentially a middle-class black man, leaves the protected class environment of a bourgeois university to become a political activist. Furthermore, he commits his energies to avenging the young man's death by raising the money for a murder contract on Corrigan. In addition, not only do we see Browning's life unfold in its changing middle-class implications but we are given an understanding of the lives of both contract killers as well: the Mafioso Don and Ishak Hod, a Polish-Russian emigre, who both function as hired killers. These men represent the irony of political corruption: earlier they have been forced by a higher authority in their separate homeland to become murderers. Williams thus creates a complex picture of how ideological forces interact with yet clash against each other.

Within all of this, again, Williams presents the urban setting which conditions the structure and form of the novel, charting the exact nature of how people experience city life. Multi-ethnicity dominates, but the American melting pot blending ethnic groups with each other is mere myth. Clearly, group cooperation is not the case in *Sons of Darkness, Sons of Light*. If anything, the social order constituting human experience is that of a post-industrial economy which places people into antagonistic, competitive human arrangements. A pattern of social relationships underlies the way people fail to fit in this urban situation. Little wonder racial conflict and urban conflagration become its ostensible subjects given the kind of social climate Williams creates.

The American novel in the nineteenth century often presents the image of the city as a negative or contaminated notion, one frequently containing the seeds of its own ultimate social, economic, and political destruction. Major poets from Emerson and Whitman to Frost and Stevens and major novelists from Cooper and Hawthorne to Faulkner—all castigated the urban setting. They found no other way but to ignore it in their work and most often, preferred to place their characters into rural geographies (Marx 163–64). Not until well into the twentieth century do we see Theodore Dreiser, Dos Passos, and James T. Farrell rediscovering the metropolis. Even in this somewhat more positive climate for thinking about the city as a likely place to locate a story, the negative imagery still in such writers as Sinclair Lewis and Upton Sinclair appears as an obtrusive, tenement-filled presence rather than an abiding and supportive setting.

Interestingly enough, Williams's *Mothersill and the Foxes* (1975) suggests an alliance with the nineteenth-century pastoral tradition. Odell Mothersill, the major figure in the novel, functions always with the urban environment as his major scenic backdrop, but he complains relentlessly about that fact. Perhaps out of Williams's own realistic intention, Cleveland and New York City are described at their worst through the voice of Odell. Little wonder that Williams resolves Odell's harangue with New York by retiring Odell at the end of the novel to the bucolic environs of the country and to traditionalist living: milk farming, family living, and an altruistic life in which he adopts a series of children unwanted by city parents.

This disjointed imagery of city life begins with Odell's first caseworker job in the Good Shepherd Foster Care Agency where he encounters homeless orphans who must be placed with families who want them. These children are products of adult hedonism, tiny seeds of an uncaring society committed to its own pleasure and concentrating on its own financial success. The children are seen by their retreating parents as unwelcomed entanglements. It is Odell's job to place these children into family situations which compensate for the loss of their parents. Ironically, with all the family rhetoric around, Odell's fate will greatly counteract the family values his agency esteems when twenty years later an adoptive mother shoots him almost fatally. Twenty years before this, they had had an illicit affair. Now she believes he is duplicating that affair with her daughter who is actually the product of the sexual tryst which she and Odell had two decades earlier. A wounded and disenchanted Odell thus retreats to the country.

Although this represents only one of Odell's many sexual encounters, he has many throughout the book. His relationships are failures, however, because of his compulsive need for female bodies and the womens' desperate need for his companionship. Each woman comes to him with a certain hunger, an expectation that he will fill an emotional vacuum which living in an urban setting without other meaningful relationships has somehow created in them. The city, the loneliness, and the alienation affirm further how even sex gets perverted into murder. After one of Odell's sexual conquests, which occurred after a party at the woman's apartment, he discovers that two of his lesbian co-workers have been smeared with jam and killed. This murder is based on a real event which occurred in New York City: the killing of famous writers, Max, and Phillip Whylie's nieces in Greenwich Village. The Greenwich Village life-style, the anti-traditional atmosphere, therefore, invites this kind of death.

Despite Odell's urban experience and his heart-hardening work in both foster care and the Peace Corps, this murder, the immediacy of having known these two people, fundamentally shakes his peace of mind, his sophisticated detachment. In one of his romantic affairs, Odell encounters someone "real": Potts, a hometown transplant and a friend of his more traditionalist and family rooted sister. Potts has been twice married and twice divorced. Her delay with regard to their first sexual encounter disturbs him until he discovers the cause: her structural blockage. Her response to this "disfigurement" is to attempt suicide. Hers is an overreaction in response to a situation relatively minor in medical annals (Suter 129). Just as Odell is the rescuer of parentless children, he is certainly the rescuer of suicidal women, particularly those with whom he has just attempted to make love. He runs through the indifferent streets of New York City, screaming for cabs that do not dare stop as the drivers see this black man carrying what they believe is the deadweight of a black woman on his back. He races for the local hospital emergency room. Williams paints a harrowing picture of these experiences and unfortunately one all too familiar to anyone who has lived in a large metropolis. Potts has swallowed an overwhelming dose of sleeping pills; Odell tries to keep her alive, desperately trying to reach a hospital.

Little wonder that after all of this we see Odell retreat to the clover-filled beauty of the countryside. Both Odell and the women he has encountered are alienated from commitment to families or to any form of social solidarity greater than that of their own needs. Their personal existence in New York City appears disassociated from the traditional institutions that rural environments can provide: church, school, orga-nizations, and other communal institutions. Instead, the desire for cultural role playing and participation and the attempt to achieve social and individual identity, all perfectly good human options, appear lost in the maze of sexual pursuits, victories, and rejections, as compen-sation for and counterforces against the indifference of the city. As in the nineteenth-century novel, Odell is a suave, debonair city person but also one who withdraws to the bucolic countryside.

Mothersill and the Foxes is one of the rare novels in which Williams uses flight to a rural setting as a solution to urban problems. This kind of closure in his novels is very unusual because it is the city rather than the country which is usually the answer to difficulty for a black writer. Given the Utopian nature of this ending, one would think this an unrealistic ending. It is a neat but not an altogether satisfac-tory ending.

After *Mothersill and the Foxes*, Williams published *The Junior Bachelor Society* (1976). One of the Bachelor's wives says:

> Some cities are like houses: they can charm you as you come upon them, without so much as your putting a foot on the threshold; others chill you, even from a distance. Such was this city. (150)

Like the organic London of a Dickens or the equally seductive and colorful Dublin of a James Joyce, this small city into which Williams places much of his story in *The Junior Bachelor Society* shapes, indeed stamps, upon its subjects it own identity. This place is no mere cata-lytic backdrop to narrative conventions. Instead, the setting, the region, leaves its mark upon the kind of blue-collar collectivist con-sciousness Williams creates—his characters feel they must escape in order to test their mettle and define a new identity against the dimen-sions of a broader world. Each one reaches spatially beyond the confines of this small city into grander urban places: those of America and Europe. But they share their essentially working-class beginnings, and their identities are first shaped by this very place.

This place with its ethnic polarities and class engulfment might well have destroyed their potential for middle-class achievement had they not been influenced by one very important human factor: Coach Chappie Davis, father figure, mentor and guide to these potential youthful delinquents who will become the city's admired bourgeois emblems of success. To thank Davis, the Bachelors return to give him a birthday party and honoring dinner which turns into a police investigation protecting a fugitive Bachelor. Williams foregrounds the social and psychological issues so emphatic in the novel: first, class mobility with all its accompanying psychological and financial insecurities for those who began in such humble circumstances; second, the adolescent expansive group collective sentiments posed against the adult, narrow, more individualistic strivings characteristic of upward social mobility; and finally, and most important of all, the endless metaphor of game competition in both the careers and personal lives of the characters. What most often informs these competitive metaphors are the latent tensions of the pattern of human relationships among eight men who have gathered together to celebrate their football coach's seventieth birthday.

These tensions recall earlier associations, experiences which Williams crafts retrospectively for each character. Hence the reader is always reminded, as Williams moves the point of view and the narration around to each voice, that the person in the present is always a conglomerate of past people and events. Although each of these Junior Bachelor Society members has accumulated many other kinds of psychological dimensions in the great progress toward adulthood, such as escape from the city and career establishment, Williams carefully explores the origins for the direction each one took in his life, thus providing neat and logical outcomes for each as he faces middle age. Surprisingly, this reunion illustrates Williams's penchant for working across a large canvas initiating portraits which are dual in nature: the tendency to project the best foot forward as well as to show off the fruits of middle-class stability and labor. The covert picture is quite another matter: compulsive bisexuality, physical deterioration, rampant infidelity, a mediocre singing career foundering on the brink of genuine failure, and misplaced blame for that failure.

Most important of all, the culminating human yet corrupt force in the story is represented by Moon. It is Moon who forces the Bachelors to examine their own morality and the values of the group caring; that is, collectivism taught to them by Chappie Davis. It is Moon who has traveled the cities of America encountering and overcoming the legal authorities with his "stable full of fillies" and his gambling. It is Moon who has gone far beyond the bourgeois respectability that each Bachelor has worked so hard to achieve, albeit one which chokes each one of them in its never ceasing demands. It is Moon whose very presence reminds them of what the treacheries in the American economic system cannot and will not do for black men. Moon, a proverbial gamesman and a player against that system, kills two policemen and still evades the law at the end of the novel. His ironic relationship to the social and legal order, his success, is what will undermine the Bachelors' best but mediocre intentions to be upstanding. By the end of the reunion, there exist a possible divorce among them, several budding extramarital affairs, genuine career dissatisfaction, and finally Moon galloping off in the sunset as the new individualistic American hero.

Central to the reality in this situation is the notion that it was the small city and its human ambience which produced these men and women in the first place. They are products of its efforts. They are survivors. However, they had to leave this place to arrive at a more successful identity in the terms of the world. This yearning for broader territory, this leaving home to find one's mettle, is common both in mainstream and black American writing. In Williams's novel, striking out for the bigger territory always comes with responsibility to the past historical circumstance, the legacy of slavery. Black characters do not set themselves toward urban freedom without the realization of their racial identity and all that legacy really requires. Generally, this observation is true for Williams's characters. History always looms heavily about them, their struggles, and efforts to overcome it.

!Click Song, Williams's novel in the 1980s, registers issues which underlie the post-industrial age living with its competitive abstractions, albeit from a black rather than a mainstream point of view. The early Puritans who came from Europe to begin their "city on the hill" hardly had a black Cato Douglass in mind as narrator of this experience. It is this incongruence of historical situation between blacks and whites in America which underlies much of the conflict in the novel. Williams examines both the historical and contemporary major cities from the perspective of class, economic, and literary competition as these prevail within the foundations of Cato's human identity. Williams constantly juxtaposes capitalism against racism, family life against isolation and death, the artistic success of a mediocre mainstream writer, Paul Cummings, against Cato's own relative failure at publishing.

Williams also uses Cato, a sophisticated and well-traveled black

middle-class American, as a prism through which to explore the insidi-
ous metaphors of competition not only in the urban setting but within
the business of publishing, book sales, and coping with editors for
whom profit rather than merit determines the selling of art. In addition, racial experience is unyielding and, while not the only fundamental of Williams's concerns, it nevertheless recurringly provides the
prism of consciousness through which Cato gauges the world of New
York City and its fiercely competitive gestalt. Just as Cato measures
the world through the racial gestalt, it continually views him through
W. E. B. Du Bois's "double consciousness." He is forever the single,
introspective black seer weighing the world and the situation and,
most important of all, attempting to understand the implications of
what his being a black writer means in this fast paced, cosmopolitan
existence, defined essentially by the economics of power.

Furthermore, Williams uses his retrospective structure to develop
his narrative by initiating the story at Paul's suicide. This gives Williams an opportunity to work backward, as he did in The Man Who
Cried I Am, to craft the growth and regressions of both Paul and
Cato. With some detail, Williams portrays their friendship and its
varying realities. While Paul hides his Jewish identity, Cato explores
his black one even more deeply. Thus Cato travels to Paris and Sydney,
to Spain and the history of the Moors, and then finally makes his
journalistic jaunt throughout the American south.

Paul as writer, as mainstream artist, and even as mediocre talent
functions as a free agent, acknowledging and then denying his Jewish
identity when he wishes or when convenient. Cato, on the other
hand, has no choice but to be the victim of slavery and of its racial
"mark of oppression." Cato's very capacity to achieve, to economically
succeed in the huge New York metropolis, is fraught with race despite
the assumed liberality of the setting. Because of race, he cannot marry
easily the woman he wants to marry, nor can he live comfortably
where he wants to live. Nor can he publish what or as much as he
wants because a black writer is not the kind of "commodity" that a
white progressive writer is in the New York publishing world.

Counterposing solutions to the vast potential for personal fragmentation and destruction in this predicament, Williams uses family life,
friendship, and the preoccupation with children, all of which become
the buffers against meaninglessness. Contrasting evidence for how important these humanly unifying experiences must be is scattered all
over the novel. Women editors use sex both as an antidote for loneliness and as a way of manipulating writer-clients. Writers drink to
drown their own personal emptiness, as well as the emotions caused
by several suicides in the novel. Jolene Bookbinder, wife to "razzle-
dazzle" black editor, Amos Bookbinder, ends her life and that of her

children because she realizes her essential insignificance to him and to the rest of the world. Part native American, part black poet, Leonard Bluesky, who cannot make the racial connection with Cato, kills himself, having walked into a Manhattan snow bank and frozen to death. The trash man collects his body the next morning like so much "morning after" debris; after all, "they are accustomed to collecting such things daily."

After these two suicides, Cato cannot help but be haunted by the potential for self-destruction built into the urban setting if one is without family or meaningful people in one's life. Cato holds closer ties to his family and community in order to sustain his own human meaning as buffers against the impersonal capitalistic machinery of everyday life in this huge city. The resolution this novel suggests lies in the reality that human fragmentation and death stalk us all if we do not heed the warnings of the fundamental values of human connection and a sense of purpose for each other.

From the earliest historical contact with the new world, black experience has been both agrarian and economically oppressed in nature. Only with the mass migration of late nineteenth century and early twentieth century did the character of black experience evolve into one of predominantly urban character. Given this particular change in the evolution of black reality, it is little wonder that Williams centers his narrative in the urban settings of both America and Europe as a way of reconfiguring a symbolic construction of black experience in his novels.

He presents no utopias, however. The metaphors of competition and struggle for economic survival color urban life; they are what Leo Marx outlines as the underlying basis of social relations given the harsh nature of this material reality as it evolves in the city. It is not surprising that these urban metaphors do not escape the consciousness of all his black central figures. Indeed they must run! Despite the imperialist legacy and despite the strangeness and unfamiliarity black characters feel in the city, it is finally in Europe that Williams grants his black characters their greatest sense of freedom and unconstricted movement. These small inconveniences are nothing when compared with the overwhelming destruction of their psyche, economic security, and viable social relations that his characters experience. Europe provides them far more than remaining here among the familiar.

NOTE

1. In his *John A. Williams,* Gilbert A. Muller outlines, in detail, the series of misperceptions surrounding "The Prix de Rome Affair" in which Williams was ini-

tially promised the literary prize by the Academy of Arts and Letters then denied it later. Essentially, the panelists had not fully read the novel until they withdrew the prize. However, Williams was never given a full explanation from any of the panelists for not having received the prize. He concluded that the prize was denied because of the book's subject matter (14–15).

WORKS CITED

Bryant, Jerry H. "John A. Williams: The Political Use of the Novel." *Critique* 16 (1975): 81–100.

Butler, Edgar. *The Urban Crisis: Problems and Prospects in America.* Santa Monica, Calif.: Goodyear, 1977.

Lynch, Kevin. "Reconsidering the Image of the City." In *Cities of the Mind: Images and Themes of the City in the Social Sciences,* edited by Robert M. Hollister and Lloyd Rodwin, 151–61. New York: Plenum Press, 1984.

Marx, Leo. "The Puzzle of Antiurbanism in Classic American Literature." In *Cities of the Mind: Images and Themes of the City in the Social Sciences,* edited by Robert M. Hollister and Lloyd Rodwin, 163–83. New York: Plenum Press, 1984.

Muller, Gilbert A. *John A. Williams.* Boston: Twayne, 1984.

Suter, Barbara. "Suicide and Women." In *Between Survival and Suicide,* edited by Herbert Krause and Benjamin B. Wolman, 129–61. New York: Gardner Press, 1976.

Walcott, Ronald. "The Early Fiction of John A. Williams." *CLA Journal* 16 (December 1972): 198–213.

Williams, John A. *!Click Song.* Boston: Houghton Mifflin, 1982.

———. *The Junior Bachelor Society.* Garden City, N.Y.: Doubleday, 1976.

———. *The Man Who Cried I Am.* Boston: Little, Brown, 1967; New York: New American Library, 1972.

———. *Mothersill and the Foxes.* Garden City, N.Y.: Doubleday, 1975.

———. *Night Song.* New York: Farrar, Straus & Cudahy, 1961; New York: Pocket Books, 1970; Chatham, N.J.: Chatham Bookseller, 1975.

———. *Sissie.* New York: Farrar, Straus & Cudahy, 1963; New York: Anchor Books, 1969; Chatham, N.J.: Chatham Bookseller, 1975.

———. *Sons of Darkness, Sons of Light: A Novel of Some Probability.* Boston: Little, Brown, 1969; New York: Pocket Books, 1970.

15

The Urban Pastoral and Labored Ease of Samuel R. Delany

DONALD M. HASSLER

ut varias usus meditando extunderet artis
"Thus practice by being self-conscious forges various arts."
—Vergil, *Georgics,* I, 133

I do not mean to say at the outset that Samuel R. Delany is exactly the urban cowboy of recent criticism and fiction; but there is something about the wonderful verbal bumps and grinds this black, male feminist, science-fiction writer has recently forged that is both so modern and so ancient. Delany may never accomplish, finally, the epic work of science fiction, which would establish the full maturity for both his own ambitious career and the often-maligned literary ghetto of science fiction; but he does seem to have set himself very consciously along the classic, Vergilian path of movement from early pastoral to middle georgic to the most ambitious forms of epic writing. And like Vergil himself, Delany's development never quite gets him beyond the solemnity and the ugly hard work of the city. Just 12 lines farther along in Vergil's poem from the motto I quote above comes the famous enigmatic tag of how "unrelenting labor conquers" the world, and this solemnity is exactly the georgic seriousness even of Aeneas. Fortunately for us as readers, Delany also is never quite simply pastoral nor eloquently epic. He is continually a city writer and a hard-working exponent of georgic labor.

Although Delany is, obviously, never as self-consciously neo-classic as a Dryden or a Pope in explaining his desire to imitate the Vergilian movement from pastoral to georgic to epic, he does echo eighteenth-century awareness of such genre expectations.[1] In particular, he has begun lately to write more and more autobiographically about his writing career and his genre intentions. Throughout his career theoretical writing about genre and the nature of science fiction has seemed to be almost as important to Delany as his fiction, which, as I argue more fully later in this essay, represents itself a rather complex-urban, georgic attitude toward writing; but most recently his theory has become more openly autobiographical. His 1988 book *The Motion of Light in Water: Sex and Science Fiction in the East Village, 1957–1965* won a Hugo Award for nonfiction writing.[2] In an earlier version of this autobiographical text that first appeared in 1983, Delany recollects about his first fictions in terms that carry distinct pastoral connotations:

> Today *The Fall of the Towers'* three volumes strike me as very naked. They show—not necessarily in the best light, either—all the preoccupations to be expected of a young man whose family two years before had merited a paragraph in a popular non-fiction best-seller, *High Society in the United States* (in a chapter on "Negro High Society"), who now lived in a Lower East Side tenement where rats leapt on the sink when you went to brush your teeth in the morning and wild dog packs roamed the stairwells. . . . I wept when I wrote the scene [one of several with autobiographical overtones that he has been describing in this long paragraph]—aware, as I wrote, as I cried, that tears were no assurance it would be more than melodrama.[3]

This pastoralism seems to reside in the nakedness and personal qualities of the young writer whereas, obviously, the harsh realities of city life already dominate both the recollections and the actual early texts of the young Delany. The *labor omnia vicit* passage in the *Georgics,* significantly, goes on to include the wonderfully connotative words *improbus et duris* where *duris* is relatively easy to read as "hard" but *improbus* means something like "disgraceful," "ignoble," or "insatiable"—certainly the ratlike quality in city life that Delany the young aristocrat encountered and then recollected.[4] In any case, the progress of Delany's writing career is clear both from his recent autobiographical work and from the publication data itself.

He was born in New York City in 1942, published his first novel when he was 19, produced five novels before he was 22 (including the trilogy *The Fall of the Towers*), had a nervous breakdown shortly after, and has gone on to become one of our most highly regarded writers of science fiction. His 1968 novel *Nova* is built around what some critics have identified as a "grail quest" narrative.[5] *The Ballad of Beta-2* (1965) also is a young man's story of a sort of literary or sociological research that carries the magic of the primitive and, even, pastoral—as does his first story *The Jewels of Aptor* (1962). Nearly all the rest of Delany's fictions, however, make use of images of the city to represent the middle style of hard work and, even, genre invention that is, in my opinion, distinctly georgic in effect. I have argued else-where that Delany's major and masterful work from 1975, *Dhalgren*, which one would think of as an epic achievement simply because it is so massive and has received so much favorable attention, carries essentially a georgic effect of tentative artistic invention and hard work. Certainly the shadowy city Bellona haunts that novel.[6] I turn my attention here to other cities in this middle period, and middle style, of Delany who has, I hope, miles yet to go in his writing career.

The very fact of a tentative, unfinished writing career, as well as a continual theoretic forging of ideas about writing carries the implica-tion of the georgic effect as opposed to what one critic of Vergil's *Georgics* has called "nostalgia for an idyllic past (or future)."[7] Vergil himself, of course, left his *Aeneid* unfinished and in both that poem and his *Georgics* maintained an extremely tentative, nearly skeptical, balanced attitude toward the major questions of both literature and belief. A modern editor of Vergil's epic writes, "[the] problem is to depict a new kind of hero, a hero for an age no longer 'heroic' . . . there is something much more human in the man who ponders, worries, negotiates. . . . This is one reason why the character of Aeneas has been frequently criticised . . . because he is insufficiently 'heroic.'"[8]

Thus if Delany's career brings to mind the neo-classic pattern of imitating Vergil in a movement from pastoral, "naked" beginnings to the more complex sophistication of georgic, the parallel grows in generality to embrace most "fallen" literature. The cities and the new hero in Delany, as we shall see, have the appearance of the future; but the reality is the old truth of georgic complexity at least as ancient as Vergil and certainly including his neo-classic imitators such as Dry-den and Pope who could go no further than mock epic. Pastoral sim-plicity may characterize the nostalgic recollections of one's beginnings in writing, from the perspective of later autobiography as in Delany. But then the most epic ambitions get mired in the georgic honesty of teeming cities, skeptical tentativeness, and unrelenting labor—or "insatiable toil" as one fine commentator insists on with regard to the *labor . . . improbus* expression.[9]

The actual label "georgic" in Latin connotes the impossible task of settling in to build something that will last as opposed to the label "nomades" (or nomads) who are pastoral wanderers.[10] Naturally, De-lany likes wandering as do all human beings when they let their minds be drawn back to primitive beginnings. But my reading of this most complex of modern science fiction writers suggests that, finally, Delany

is a builder of walls and a teller of the fallen hero in the city. And in
this program he is, incidentally and perhaps consciously, Vergilian and
Augustan. In fact, many of his readers have commented on exactly
this "insatiable" desire Delany seems to have to champion real-life
details, even important social and political issues, in his futuristic
fictions—and lately in theory and autobiography. In a recent study of
Delany's deconstruction of rock music (he himself performed semi-
professionally at East Village coffee houses in the sixties) in *The Einstein Intersection* (1967), Takayuki Tatsumi writes:

> Delany even disclosed his willingness to write essays about his sex life, his
> life as a black American, his experiences with psychotherapy and eventual
> hospitalization, his critical encounters, and his film production. Delany's
> life, shining prismatically, can aptly be called "multiplex" if we apply the
> Delanian term which strongly impressed me in one of his earlier novels,
> *Empire Star* (1966).[11]

When Delany toys with his continual theoretical effort to characterize science fiction itself as a "multiplex" within the pages of a fiction, as Tatsumi notes, he is behaving in a particularly georgic manner.
He is laboring at a continuing task, and he is working tentatively
because the exigencies of the fictional context dictate that no definitive
answer can be reached. In fact, the georgic interweaving of such profound questions into the multiplex of a fiction itself, often a fiction
of a city, makes exactly the proper statement about the tentative,
accumulative, and ever-evolving nature of such important matters of
epistemology and belief. Hence science fiction, as Delany writes it, is
particularly philosophic.

In addition to literary theory, Delany is very serious about work
(labor) and about the complex networks that frame issues such as
sexuality, racism, and, most generally, city building itself in our society. He is probably a Marxist but too aware, I think, of georgic contin-
gencies (the multiplex of science fiction) to be only a Marxist. Here is
a wonderfully rich passage gleaned, again, from his autobiographical/
theoretical writing; and it might be read as more doctrinaire than his
ideas embedded in fiction except for the fact that the shifting, marginal
texture of his nonfiction (he glosses, quotes himself, and adds margina-
lia to his own texts). He also defies straightline exposition in favor of
the georgic maze, much like an evolving city:

> In a depressingly real sense, the Marxist glorification of work for its
> own sake, coupled with the naive assumption that as long as everybody
> is working *hard*, all sexual "problems" will disappear, i.e., reduce to a
> pastoral (and suspiciously bourgeois) vision of respectful, shy, young work

ing men getting up the nerve to propose to respectful, shy, young working women, who must get up the nerve to respond, quiveringly, "Yes" (both, finally, taking courage from the fact that they are serving the state—the Marxist equivalent of "doing it for Old Glory"?), is historically. . . . The entire template, Marxist and Capitalist, is a pre-Freudian disaster area which Freud's own inability to distinguish between sensuality, sexuality, biological gender, and sex role socialization has done as much to perpetuate in the West as his basic discovery of the unconscious, sexual repression, transference, and infantile sexuality have prepared the groundwork to alleviate.[12]

So Delany likes Freud, and he does not like Freud. Even though this essay is dedicated to the relatively simple task of exploring the meaning of the city for Delany, which I read as a set of georgic images and implications, and not to exploring love/hate complexities of tone, the tonal ambivalences in the intricate passage just quoted, dealing with the necessary intellectual giants of our time, may hint at the psychological depths we encounter just in reading city images in Delany. Again, from the recollections he has undertaken to set down for us about the beginnings of his writing career (when he was first married to Marilyn Hacker and yet actively gay, when he was wrestling with issues of racism, poverty, and creativity in New York City), we come across an account of what he calls, this time, a dream. It is firmly written and hardly a dream account; rather an anticipatory multiplex of much of his science fiction that was written down, of course, in this autobiographical text *after* the science fiction had been published:

With such thoughts, I turned to lie down on the daybed in the shadowed living room, to sink, tingling with hyperawareness (once again), into the luminous evening waterfront of a primitive city, to climb, dripping, from the river into the ruined streets of an abandoned futuristic metropolis, to toil through glimmering jungles alive with violet sunsets and red-bugs and ghouls, above which soared ivory and onyx vampires and in whose rivers dwelt a slimy aquatic race, jungles where I watched a man turn into a wolf while I tramped past moss-gown temples to the foot of a volcano abroil on the night, and where great violence was done to a four-armed child, which woke me (again), sharply and shockingly, in the dim tenement.[13]

I think that Delany's "primitive city" here is most successfully depicted as the "autumnal city" Bellona in *Dhalgren*. I have written about that masterful work elsewhere, and there are other manifestations of the city.[14] In fact, the novel that Delany was working on at the same time as *Dhalgren* contains, also, a Bellona; but this one is found on Mars and is much less mysterious, foggy, or symbolic than either the dream city or the autumnal city. Thus not only in the Dhalgren to Triton complex but also throughout his fictions similar cityscapes keep coming back. Some of them such as Istanbul, Paris, and New York (see his frequently anthologized short story "Aye, and Gomorrah . . .") have our familiar names. Others like Bellona and Branning-at-sea in The Einstein Intersection are more mysterious and filled with symbols. But these cities are, indeed, multiplex. Here is a typical description of a sector in a city, this one from Triton (1976), where variety, even deviant behavior flourishes: "most cities develop, of necessity, such a neighborhood. . . . These sectors fulfilled a complex range of functions in the cities' psychological, political, and economic ecology. Problems a few conservative, Earth-bound thinkers feared must come, didn't."[15]

Even more "liberal" and issue-oriented is Delany's most recent science fiction novel, Stars in My Pocket like Grains of Sand (1984). This book is promised by Delany as the first of what he calls an "SF diptych" in which the announced title of the second is particularly appropriate for this georgic theme of the real-life city: The Splendor and Misery of Bodies, of Cities.[16] The second part is late appearing, however, and Delany has gone on to a set of fantasy novels. Nevertheless, this 1984 text, though, in my opinion, not as successful in its complexities and resonances as Dhalgren, is a prime example of how well science fictional themes of technological advance, in particular, fit the ancient georgic mode of hard work, tentativeness, and "issues." Near the end of the story, Delany's postmodern narrator of sexual and social virtuosity almost beyond belief declared explicitly that "the dawn of space travel is the dawn of woman."[17] The simple statement comes in the midst of a long linguistic discussion, so characteristic of Delany, about how the metaphors in science fiction can have literal, nearly technological meanings; and what it refers to is the dominant theme in this novel of extrapolating future sexual experimentation and development. Delany here is farming, or city building, on the grandest Vergilian scale. An earlier statement in this novel, again set in quotation marks to indicate that the story is as much about the elements of story themselves as about anything else, sets forth even more clearly the program of science fiction: "Thus: 'There is an alien life form that travels between stars' is simply another little-known fact—because in our human universe, of necessity, all facts are as little known as the works of great poets."[18]

Perhaps now it is clear the way in which the usual conventions and environments of science fiction (hard extrapolations from "fact" and a serious concern with "city" issues as opposed to the more free-wheeling and playful imaginativeness of fantasy) are themselves descended from the Vergilian solemness of georgic. The mode is never that simple, however, both in its ancient form and in the work of Delany. Here is part of the conclusion from a recent booklength study of the original *Georgics*:

> In sum, while the poem purports to be didactic and to teach *praecepta*, it embodies, in fact, a whole range of values that function in tension with the conventional, material, and Iron Age values upon which a georgic poem might be expected to be based. The poem privileges mystery, not solution; complexity and ambiguity, not certainty. The overall effect of this poem is to highlight the mysteries of existence, to challenge and even to transcend the values of the technological mode that it ostensibly accepts and endorses.[19]

When Delany writes as a science fiction writer and as a serious literary theorist or autobiographer, he works hard at the extrapolations and at the tentative progressive steps forward. This is genuinely a "middle style" or mode, and I think the labor (and even "insatiable" ugliness of it at times) is Delany's finest contribution. He is a black American writer about cities, and this is his solemn Vergilian inheritance. But like Vergil he is, also, essentially a poet; and so the solemn labor carries with it as well the labored ease (a hint of residual pastoralism) of what the classicist I quoted above calls in the title to her book *The Poet's Truth*. Not only has Delany produced recently a number of fantasy novels and seemed to neglect what we usually label "hard science fiction" but also the "ghouls" in that 1961 dream of his "primitive city" and the wonderful, fey dragons in a novel such as *The Einstein Intersection* indicate that he is never merely solemn and a worker at issues.

Rather, the poet's truth of labored ease always acknowledges that both the issues and the answers, no doubt, carry within them a large portion of mystery that can never be teased out either tentatively or laboriously. I do not believe that any sensible writer, either a Delany or a Vergil—and certainly not a Samuel Johnson—is totally comfortable with such mystery.[20] Hence the continual reappearance of georgic effects and of the city building in literature that finds its latest manifestation in science fiction. But apparently the true poets write about mysteries when the georgic will not do. I conclude this essay on Delany and the georgic with a wonderful passage that he wrote into *The Einstein Intersection*, that early science fiction novel which deconstructs rock music along with other city institutions. The narrator-hero is being told about his ancestry and the geography of where he came from; and the story is a tentative, unfolding truth as well as a lyric mystery suggestive both of New Testament Christianity and of Einstein:

> . . . it's changing, Lobey. It's not the same. Some people walk under the sun and accept that change, others close their eyes, clap their hands to their ears and deny the world with their tongues. Most snicker, giggle, jeer and point when they think no one else is looking—that is how humans acted throughout their history. We have taken over their abandoned world, and something new is happening to the fragments, something we can't even define with mankind's leftover vocabulary. You must take its importance exactly as that: it is indefinable; you are involved in it; it is wonderful, fearful, deep, ineffable to your explanations, opaque to your efforts to see through it; yet it demands you take journeys, defines your stopping and starting points, can propel you with love and hate, even to seek death for Kid Death. . . . There are an infinite number of true things in the world with no way of ascertaining their truth. Einstein defined the extent of the rational. . . . And the world and humanity began to change. And from the other side of the universe, we were drawn slowly here.[21]

NOTES

1. See my essay "Dhalgren, The Beggar's Opera, and Georgic: Implications for the Nature of Genre," Extrapolation 30 (Winter 1989): 332–38.

2. The Hugo Award is given annually at the World Science Fiction Convention in a number of categories. It is a recognition of high prestige in the field.

3. Samuel R. Delany, The Straits of Messina (Seattle: Serconia Press, 1989): 136–37. This passage was first published in a shorter form in New Moon 1 (Spring 1983) and a longer version in the award-winning text mentioned above The Motion of Light in Water: Sex and Science Fiction Writing in the East Village, 1957–1965 (New York: Arbor House, 1988).

4. Virgil, Georgics, books I–II, ed. Richard F. Thomas (Cambridge: Cambridge University Press, 1988) 41. I use this edition for the epigraph to this essay as well. Both spellings of Vergil's name are found; I prefer the one closest to his own Latin spelling of Vergilius.

5. See in particular Sandra Miesel, "Samuel R. Delany's Use of Myth in Nova," Extrapolation 12, no. 1 (1972): 86–93.

6. See my 1989 Extrapolation essay cited above in note 1.

7. John Chalker, The English Georgics: A Study of the Development of a Form (Baltimore: Johns Hopkins University Press, 1969), 106.

8. R. D. Williams, Introduction to The Aeneid of Virgil (London: Macmillan, 1972), xxii–xxiii.

9. Richard F. Thomas, Commentary to his edition of the Georgics cited above in note 4, p. 93.

10. C. T. Lewis and C. Short, A Latin Dictionary (Oxford: Oxford University Press, 1879); see under "georgi."

11. Takayuki Tatsumi, "The Decomposition of Rock and Roll: Samuel Delany's The Einstein Intersection," Extrapolation 28 (Fall 1987): 269.

12. Delany, The Straits of Messina, 55.

13. Ibid.

14. See note 1 above.

15. Delany, *Triton* (New York: Bantam, 1976), 9.

16. Delany, *Stars in My Pocket like Grains of Sand* (New York: Bantam, 1984). See "Writer's Note" in front matter.

17. Ibid., 359.

18. Ibid., 139.

19. Christine Perkell, *The Poet's Truth: A Study of the Poet in Virgil's Georgics* (Berkeley: University of California Press, 1989), 190.

20. Johnson holds forth wonderfully on what he calls "diseases of imagination"— particularly in *Rasselas* (1759)—but other places as well.

21. Delany, *The Einstein Intersection* (New York: Ace Books, 1967),116–17. Note how the same theme of "more things than we can know," which is an echo of Horatio's comment to Hamlet, appears in the 1984 Delany text cited above in note 18.

16

The Inner and Outer City: A Study of the Landscape of the Imagination in Black Drama

ROBERT L. TENER

Whether real or a fictive representation, the city has existed as "an archetype of the human imagination" seemingly forever. Sometimes it has been seen as the Heavenly City, the City of God[1] or more recently as a machine, "a humming, smoking, ever-changing contrap-tion."[2] Most often it is a living entity which has absorbed both its secular aspects as well as its sacred concerns. Its counterpart is nature against whose fictional analogue, as Joyce Carol Oates says, fictional persons "enact their representative struggles with those values the City embodies."[3] This is especially true of black American drama. One of the major views of the fictive city to emerge in the decade of the sixties in African-American drama is that it is no place to be somebody. For those fictional blacks who appear in the plays of Ed Bullins, Amiri Baraka (LeRoi Jones), Charles Gordone, Adrienne Ken-nedy, and Lorraine Hansberry,[4] the soul has apparently gone out of the city, its structures, and even its streets, producing a demonic world.[5] This fact is so apparent that there is a discrepancy between the city as environment in black drama and the city as memory in black autobiography.

The patterning of a city, vast and amorphous as it may be, reflects the soul of its civilizations. For blacks the city presents the fictional landscape of the imagination. They inhabit the city but lay no claim to it. Dispossessed, disenfranchised, without power, they did not historically make the American city.[6] This historical fact affects and makes more complex the poorly understood dramatic landscape, that fictive analogue to real cities; it appears like a box within a box remi-niscent of the ancient Chinese puzzle, or perhaps more literally, it resembles an oasis within a desert contained by a large sprawling white structure.

The city in the black drama of the sixties is first of all a metaphorical environment, a dramatic setting which in its larger aspects looms dark and threatening for the Curts, Ricks, Cliffs, Lous, and Rays whom Ed Bullins creates[7]; angry and filled with war and death for the Clays and Walkers or even loss of love for the Footes Amiri Baraka imagines[8]; a place of frustration dominated by white ideals, rules, and faith for the Shes Adrienne Kennedy describes[9]; an arena of drugs, gangs, and unemployment for the Gabe Gabriels of Charles Gordone[10]; or even a place for dreams which don't have to dry up in the sun for Lorraine Hansberry's characters.[11]

In general the large fictive city in black drama is in the industrial North, a Chicago, a New York, a Philadelphia, or a Los Angeles, clearly non-rural; it offers no soul or regenerative qualities for its black inhabitants. It sets physical limits where they can live and work and dream. It surrounds the small oasis street where Cliff and Lou live[12]; it seems removed but omnipresent for Clara in the knowledge and attitudes that she brings from her work at the hospital[13]; it is acknowledged by Clay in Lula's presence and stands represented as the school with its toilets for Footes and his gang.[14] It is historically white and segregationist in its literature and culture for She[15]; it is something material, a yard, a white neighborhood for Lena Younger and her family when they wish to move.[16]

Above all, this industrial, northern, or southwestern environment sets limits on the life patterns and imaginations of its black inhabitants. It establishes a dramatic metaphorical background which embodies values that the black fictive agents struggle against. As part of that conflict much of their living takes place in a smaller setting, not quite a city within a city. Sometimes it is more than just a ghetto; it is what Toni Morrison calls a village.[17] Sometimes it is Harlem or the South Side in Chicago; other times the immediate environment is a city block, like Derby Street in *In the Wine Time*, where the soul has not yet departed and where the white man enters only through such personas as the police or other representatives of white institutions. Under these conditions white values, though felt, are always struggled against.

Clearly the larger white city is something to avoid, to leave, to escape, or even to tear down. As Curt says in *Goin' a Buffalo*, "Man, this ain't a world we built so why should we try to fit in it? We have to make it over the best we can ... and we are the ones to do it" (69). Curt and Pandora's apartment in Los Angeles is a small surrealistic oasis of white and red colors mixed with dreams set within a white peopled world with police and jails for men like Curt.[18] The couple keep their doors locked because they always face the threat of police disguised as ghetto people who try to trap the Curts of this world. Some like Art, whom Curt met in jail, are awaiting trial for murder; some sell drugs; even some of the women face jail records as whores. Their apartment, clean but not totally domestic (they eat fast food, not prepared dinners), is a temporary oasis wherein they restore their emotional energies and can dream of escaping to Buffalo, their eastern hope.

Derby Street in *In the Wine Time* presents the same kind of setting. It is the little village world of love and socializing for Lou and Cliff where they hope, not where they realize their desires. Cliff tells Ray the world is yours. But Ray is young and can leave the street; Cliff does not have that immediate freedom. As Ed Bullins begins this rich play, he offers a prologue about the beautiful girl on the avenue whom Ray sees and wants to follow. She is the dream, the future for a young boy when he grows up, the poetry of his potentiality.[19] But this lyrical scene is set against the jibes of the street boys and the ugly physicality of the city which is alien to the lyrical sexuality of life. For Cliff and Lou the street is sometimes like a tunnel leading to despair. Protecting Ray from the white police after Ray has killed Red in a knife fight, Cliff accepts the blame and must go to prison and leave his wife. For him the only movement away from the street with all of its small town qualities is either back to the Navy or to prison; for Lou, it is either to the streets or to another man.

In Baraka's *The Toilet* the small temporarily comfortable environ-ment where most of the living occurs is the ugly hallways and toilets of the inner city school. Here Footes rules his gang. Yet in this place which by its very name seems to be alien to love, Footes finds love with a white boy Karolis. Limited by the larger white environment, the school is localized by the gang into a place of moderate safety wherein they conduct business. Here also they spend their adolescent energies and confusions as they begin their passage from boyhood into manhood.[20] Ironically, the toilet is not a pretty girl walking by. Like the street or apartment, the toilet becomes a positional source of iden-tity and power in all of its manifest filth and degradation, a mythic area neglected by whites where black boys find an existential power and freedom.

This concept is drastically altered, however, in two of Baraka's other plays, *Dutchman* and *The Slave*. In both of these dramas there is no immediate setting, dramatic space, where blacks live and have some degree of safety. Instead the subway, a dramatic metaphor of the white world, provides the domain for violence and death. Lula, a metaphorical Eve, filled with the defects of white liberalism and sex-ism, kills Clay, a black man trying to escape blackness by being white in dress and education.[21] In *The Slave* the setting is the home of a white professor; it is situated in a city under attack by blacks who bomb the area daily. The movement of the urban setting for Baraka seems to be from the toilet to subway to a home under bombardment as though his fictitious environments reflect the history of black people separated as it were by a concentration camp ghetto barbed wire from their freedom. As Walker says, "We live where we are, and seek nothing but ourselves" (43), but "sometimes the place and twist of what we are will push and string, and what the crust of our stance has become will ring in our ears and shatter that piece of our eyes that is never closed" (45).

For She there is no inner city, no Derby street, no fictional village setting for her to be in the wine time. Every place in the city for this educated school teacher of white man's English literature is a place of frustration and personal hell that denies fullness and completion to its educated mulatto women; it denies them a black history taught in the colleges; it denies them a black religion while it forces them into a version of white Christianity; it denies them as mulattos even acceptable parents.[22] For She, the city is a place of white man's dreams, values, religions, education, and history. It offers her a chance to ride the subway, pick up a stray black man or two, and sink further into her own confusions and temporary accommodations.

Only one positive note appears in this overview of the city as a dramatic environment. In Lorraine Hansberry's *A Raisin in the Sun* the immediate setting, as in Ed Bullins's plays, is a small area, an apartment, where the family of five live and which all are anxious to leave, each to pursue his or her own dreams. But it is Lena's dream, like Cliff's in *In the Wine Time*, that there is a need to escape, to find a place in the sun. For Lena Younger the sun is literally in Chicago; for Cliff it is always elsewhere. For a moment in the black drama that began to emerge in the decade of the sixties another possible direction appeared for that escape, into a more pastoral setting, into the imagination of the suburbs. In such a setting that is implicit in *A Raisin in the Sun,* Hansberry was probably reflecting the movement of white America to the suburbs, that greening of America that occurred because many felt that cities were vast and ugly places one should leave if one wanted to bring up one's children properly. But Lena Younger's hope only catches a piece of that larger movement. Her vision is not to move into the suburbs but simply to move into a home with a larger yard where Travis could play and where her plants could find more sun.

The city, the larger environment surrounding the smaller domain, remains an always dark (one should say white) and threatening agent, fictional in the plays but representing the overall white value system and its institutions geared to those values; it stands for a struggle to achieve freedom of the mind and body. In the black drama of the sixties it is an oppressive agent, whether actively or passively; it defines and makes a man or woman. Whether it be the macro- or the micro-environment, it often presents a desolate and defiled landscape of the mind. It seems to offer an escape to a middle scene which often turns out to be a purgatory between heaven and hell.

In Ed Bullins's plays the immediate landscape, if interior, is clean and neat as in *Goin' a Buffalo, Clara's Ole Man,* and *The Duplex.*[23] If it is the street, as in *In the Wine Time,* it is dirty and desolate, defiled by garbage and junk. In Baraka's *The Toilet* it is obviously the high school restroom with its typical stench and overpowering associations. Usually in Baraka's plays whether the environment be exterior or interior, it does not reflect a physical dirt. The same characteristic applies to the dramatic landscapes of Adrienne Kennedy and Lorraine Hansberry.

On the other hand, this small city within a city, for all, except Hansberry, is a metaphorical container for violence, drugs, death. One has to ask why. Is it because of the outer white city or is it the result of some other cause, like a lack of racial identity? On the surface it is an impersonal yet clearly defined inner city. The drugs and gangs there are black-related. Curt and Rich and Art in *Goin' a Buffalo* dabble in drugs and always live on the fringe of police brutality. They make friends in jail; they plan petty crimes; they are aware of other black groups such as the Black Muslims.

In *In the Wine Time* Red and Bama form a small gang that bullies its way up and down the street taking advantage of the girls and putting pressure on Ray, urinating in his wine and taking his girl friend away. To their immediate quarrels the knife offers the only answer. In *Clara's Ole Man,* a gang, obedient to Big Girl, beats up on Jack. Gangs seem thus to characterize the fictive domain of the Blacks as in *The Toilet* where a gang captures Karolis and tries to force him to fight Footes.

Kennedy and Hansberry create a different inner city. Theirs is almost white, especially Hansberry's, without the presence of gangs, knives, and excessive drinking. Yet *The Owl Answers* is filled with the dark hotel rooms She takes her men to. She rides to find men, and with surrealistic ease moves into the mind of She to explore her religious identity problems. In this play the city seems to be an extension of the minds of the fictive characters and reflects their problems rather than represents an outward reality in which they live.

With all of these playwrights, however, the inner city, regardless of its village-like quality, represents something from which the characters still need to escape. Curt and Pandora plan to leave their apartment for Buffalo; it seems to be like a tunnel or canyon or even a hole. As Curt says, he wants to "get out of this hole" (31), and then he will feel free. In *In the Wine Time* Cliff needs to leave the street. He feels anger at it (114). He tells his nephew of the need to escape into the bigger world. But that need to leave restrictive environments seems to be reserved by Ed Bullins for his male characters. Lou does not feel the same desire that Cliff does, nor does Big Girl in *Clara's Ole Man*. Instead, Big Girl rules violence with violence. In Baraka's three plays the city also does not reflect the overpowering desire to move. Yet in Hansberry's *A Raisin in the Sun*, the immediate setting reflects Lena Younger's desire to escape its limitations and take her family with her. In *The Owl Answers* the city seems to present insurmountable problems for She from which there is no alternative world, establishing as it were the troubled landscape of her own mind from which She could never break free.

One of the reasons there is a need to get out of the city is its tendency to corrupt its inhabitants. It is a kind of hell for Cliff who is dissatisfied with what he is in *In the Wine Time*. In this sense the city also defines or makes a man, gives him strength and status or destroys him. Emotionally alone, Cliff is dissatisfied with Derby Street and its people; he calls them names, dislikes the dirty graffiti, the tattered posters, the sense of nowhere to go except down. For him it is a small town with everyone knowing everyone's business. It is where one works for almost nothing and loses one's self-respect; it is the place where Cliff doesn't want any children until he can afford them because he is "Dollar-an-hour Dawson" (137). On Derby Street the street language is always vaguely threatening, veiled, contentious, and the women wait for their men.

In *Goin' a Buffalo*, the inner city reflected in the life style of Curt, Rich, and Pandora defines their friends and allows them only limited ways to earn a living, from the women doing their tricks on the street to the men selling drugs. Even where Pandora works, the reality of the Strips Club is the domain of whores, and "the men should wonder if the habitat of whores is not indeed the same region as their creatures of private myth, dream, and fantasy" (48). In defining their relationships and identities, the city forces its inhabitants to wait. Art waits (56); Curt and Rich wait for some Godot of events to occur. Art says "the whole world will come to you if you just sit back and be ready for it" (56). For Cliff the waiting is for a future that will not recover the past; for Lena Younger and She, the waiting is to find themselves; even Gabe Gabriel waits to find a job as actor or playwright.

If the city defines its men and establishes their limitations, it also presents rebellious characters ranging from Lena, who won't remain in her small apartment despite white opposition, to Walker, who leads an army of blacks to attack the white city. For Bullins this aspect of the city appears as a chessboard of moves, an intellectual game, as Curt and Art match private conflicts with public struggles against the white world.

If the city is the landscape of the black imagination, it offers a man in *In the Wine Time* the chance to drink and get sick on wine, to socialize in the summer with memory, friends, and acquaintances; it brings Walter to the depths of despair as it cheats him of a chance to get rich in the liquor store business; it denies Gabe the opportunity to be a complete artist. Perhaps in the long run the city is even harsher on its women. In *Goin' a Buffalo* it brings a woman to give her body to get her fix and murder every day (59). It causes her pimp to keep her needing him. That is all she can look forward to. Baraka's fictive city has no immediate female characters; his city is populated with men who talk about their women or girlfriends and play the dozens as teen-agers. Baraka does not allow female characters in those plays where his male characters struggle to find their identities and self-respect.

The city clearly offers opportunities to She to degrade herself and get lost in her desperate search for her identity. If it is a city of literary importance like London, then it rejects her through its white structures; if it is New York, then it merely offers her opportunities to search desperately but not to satisfy her hungers. In short, the city offers no positive images or means of identification for She. In *A Raisin in the Sun*, the city has brought two boyfriends to Beneatha, one from a wealthy family and one from Africa; it offers her the opportunity for a college education to be a medical doctor. Most of all, however, the city offers her mother Lena a chance to return to the sun and garden of her dreams. Only in this play is there a touch of the pastoral myth associated positively with the city. In all the other plays nature is absent except for its harsh representation as winter in Bullins's *In New England Winter*.[24] While the larger city provides Walter Younger with his job as chauffeur as it takes away his self-respect, it also provides the opportunity for his momentary escape through driving to see the factory buildings or to go out into the country and see farms. Tucked into this play is the rural myth of America associating the green land with a richer personal growth.

One can postulate a large city, the white structure; then a middle territory, the ghetto for blacks; and then within this an inner or private landscape such as an apartment, Derby Street, a high school restroom, or a hotel room. All of these act like a holding station for their inhabitants, a place where they can wait, and where there appears to be temporary safety. At best, they represent the characters' accommodations with daily living. But, most importantly, they are where they start to dream, to exist, and even to share. In the black drama that emerged in the sixties, the city is not cast in the role of the heavenly city or even as that warm cultural repository of childhood memories so often pictured with nostalgia in Jewish literature, nor is it the rich teeming life of Harlem that Langston Hughes writes about in his autobiographies.[25] But it is the place of dreams, where they start, take form, acquire energy, and then launch out into oblivion.

As Lawrence Ferlinghetti says in "Modern Poetry Is Prose," writing about our "soul-less civilization" and its architecture,

> And so wails today a still wild voice
> inside of us
> a still insurgent voice
> lost among machines and insane nationalisms
> still longing to break out
> still longing for the distant nightingale
> that stops and begins again
> stops
> and begins again
> stops
> and resumes again
> It is the bird singing that makes us happy.[26]

However pessimistic or destructive the city and its aspects are in black drama, it reflects a construction of the playwrights; they put their dreams in it; they create images, the dramatic metaphors that suggest their fictive environments are still a symbol of the emotional and intellectual movement of blacks. Perhaps it still contains some aura of the sacred, of possibilities to be dreamed and achieved for writers such as Bullins to associate dreams with it, even if it is not in his plays or in other dramas an end in itself. For Baraka, Walker in The Slave is willing to fight and indeed leads a revolution to retake the city. But it is the city that sets limits, physical and intellectual, on its blacks. And because of that necessary push like a Faustian-Mephistophelian nudge, the fictive blacks dream and wish to move beyond those limits which they feel, like Cliff and Curt in Bullins's plays, but which they did not set for themselves.

First of all, the city enables its inhabitants to transcend its limits. That transcendence seems to be more than a dream; it is a possibility, one of those future directions or worlds open on the basis of choice and opportunity. Bullins creates a visual image of that possibility as a beautiful young woman. As the narrator says,

> She passed the corner every evening during my last wine time, wearing a light summer dress with big pockets, in small ballerina slippers, swinging her head back and to the side all special-like, hearing a private melody singing in her head . . . On these days her yellows and pinks and whites would flash out from the smoked walls, beckoning me to hurry to see the lights in her eyes before they fleeted away above the single smile. (103)

She tells the narrator, Ray, that she loves him, though she is years older than he is and when he is ready she says he can come find her. He asks where; she replies, "Out in the world, little boy, out in the world. Remember, when you're ready, all you have to do is leave this place and come to me, I'll be waiting. All you'll need to do is search" (105). Ray's uncle Cliff also keeps telling Ray that he must leave Derby Street, that cozy village domain where in the evening wine time they gather on the front stoop to Lou and Cliff's place.

For Bullins the wine time seems to be an ambivalent metaphor. It has its associations with the gods, not necessarily with the Greek Dionysus, but clearly with some divinity that allows blacks their immortal longings. It is both an escape from the oppressiveness of the immediate present and an indicator of a freer other time, other place. Remembering the past, Ray the narrator says,

> Summer and Cliff and Lou and me together—all poured from the same brew, all hating each other and loving, and consuming and never forgiving—but not letting go of the circle until the earth swung again into winter, bringing me closer to manhood and the freedom to do all the things that I had done for the past three summers.
>
> We were the group, the gang. Cliff and Lou entangled within their union, soon to have Baby Man, and Henrietta, and Stinky, and Debra, and maybe who knows who by now. Summer and me wrapped in our embrace like lovers . . . My coterie and my friend . . . (104)

The image Ed Bullins creates is ambivalent because it generates with nostalgia aspects of the anarchic, the illiterate, the primitive which E. E. Cummings sees as opposed to social order but echoing individualism.[27] The movement of the vision is outward from the presentness of the city into future time and setting.

This movement also is implicit in Baraka's *The Toilet* and *The Slave*. In *The Toilet* it emerges in the final visual image that he creates. Despite the status within the gang that Footes has as the leader, despite his being the smallest physically, he is the emerging intellectual who leads them by virtue of his rational powers to control emotions. But his relationship with the gang is set in the immediate present of the small stinking portion of the city allotted to these teen-age boys. He has their respect, their grudging willingness to follow his decisions. What he does have is their love and sharing. That comes, despite their mockery of it and their embarrassment caused by their own emerging sexuality, only at the end when Footes returns to the rest-room, opens the door, stares at the beaten Karolis, "looks quickly over his shoulder, then runs and kneels before the body, weeping and cradling the head in his arms" (62). The curious use of the definite article adds to the power of the visual metaphor and emphasizes the ambivalence of the image. The present denies humanity and dreams, makes body and head impersonal object things; the future, separate from the immediate ties which lie behind one's shoulder, allows one to transcend objects and cradle love. Even Walker, leading his army in the bombardment of the present city, can transcend those physical limitations and create a new city, an architecture in his image filled with his love for his two daughters.

Like Bullins, Baraka uses a character, Walker, as the narrator who appears in the beginning as an old field slave looking back at the emotional depths of what happens in the present time of the play's action. This image suggests the circularity of things and their inevitability as though Walker had repeated his historical self. Walker begins by saying,

> Whatever the core of our lives. Whatever the deceit. We live where we are, and seek nothing but ourselves. We are liars, and we are murderers. We invent death for others. Stop their pulses publicly. Stone possible lovers with heavy worlds we think are ideas . . . and know, even before these shapes are realized, that these worlds, these depths or heights we fly smoothly, as in a dream, or slighter, when we stare dumbly into space, leaving our eyes just behind a last quick moving bird, then sometimes the place and twist of what we are will push and sting, and what the crust of our stance has become will ring in our ears and shatter that piece of our eyes that is never closed. (43)

But the ideas, the vision of other futures, need to be examined, to be lived rightly or wrongly. That is how one finds oneself. In the present Walker finds the town that he and his army are blowing apart is "shitty"; it needs to be flattened (49). As Walker tells Grace, his former wife, he did "come into the world pointed in the right direc-tion" (53). What is the "right direction"? The aural image begins at the literal level, a proper birth for a baby, not breached. But is that auspicious beginning symbolic of the direction the body and mind take thereafter? By ironical implication, Walker says no. Then what is the right direction? For Walker? For blacks? For the Rays and Cliffs? Is it the direction toward manhood that both Bullins and Baraka imply in their plays? Is it the way into a different transcendent world created in their architectural image? Is it an act of role playing, accepting the world, the future, as a play? If so, then does one act out a part historically already determined? Baraka and Bullins both seem to imply that the answer to this question is yes.

Walker as a field slave looks back on the fighting events of his younger days. Has he lost the battle? Why is he an old field hand? How are we to interpret that visual and aural image? Is it that the act of transcending the present can be done only in dramatic images and thus these images are always uncertain and subject to the ironical drift of historical processes? Certainly for Cliff that drift is not into any act of transcendency. He goes to prison because he says that he killed Red, his sacrifice to save the future for Ray. But that leaves Lou without a husband and she is pregnant. His future section of the city of heavenly dreams will be a prison cell as it will be for Curt and Rich.

Bullins re-examines that future for Cliff in In New England Winter. Cliff is now 29, "large, husky, going to fat . . . a hint of a subdued swagger and worldliness remains" (130). The narrator is Steve, Cliff's half-brother, who is a "brooding" but thinking man (130). Their present is to be involved in robbing a finance company. Lou is far in the past for Cliff. Steve says of the coming event,

> we . . . drove with brood hanging close to our bodies blended with the sweat . . . and Indian summer rode with us across the city, a spent brave, a savage to the last, causing me visions of winter in New England. (131)

This is a curious image. The term "Indian summer," despite references extended to "brave" and "savage," carries with it its more original sense of false summer, of false hope and cues, false transcendence. Cliff has come full circle in the rhythms of the earth and the history of his personal life. He has left the city in In the Wine Time, left his prison cell, but has not been able to transcend the limits set by the larger city. It is Steve's past that we see as the play unfolds, not Cliff's future. Throughout the play Steve narrates from the future outside the immediate drama,

> Our futures loomed bitter and less bearable than the snowdrifts blocking the alleys below; but our fears seared, raging about our souls, fanning a combustion of brutality. As my manhood leaked away upon the wintry

streets by day, she cemented together my backbone under the patched quilt through the long long icy nights. (132–33)

As in a play, they rehearse for the finance company job; they need to be sharp for, as Steve says, "the scene we gonna make tomorrow" (134). For Cliff that scene suggests that he has nowhere to go, no future, no past, only the present and its limits. For him, Lou was a long way ago, in another play, another time, a different place. As Cliff says,

> If it was a thousand years it would be like this morning. . . . I sat in a cell . . . I sat in a cell one day draggin' its behind after the other . . . waitin' to get out . . . waitin' to see her, to touch her . . . smell and taste her. . . . And I was in prison for years. . . . Hahh! . . . She didn't even send me a letter to tell me. (138)

The dream away from the time and place of the immediate city in this play is Steve's, not Cliff's. Why? It is almost as though Steve is some extension of Ray, via Ed Bullins, carrying a vague hint of family ties to Cliff like a passage of a dream from the older to the younger generation. Certainly Steve has been dreaming with his girl Liz. Liz tells Carrie,

> The world is ours: thus sayest my black lord and master, Steve. . . . And Steve's mine and our baby's. If our baby's made yet, and if he's not made already then we'll make him tonight . . . or tomorrow night . . . or while the snow falls and we drink muscatel and I sing to him and he reads to me and we love. Oh, we must love quick . . . quick and hot and hard . . . for they might come for him . . . they might come to steal him away. Steal his blackness . . . steal his spirit and soul . . . steal his manhood and make him not mine . . . nor his son's to be. (150)

Steve tells Cliff that he lives to win, and in their discussion Cliff says that he "can't break through" (162).

But in the events to come, as Bullins creates them, even for Steve there is no real transcendence. Liz breaks from him. And through their quarrel and hurt, Steve cries,

> Madness madness madness . . . God, I can't take this. . . . I can't live this one out. It can't be *this* way. This isn't it . . . there must be order . . . perfection . . . there must be form . . . there must be reason and abso-lutes. . . . There can't be only madness and reaching out and never touch-ing the sides . . . everyone can be felt, can't they? There *has* to be something for me besides this emptiness . . . this living death . . . this white coldness. . . . (167)

The "sides" are that sense of the larger white box, the macro city, that has set the limits which Steve wanted to transcend but could not. The cluster of images from "sides" to "white coldness" suggests that historical limitations which are always attached to the dream. For Cliff it was Steve who took Lou away in the past; in the present, Cliff has forgiven Steve who finds Cliff always his big brother. After they rob the finance company, they go north into their New England winter.

The city as dream, as the world-is-yours concept, is also the impulse to withdraw into the dream self. It represents a withdrawal into what seems to help define one, there to gather energy and then move on to give that dream-image a reality. If this idea does not seem to be possible in Baraka's and Bullins's plays because of the historical limits set by the larger white city, it does seem possible for Lena and Ruth and Beneatha in *A Raisin in the Sun*. Yet one has to question its accuracy or its possibility of actual achievement. Lena, Ruth, Beneatha, and Walter are clearly pro-urban. Their visions originate within the city, and they expect or hope to find fulfillment there. As Toni Morrison has so aptly put it, the dramatic images that Hansberry creates of the Younger family reflects the desire to be accepted within the larger city, to be individually free there, to seek "entrance in and associations with the very institutions" often derided by whites (38). The rewards of moving into a white middle-class neighborhood are those that prove the stereotype wrong (38). But something is missing from that inner movement, even if Baraka and Bullins are wrong. There is "a marked and poignant absence of some vital element of city life that is all the more startling because of the presence of this same element or quality in their description of rural or village settings" (39). As Toni Morrison continues, what is missing is the presence of the ancestor.

At the moment when all of Lena's, Ruth's, and Beneatha's dreams seem dashed because of Walter's reckless investment of the insurance money (no separate room for Ruth and Walter, no larger home with a yard and sun for Lena, no medical school for Beneatha), Asagai proposes marriage to Beneatha. He wants her to go back with him to Nigeria where, as he says,

> Nigeria. Home. . . . I will show you our mountains and our stars; and give you cool drinks from gourds and teach you the old songs and the ways of our people—and, in time, we will pretend that—(*Very softly*)—you have only been away for a day—. (116)

It is the old ways, "old songs," "old people" that he offers and it does confuse Beneatha. For what the Younger family really wants, despite the fact that it will be purchased with the monetary value of a man's life after he is dead, is a home with a yard, to be part of that greener America. Ironically, the dramatic movement, the escape from their inner village apartment where they were so close and where in confrontation with the white Linder, Walter acquires some dignity as a man (a sop for the black male?), is into the larger white city wherein Ruth will still be a maid in a white woman's house and Walter will still be the chauffeur for a white man. The city lacks the black soul that began to emerge in the decade of the sixties.

The city that provides the impulse to withdraw into oneself can either represent the withdrawal into racial memories or into the white vision. The Younger family withdrew into the white system, into the illusion that the larger white environment being closer to the sun would make available an inner freedom and fulfillment. This interpretation is certainly not true for the fictive world Adrienne Kennedy creates in *The Owl Answers*. In this play special aspects of the city, drawn from the wide world and from time itself, become a collage of oneness: the New York subway being also the tower of London being a Harlem hotel room being St. Peter's. The mind constructs through its imaginary images its inner vision, making a new creative truth of power out of more realistic material. For She there is no escape, no physical movement, into another city, no Buffalo to encapsulate her dreams, no inner white neighborhood to move into. Her direction through drama is into the intellectual historical past of the English literature teacher visiting London and the birthplaces of white literary persons. But this is a visit more of honor than of search for identity. Equally ambivalent is her visit to Harlem hotel rooms with black men and her riding the subways hunting for black men. Her search grows out of her emotional chaos, not out of her rational thought. For She the city and its symbols are manifested through external events which are submerged within her personal desires.

This view of the city and the emotional and intellectual effects of its institutions, forms, and forces on a young woman creates a powerful dramatic metaphor, a theater of the mind. Reflecting this view, Kennedy assigns a speech of great poignancy to She:

I who am the ancestor of Shakespeare, Chaucer, and William the Conqueror, I went to London the Queen Elizabeth, London they all said, who ever heard of anybody going to London but I went. I stayed in my cabin the whole crossing, solitary, I was the only Negro there. I read books on subjects like the History of London, the Life of Anne Boleyn, Mary Queen of Scots, and Sonnets. When I wasn't in the cabin I wrapped myself in a great sweater and sat over the dark desks in the writing room and wrote my father. I wrote him every day of my journey. . . . I was married once briefly. On my wedding day the Reverend's Wife came to me and said when I see Marys I cry for their deaths, when I see brides, Clara, I cry for their deaths. But the past years I've spent teaching alone in Savannah. And alone I'm almost thirty-four, I who am the ancestor of somebody that cooked for somebody and William the Conqueror. . . . You must know how it is to be filled with yearning. (761)

At last She withdraws into herself, and in a moment of self-immolation, confused by the various identities the city has encumbered her with through its white-black minister and wife, its black-white religion, its bastardy laws, she tries to kill the black man she has picked up. Failing in that, she falls back onto the altar of her burning bed, and almost resembling the owl who calls one's name, she gasps out the final sounds of the play "Ow . . . oww" (764). It is a powerful image that Kennedy has created. But some of its strength derives from the need to find one's place, one's position within a city of human beings, not within a white city that blacks did not help create.

The escape into oneself from the city and its limitations on identity seem sometimes, as with Walter Younger, to partake of a drifting into the white man's ways of making money, into a world capitalism wherein all problems of power and especially of identity would be resolved with money. Lost in these plays is the wonder at the mere fact of being alive in a large city; there is even no awe induced by the possibilities of personal enrichment which a city can offer. In *No Place to Be Somebody,* Gabe is the narrator; the immediate environment is Johnny's bar in New York City. Gabe is a playwright and he narrates the events of the play. As he begins he picks up a Bible, a visual representative of white Christianity, and says while turning the pages, "Gabriel! Gabriel! Make this man understand the vision! So He came near where I stood! And when He came, I was frightened and fell upon my face!" (3). But the dominant dream or vision in the play is to make money, compounded of Sweets's knowledge, Johnny's greed, and the Italian gangsters. Throughout the play Gabe intrudes at the beginning of acts and scenes with his poetry to define what being black is:

> It's buyin'
> What you don't want, beggin' what you don't
> Need! An' stealin' what is yo's by rights!
> Yes! They's mo' to bein' black than meets the
> Eye!
> It's all the stuff that nobody wants but
> Cain't live without!

It's the body that keeps us standin'! The
Soul that keeps us goin'! An' the spirit
That'll take us thooo! (80)

In the end Sweets and Johnny die. Johnny wants to use his inheritance from his friend Sweets in a blackmail scheme to make money in his private war with the white man. In the ensuing quarrel because Gabe does not want such a war, Gabe shoots and kills Johnny. Ironically, everything comes to naught in the end. For the epilogue, Gabe enters dressed as a woman in mourning for her dead black men. She/ he mourns the passing of a people dying, "of a people dying into that new life. A people whose identity could only be measured by the struggle, the dehumanization, the degradation they suffered ... Of a people dying into that new life" (115).

Although the world belongs to the young people as the stereotyped commencement address used to mouth, its cities do not. For Walker and Clay and Cliff Dawson the city is a place of lies, deceptions, myths, a no-man's-land, as well as a focal point for violence. In Baraka's terms both of his creations, Walker and Clay, have rejected the city as a place to dream and create. The rightness of a thing, of a need, lies in the act, as Walker says (75), an idea prophetic of the movie Do the Right Thing.

At the beginning of the second act in No Place to Be Somebody, Gabe, who is drunk, sings a song that expresses the deeper sense of what a city means in its limitations, forces, and dreams to the black imagination:

> So we grew up clean and keen!
> And all our clean-white neighbors
> Said we had earned the right to go
> Out into the clean-white world
> And be accepted as clean-white people!
> But we soon learned,
> The world was not clean and white!
> With all of its powders and soaps!
> And we learned too that no matter how
> Much the world scrubbed,
> The world was getting no cleaner!
> Most of all!
> We saw that no matter how much or how
> Hard we scrubbed,
> It was only making us blacker!
> So back we came to that dirty-black slum!
> So back we came to that dirty-black slum!
> To the hovels, the filth and the garbage!

> Came back to those dirty-black people!
> Away from those clean-white people!
> That clean, white anti-septic world!
> That scrubs and scrubs and scrubs! (47)

If the place where the fictive blacks are pushes and stings, to para-phrase Walker (45), it does so because the city is a rebus, twisting and turning in on itself, concealing fears behind dreams and visions under the hatred. Where in some historical sense, at least for whites, the city has acted in the western world as a mediator between the human order and the natural order,[28] between the world of the mind's inner reality that names and organizes human existence and the outer world all life occupies with limited awareness, it does not function as a doorway for the black imagination in the black drama of the sixties. Bullins's dramas depict perhaps the best image of the fictive city with its occasional village-like qualities for blacks. The city establishes a network of social arrangements, becomes an arena for play or violence, provides the flux and form for financial orders, creates the need for tribal forms such as the gang, and pushes its family men to the periph-ery. But all of this occurs within a larger more pervasive and powerful structure that does not mediate between whites and blacks.

A sense of sadness, of poignancy, runs through the images of the city developed in the black drama of the sixties. It enacts a future that is no future for the Cliffs and Lous, the Clays, the Walkers, the Gabes, the Shes. The chemistry of that fictive domain seems static; its frame of choices limited, compelling its inhabitants into certain idealizations or realizations of its possibilities. Perhaps, if one follows Bullins, Baraka, and Kennedy too closely, there is even the sense that the city is some diabolical instrument or machine for killing that even as it possesses its inhabitants it sets out to destroy them. It prevents the full realization of what it means to be human. Perhaps Dante was right in figuring Hell as a walled city.

NOTES

1. Joyce Carol Oates, "Imaginary Cities: America," *Literature and the Urban Experience*, ed. Michael C. Jaye and Ann Chalmers Watts (New Brunswick, N.J.: Rutgers University Press, 1981), 11.

2. Christopher Rand, "Los Angeles: The Ultimate City," *City Life*, ed. Oscar Shoenfeld and Helene MacLean (New York: Grossman, 1969), 492.

3. Oates, "Imaginary Cities," 12

4. See LeRoi Jones, *Dutchman* and *The Slave* (New York: William Morrow, 1964); LeRoi Jones, *The Baptism* and *The Toilet* (New York: Grove Press, 1966); Ed Bullins, *Five Plays* (Indianapolis: Bobbs-Merrill, 1968); Charles Gordone, *No Place*

to Be Somebody (Indianapolis: Bobbs-Merrill, 1969); Adrienne Kennedy, The Owl Answers in Black Theater, U. S. A., ed. James V. Hatch (New York: Free Press, 1974); Lorraine Hansberry, A Raisin in the Sun (New York: New American Library, 1959).

5. Joyce Carol Oates, in referring to the cites of the late nineteenth- and early twentieth-century writers, says "the City is a place in which human beings die as a consequence of the unspeakable conditions of slum life and actual mistreatment by employers or by one another" (12).

6. Toni Morrison, "City Limits, Village Values: Concepts of the Neighborhood in Black Fiction," Literature and the Urban Experience, 35.

7. Bullins, Goin' a Buffalo and In the Wine Time.

8. Jones, Dutchman, The Slave, The Toilet.

9. Kennedy, The Owl Answers.

10. Gordone, No Place to Be Somebody.

11. Hansberry, A Raisin in the Sun.

12. Bullins, In the Wine Time.

13. Bullins, Clara's Ole Man.

14. Jones, The Toilet.

15. Kennedy, The Owl Answers.

16. Hansberry, A Raisin in the Sun.

17. Morrison, "City Limits," 38.

18. See Robert L. Tener, "Pandora's Box: A Study of Ed Bullins' Dramas," CLA Journal 19 (June 1976): 533–44.

19. Geneviève Fabre, Drumbeats, Masks and Metaphor (Cambridge: Harvard University Press, 1983). She says "the young woman is associated with summer, the summer of life constantly referred to in the play, that season of the year when the street and the neighborhood come fully alive" (177).

20. See Robert L. Tener, "The Corrupted Warrior Heroes: Amiri Baraka's The Toilet," in Imamu Amiri Baraka (LeRoi Jones): A Collection of Critical Essays, ed. Kimberly W. Benston (Englewood Cliffs, N.J.: Prentice-Hall, 1978), 148–56.

21. See Robert L. Tener, "Role Playing as a Dutchman," Studies in Black Literature 3 (Autumn 1972): 17–21.

22. See Robert L. Tener, "Theatre of Identity: Adrienne Kennedy's Portrait of the Black Woman," Studies in Black Literature 6 (Summer 1975): 1–5.

23. Ed Bullins, The Duplex (New York: William Morrow, 1971).

24. Ed Bullins, In New England Winter, in New Plays from the Black Theatre, ed. Ed Bullins (New York: Bantam Books, 1969).

25. Langston Hughes, I Wonder As I Wander (New York: Hill & Wang, 1963) and The Big Sea (New York: Hill & Wang, 1963).

26. Lawrence Ferlinghetti, "Modern Poetry Is Prose (But It Is Saying Plenty)," in Literature and the Urban Experience, 9.

27. See Morrison, "City Limits," 36.

28. Ihab Hassan, "Cities of Mind, Urban Words: The Dematerialization of Metropolis in Contemporary American Fiction," in Literature and the Urban Experience, 95.

Contributors

Yoshinobu Hakutani, Professor of English at Kent State University in Ohio, has written on American literature and other subjects. Among his books are *Critical Essays on Richard Wright, Selected English Writings of Yone Noguchi: An East-West Literary Assimilation, Young Dreiser: A Critical Study,* and *Selected Magazine Articles of Theodore Dreiser: Life and Art in the American 1890s,* for which he received a *Choice* award in 1987.

Robert Butler is Professor of English at Canisius College in Buffalo, New York. The author of *Native Son: The Emergence of a New Black Hero* (1991), he also has written many articles on Richard Wright, Ralph Ellison, Toni Morrison, Alice Walker, and other African-American topics in such journals as *Centennial Review, Black American Literature Forum, African American Review, MELUS,* and *CLA Journal.*

Donald B. Gibson has performed most of his professional activities at Rutgers University, where he is Professor of English and Director of Composition. He has written or edited many books on American literature. His recent publications include *The Red Badge of Courage: Redefining the Hero* (1988) and *W. E. B. Du Bois: The Souls of Black Folk* (1989).

Jack B. Moore is Professor and Chair of American Studies at the University of South Florida. He has written extensively on African-American literature and edited, with Michel Fabre, a special issue on Richard Wright for the *Mississippi Quarterly* (1989).

Eberhard Brüning is Professor Emeritus, former Chair of American Studies at the Universität Leipzig in Germany. In addition to being the author of many publications, he was editor of *Zeitschrift für Anglistik und Amerikanistik.*

Michel Fabre, Professor of American and African-American Studies at the Université de la Sorbonne Nouvelle, Paris, has taught at King's

College (London), Wellesley College, Harvard University, University of Iowa, and University of Mississippi. Among his books are *Les Noirs Américains, Planteurs et Esclaves, The Unfinished Quest of Richard Wright, F. Scott Fitzgerald, The World of Richard Wright,* and *From Harlem to the Seine.*

JOHN CONDER, Professor of English at Vanderbilt University, is the author of *A Formula of His Own: Henry Adams's Literary Experiment* and *Naturalism in American Fiction: The Classic Phase.*

FRED L. STANDLEY is the Daisy Parker Flory Alumni Professor of English at Florida State University. Writing extensively on James Baldwin, he has recently published, with Louis H. Pratt, *Conversations with James Baldwin* (1989).

JOCELYN CHADWICK-JOSHUA is an Assistant Professor of English at the University of North Texas in Denton, Texas. She has co-authored two books and is currently working on a scholarly book, *A Spoke in the Human Wheel: Nineteenth-Century African-American Periodicals and Their Rhetoric of Freedom.* She has also published articles in her area of specialization, nineteenth-century American literature, women's studies, and rhetoric.

MICHAEL F. LYNCH, Assistant Professor of English, Kent State University-Trumbull, has taught at the University of Akron and the Notre Dame College of Ohio. He is the author of *Creative Revolt: A Study of Wright, Ellison, and Dostoevsky.*

LARRY R. ANDREWS, Dean of the Honors College and Associate Professor of English and Comparative Literature at Kent State University, has taught at Volgograd State University in Soviet Russia and the University of Warsaw. He has published articles on Slavic literature as well as on African-American literature in such journals as *Neophilologus, Comparative Literature, Contemporary Literature,* and *CLA Journal.*

PRISCILLA R. RAMSEY is Associate Professor of Afro-American Studies at Howard University. She has written about Ethelbert Miller, Maya Angelou, Nella Larsen, Charles Chesnutt, James Baldwin, and many other African-American literary topics.

DONALD M. HASSLER, Professor and Director of Graduate Studies in English at Kent State University, is editor of *Extrapolation,* a journal of science fiction. He is the author of several books including *Erasmus Darwin, Comic Tones in Science Fiction,* and *Hal Clement.*

ROBERT L. TENER is Professor Emeritus and former Director of Graduate Studies in English at Kent State University. He has published numerous poems, many of them collected in, with Lloyd Mills, *Laughter and Dry Mockery: Satires* and in *A Dialogue of Marriage: The First Thousand Days.* In addition to writing *Phoenix Riddle: A Study of Drama,* he has written articles on Amiri Baraka, Ed Bullins, and Adrienne Kennedy.

Index